Digital Technologies and the Law of Obligations

Digital Technologies and the Law of Obligations critically examines the emergence of new digital technologies and the challenges they pose to the traditional law of obligations, and discusses the extent to which existing contract and tort law rules and doctrines are equipped to meet these new challenges.

This book covers various contract and tort law issues raised by emerging technologies – including distributed ledger technology, blockchain-based smart contracts, and artificial intelligence – as well as by the evolution of the internet into a participative web fuelled by user-generated content, and by the rise of the modern-day collaborative economy facilitated by digital technologies. Chapters address these topics from the perspective of both the common law and the civil law tradition. While mostly focused on the current state of affairs and recent debates and initiatives within the European Union regulatory framework, contributors also discuss the central themes from the perspective of the national law of obligations, examining the adaptability of existing legal doctrines to contemporary challenges, addressing the occasional legislative attempts to deal with the private law aspects of these challenges, and pointing to issues where legislative interventions would be most welcomed. Case studies are drawn from the United States, Singapore, and other parts of the common law world.

Digital Technologies and the Law of Obligations will be of interest to legal scholars and researchers in the fields of contract law, tort law, and digital law, as well as to legal practitioners and members of law reform bodies.

Zvonimir Slakoper is a Full Professor of Civil Law and the Head of the Department of Civil Law at the University of Rijeka, Faculty of Law, and a Full Professor of Commercial Law at the University of Zagreb, Faculty of Economics and Business. His expertise covers the law of obligations, especially banking contracts, and company law, and he has written, co-authored, and edited several books, including university textbooks, and many journal articles in these fields.

Ivan Tot is an Assistant Professor of Commercial Law at the University of Zagreb, Faculty of Economics and Business. His research mainly focuses on the law of obligations, banking law, and European contract law. He is a Co-Chair of the ELI Croatian Hub.

Digital Technologies and the Law of Obligations

Edited by
Zvonimir Slakoper and Ivan Tot

Routledge
Taylor & Francis Group
LONDON AND NEW YORK

First published 2022
by Routledge
2 Park Square, Milton Park, Abingdon, Oxon OX14 4RN

and by Routledge
605 Third Avenue, New York, NY 10158

Routledge is an imprint of the Taylor & Francis Group, an informa business

British Library Cataloguing-in-Publication Data
A catalogue record for this book is available from the British Library

Library of Congress Cataloging-in-Publication Data
Names: Zagreb International Conference on the Law of Obligations (1 : 2019 : Zagreb, Croatia) | Slakoper, Zvonimir, editor. | Tot, Ivan, 1983-editor. | Sveučilište u Zagrebu, sponsoring body.
Title: Digital technologies and the law of obligations / edited by Zvonimir Slakoper and Ivan Tot.
Description: Abingdon, Oxon ; New York, NY : Routledge, an imprint of the Taylor & Francis Group, an Informa Business, 2022. | "This book is one of the several planned volumes that grew out of the 'Zagreb International Conference on the Law of Obligations', organized by the Department of Law at the University of Zagreb, Faculty of Economics and Business (FEB Zagreb), and held in Zagreb on 12-13 December 2019."—ECIP preface. | Includes bibliographical references and index.
Identifiers: LCCN 2021010336 (print) | LCCN 2021010337 (ebook) | ISBN 9780367512705 (hardback) | ISBN 9781032065038 (paperback) | ISBN 9781003080596 (ebook)
Subjects: LCSH: Obligations (Law)—Congresses. | Electronic commerce—Law and legislation—Congresses. | Digital media—Law and legislation—Congresses.
Classification: LCC K830.A6 D54 2022 (print) | LCC K830.A6 (ebook) | DDC 346.02—dc23
LC record available at https://lccn.loc.gov/2021010336
LC ebook record available at https://lccn.loc.gov/2021010337

ISBN: 978-0-367-51270-5 (hbk)
ISBN: 978-1-032-06503-8 (pbk)
ISBN: 978-1-003-08059-6 (ebk)

DOI: 10.4324/9781003080596

Typeset in Bembo
by codeMantra

Contents

Table of cases

Australia

Canada

European Union

Poland

Singapore

United Kingdom

United States

Table of legislation

European Union

Directives

Recommendations

Regulations

Treaties

Slovenia

Obligations Code (*Obligacijski zakonik*), *UL RS* 97/2007, 64/2016, 20/2018 *39*

Art 6(2) *39*
131 *39*

United Kingdom

Automated and Electric Vehicles Act 2018 *112*
Insolvency Act 1986 *73*

s 74(2)(d) *73*

United Nations

International Covenant on Civil and Political Rights (adopted 16 December 1966, entered into force 23 March 1976) 999 *UNTS* 171 *176–77*

Art 17 *176*

UNCITRAL Model Law on Electronic Commerce (United Nations 1996) *129, 136–38, 141–42*

Art 13 *137, 141*

United Nations Convention on the Use of Electronic Communications in International Contracts (adopted 23 November 2005, entered into force 1 March 2013) 2898 *UNTS* 3 *136, 138*

Art 12 *137–38*

Universal Declaration of Human Rights (adopted 10 December 1948) UNGA Res 217 A(III) *176*

Art 12 *176*

United States

Arizona Revised Statutes

ARS § 44–7061 C *128*

Delaware Code

8 Del C 1953, § 224 *86*

Tennessee Code

TN Code § 47-10-201(2) *128*
§ 47-10-202 *129*

Uniform Acts

US Code

Preface

Over the last two decades, global society has witnessed accelerated technological developments in the still ongoing 'digital revolution', the emergence of new digital technologies characterized by increased automation and interconnectedness which has marked the beginning of the 'fourth industrial revolution', as well as the economic transformation triggered and powered by innovations in the digital arena. The rapid technological change, development of new products, services, and business models, and the expansion of the platform economy present numerous regulatory challenges in various fields of public and private law, both at the national and supranational level. This book deals with the interactions of the evolving digital environment and the law of obligations and covers various contract and tort law issues raised by the new and emerging digital technologies (e.g. distributed ledger technology, blockchain-based smart contracts, and artificial intelligence), as well as by the evolution of the internet into a participative web fuelled by user-generated content, and by the rise of the modern-day collaborative economy facilitated by digital technologies.

This book is one of the several planned volumes that grew out of the Zagreb International Conference on the Law of Obligations, organized by the Department of Law at the University of Zagreb, Faculty of Economics and Business (FEB Zagreb), and held in Zagreb on 12–13 December 2019. One of the five main topics of the conference dealt with the law of obligations aspects of the new and emerging digital technologies and contemporary social phenomena under the heading 'The Contemporary Challenges to the Law of Obligations'. The central theme addressed within this conference topic was whether the existing rules and doctrines in the national law of obligations provide the answers to the questions raised by digital technologies, or whether an appropriate modification of existing rules or the creation of entirely new rules is needed to address the challenges posed by the digital technologies. The contributions collected in this volume are mostly based on the early drafts of papers presented at the conference under this topic.

As heads of the conference scientific and organizing committees, we are grateful to our partners who supported the Department of Law at the FEB Zagreb in the organization of the conference: the UNCITRAL Secretariat and the ELI Global Private Law Special Interest Group. We would also like to thank the members of the conference scientific and organizing committees, conference speakers, and other participants.

As editors of this volume, we would like to thank the contributors to this volume for their hard work on the book chapters during the unprecedented and challenging times of the global pandemic. We are grateful to everyone at Routledge who supported this project and contributed to the production process, particularly to Siobhán Poole, Cathy Henderson, Lizzie Cox and Henry Strang, and to our copyeditor Katherine Laidler. We are especially indebted to Siobhán Poole for believing in the project at its proposal and supporting us ever since.

Zvonimir Slakoper and Ivan Tot

Abbreviations

AI	artificial intelligence
AIA	Artificial Intelligence Act (European Union)
AI&L	*Artificial Intelligence and Law*
Ariz L Rev	*Arizona Law Review*
ARS	Arizona Revised Statutes
BBLLC	blockchain-based limited liability company
Berkeley Tech LJ	*Berkeley Technology Law Journal*
BGBl	*Bundesgesetzblatt* (Official Gazette of the Federal Republic of Germany)
Bracton LJ	*Bracton Law Journal*
Brook J Corp Fin & Com L	*Brooklyn Journal of Corporate, Financial and Commercial Law*
Brook L Rev	*Brooklyn Law Review*
BU J Sci & Tech L	*Boston University Journal of Science and Technology Law*
Buff L Rev	*Buffalo Law Review*
Bull Inst Class Stud	*Bulletin of the Institute of Classical Studies*
Bus Horiz	*Business Horizons*
C&SLJ	*Company and Securities Law Journal*
Cal L Rev Circ	*California Law Review Circuit*
Can J Comp & Contemp L	*Canadian Journal of Comparative and Contemporary Law*
Cap U L Rev	*Capital University Law Review*
Cardozo Arts & Ent LJ	*Cardozo Arts & Entertainment Law Journal*
Cardozo L Rev	*Cardozo Law Review*
CDA	Communications Decency Act (United States)
CERCLA 1980	Comprehensive Environmental Response, Compensation and Liability Act 1980 (United States)
Charleston L Rev	*Charleston Law Review*
Chinese (Taiwan) YB Intl L & Aff	*Chinese (Taiwan) Yearbook of International Law and Affairs*

CISG	United Nations Convention on Contracts for the International Sale of Goods
CJEU	Court of Justice of the European Union (the judicial institution)
CLJ	*Cambridge Law Journal*
CLP	*Current Legal Problems*
CLR	*California Law Review*
CLS Rev	*Computer Law & Security Review*
CLWR	*Common Law World Review*
CML Rev	*Common Market Law Review*
Colum JL & Arts	*Columbia Journal of Law & the Arts*
Comm Law	*Communications Lawyer*
Commun ACM	*Communications of the ACM*
Computer L & Secur Rep	*Computer Law and Security Report*
Conn L Rev	*Connecticut Law Review*
CUECIC	United Nations Convention on the Use of Electronic Communications in International Contracts
CUP	Cambridge University Press
Curr Issues Tour	*Current Issues in Tourism*
DAO	decentralized autonomous organization
DCFR	Draft Common Frame of Reference
Del C	Delaware Code
DePaul L Rev	*DePaul Law Review*
Dike	*Dike – Rivista di storia del diritto greco ed ellenistico* (Italy)
DLT	distributed ledger technology
DMA	Digital Markets Act (European Union)
DMCA	Digital Millennium Copyright Act (United States)
DSA	Digital Services Act (European Union)
Duke LJ	*Duke Law Journal*
DzU	*Dziennik Ustaw* (Official Gazette of the Republic of Poland)
EBOR	*European Business Organization Law Review*
ECFR	*European Company and Financial Law Review*
ECHR	Convention for the Protection of Human Rights and Fundamental Freedoms (European Convention on Human Rights)
ECJ	Court of Justice (at the CJEU)
ECLI	European Case Law Identifier
ECR	*European Court Reports*
Electron Commer Res	*Electronic Commerce Research*
ELI	European Law Institute
ERCL	*European Review of Contract Law*
ERPL	*European Review of Private Law*

EuCML	*Journal of European Consumer and Market Law*
Fordham Intl LJ	*Fordham International Law Journal*
Fordham L Rev	*Fordham Law Review*
GDPR	General Data Protection Regulation (EU)
Geo L Tech Rev	*Georgetown Law Technology Review*
Golden Gate U Envtl LJ	*Golden Gate University Environmental Law Journal*
GU	*Gazetta Ufficiale* (Official Gazzette of the Italian Republic)
Harv Bus Rev	*Harvard Business Review*
Harv JL & Tech	*Harvard Journal of Law & Technology*
Hastings Sci & Tech LJ	*Hastings Science and Technology Law Journal*
Hous Bus & Tax LJ	*Houston Business and Tax Law Journal*
HUP	Harvard University Press
I & CTL	*Information & Communications Technology Law*
ICLQ	*International & Comparative Law Quarterly*
IEEE Trans Inf Theory	*IEEE Transactions on Information Theory*
IIoT	industrial internet of things
IJLIT	*International Journal of Law and Information Technology*
Int J	*Health Serv International Journal of Health Services*
Internet Pol'y Rev	*Internet Policy Review*
IoT	internet of things
IP	intellectual property
ISP	internet service provider
Ita LJ	*The Italian Law Journal*
J Bus & Tech L	*Journal of Business & Technology Law*
J Corp L	*Journal of Corporation Law*
J Eur Econ Assoc	*Journal of the European Economic Association*
J Prof Neglig	*Journal of Professional Negligence*
J Tort L	*Journal of Tort Law*
J Travel Tour Mark	*Journal of Travel & Tourism Marketing*
J World Bus	*Journal of World Business*
JCL	*Journal of Contract Law*
JCLS	*Journal of Corporate Law Studies*
JETL	*Journal of European Tort Law*
JILT	*Journal of Information, Law & Technology*
JIPITEC	*Journal of Intellectual Property, Information Technology and E-Commerce Law*
JL & Innovation	*Journal of Law & Innovation*
KF	key findings of the NTF Report (European Union)
KSH	Polish Code of Commercial Companies (*Kodeks spółek handlowycheven*)

La L Rev	*Louisiana Law Review*
Law Innov Technol	*Law, Innovation and Technology*
LGBl	*Liechtensteinisches Landesgesetzblatt* (Official Gazzette of the Principality of Lichtenstein)
LLC	limited liability company
LMCLQ	*Lloyd's Maritime and Commercial Law Quarterly*
LQR	*Law Quarterly Review*
LS	*Legal Studies*
MiCA	markets in crypto-assets
MJ	*Maastricht Journal of European and Comparative Law*
Mkt & Competition L Rev	*Market and Competition Law Review*
MLEC	UNCITRAL Model Law on Electronic Commerce
MLR	*Modern Law Review*
Nat Resources J	*Natural Resources Journal*
NC L Rev	*North Carolina Law Review*
Neb L Rev	*Nebraska Law Review*
NN	*Narodne novine* (Official Gazette of the Republic of Croatia)
NPFC	National Pollution Funds Center (United States)
NTF	European Commission Expert Group on Liability and New Technologies – New Technologies Formation
Nw U L Rev	*Northwestern University Law Review*
OECD	Organisation for Economic Co-operation and Development
Ohio St LJ	*Ohio State Law Journal*
OJ	*Official Journal of the European Union*
OPA 1990	Oil Pollution Act 1990 (United States)
OSLFT	Oil Spill Liability Trust Fund (United States)
OSP	online service provider
OUP	Oxford University Press
OZ	Slovenian Obligations Code (*Obligacijski zakonik*)
P2B	platform-to-business
P2P	peer-to-peer
PECL	Principles of European Contract Law
Pepp L Rev	*Pepperdine Law Review*
PETL	Principles of European Tort Law
PLD	Product Liability Directive (EU)
PLDF	European Commission Expert Group on Liability and New Technologies – Product Liability Directive Formation
Probate Prop	*Probate and Property*
Real Prop Tr & Est LJ	*Real Property, Trust and Estate Law Journal*
S & LS	*Social & Legal Studies*

S Ac LJ	*Singapore Academy of Law Journal*
S Cal L Rev	*Southern California Law Review*
Santa Clara High Tech LJ	*Santa Clara High Technology Law Journal*
Savannah L Rev	*Savannah Law Review*
SCA	Stored Communications Act (United States)
SCRIPTed	*SCRIPTed – A Journal of Law, Technology & Society*
Seton Hall L Rev	*Seton Hall Law Review*
Singapore Econ Rev	*Singapore Economic Review*
Stanford J Blockchain L & Pol'y	*Stanford Journal of Blockchain Law & Policy*
Stan L Rev	*Stanford Law Review*
Stan Tech L Rev	*Stanford Technology Law Review*
Strateg Manag J	*Strategic Management Journal*
Stud Cywilis	*Studia Cywilistyczne* (Poland)
Sw L Rev	*Southwestern Law Review*
Syd LR	*Sydney Law Review*
Syracuse Sci & Tech L Rep	*Syracuse Science and Technology Law Reporter*
Tenn J Bus L	*Transactions: The Tennessee Journal of Business Law*
TFEU	Treaty on the Functioning of the European Union
TLJ	*Torts Law Journal* (Australia)
TN Code	Tennessee Code
Tort L Rev	*Tort Law Review*
TOS	terms of service
Tul Mar LJ	*Tulane Maritime Law Journal*
U Chi L Rev Online	*University of Chicago Law Review Online*
U Colo L Rev	*University of Colorado Law Review*
U Ill JL Tech & Pol'y	*University of Illionois Journal of Law, Technology & Policy*
U Ill L Rev	*University of Illinois Law Review*
UCITA	Uniform Computer Information Transaction Act (United States)
UL RS	*Uradni list Republike Slovenije* (Official Gazette of the Republic of Slovenia)
UNCITRAL	United Nations Commission on International Trade Law
UNGA	General Assembly of the United Nations
UNIDROIT	International Institute for the Unification of Private Law
UNTS	*United Nations Treaty Series*
UPICC	UNIDROIT Principles of International Commercial Contracts
USC	United States Code
UTLJ	*University of Toronto Law Journal*

Va L Rev	*Virginia Law Review*
Val U L Rev	*Valparaiso University Law Review*
Vand L Rev	*Vanderbilt Law Review*
VSA	Vermont Statutes Annotated
Wash & Lee L Rev	*Washington and Lee Law Review*
Wash & Lee L Rev Online	*Washington and Lee Law Review Online*
Wash L Rev	*Washington Law Review*
Yale LJ	*Yale Law Journal*
ZAPDSP	Croatian Copyright and Related Rights Act (*Zakon o autorskom pravu i srodnim pravima*)
Zbor Prav Fak Rijeka	*Zbornik Pravnog fakulteta Sveučilišta u Rijeci* (Croatia)
Zbor Prav Fak Zagreb	*Zbornik Pravnog fakulteta u Zagrebu* (Croatia)
Zbor Rad Prav Fak Split	*Zbornik radova Pravnog fakulteta u Splitu* (Croatia)
ZOO	Croatian Obligations Act (*Zakon o obveznim odnosima*)
ZVDSP	Croatian Act on Ownership and Other Real Rights (*Zakon o vlasništvu i drugim stvarnim pravima*)

Notes on contributors

Matija Damjan is an Assistant Professor of Civil and Commercial Law at the University of Ljubljana, Faculty of Law, and the Secretary-General of the Faculty's Institute for Comparative Law, where he is also active as a researcher. In his work, he primarily focuses on the areas of civil law, intellectual property law, and information society law, and he has authored more than thirty scientific articles discussing issues in these fields. He is also the author or co-author of several scientific monographs and co-author of several draft proposals of legislative acts. He is currently engaged in long-term research projects on the legal challenges of the information society and the modernization of the insurance contract regulatory framework.

Kosjenka Dumančić is an Associate Professor of Commercial Law, Vice-Dean for international relations and projects, and the Head of Institute for Euro-Asian Studies at the University of Zagreb, Faculty of Economics and Business. Her research interests are in the fields of European company law, European internal market law, and collaborative economy. Currently, she is actively involved in an EU-funded Erasmus+ COLECO Project which aims to examine the impacts of the collaborative economy in Europe, focusing on peer-to-peer accommodation platforms.

Mateja Durovic is a Reader in Contract and Commercial Law and Deputy Director of the Centre for Technology, Ethics, Law and Society (TELOS), at King's College London, The Dickson Poon School of Law. His expertise covers consumer law and contract law, and he has published widely in these areas in leading law journals and with prominent international publishers. He is a member of the European Law Institute, Society of Legal Scholars, and Society for European Contract Law.

Andrea Faraci is an Italian qualified lawyer and an independent scholar. His research interests include philosophy of law, ancient and contemporary contract law, particularly general clauses, contractor's defence, and abuse of law.

Dino Gliha is an Attorney-at-law in the Joint Law Office Dr. sc. Marković, Grbavac & Gliha in Zagreb, and a PhD student at the University of Zagreb,

Faculty of Law. His areas of expertise are corporate and commercial law, intellectual property, and competition law. He is currently writing a PhD thesis in the field of interaction between copyright and competition law with a special focus on the digital market. His research interests also include the implementation of the law to newly developed technologies and the application of technologies to the legal system.

Dubravka Klasiček is an Associate Professor and the Head of the Civil Law Chair at the University J. J. Strossmayer in Osijek, Faculty of Law. She defended her doctoral thesis 'Forced share as a limitation of freedom of testation' at the University of Zagreb, Faculty of Law in 2011. Independently and as co-author, she has published numerous scientific and professional papers and has participated in national and international scientific conferences. Her main field of expertise is succession law and the law of obligations.

Nicholas Liu is a Lecturer of Law at the Singapore Management University, School of Law. He holds a JD (*summa cum laude*) from the Singapore Management University and a BA (Honours, First Class) in English Literature from the National University of Singapore.

Luigi Lonardo is a Lecturer in Law at University College Cork and Visiting Lecturer of European Foreign Security and Defence Policy at Sciences Po Paris. His research focuses on interdisciplinary approaches to the EU's foreign policy and draws from law, international relations and EU integration theory, political theory, and contemporary European history.

Sandra Marković is an Attorney-at-law in the Joint Law Office Dr. sc. Marković, Grbavac & Gliha in Zagreb. Previously she worked for more than twenty years at the Constitutional Court of the Republic of Croatia as Head of Legal Advisory Division and Senior Constitutional Court Legal Advisor. Since 2013 she has also been an Associate Lecturer at the University of Zagreb, Faculty of Law, Department of Constitutional Law. She holds a PhD degree from the University of Zagreb, Faculty of Law. Her expertise and research interests are in the fields of constitutional law and human rights.

Marcin Mazgaj is an Assistant Professor of Law at the Pedagogical University of Cracow, Institute of Law, Administration, and Economics, and an attorney-at-law and partner in the law firm JWMS Jakubowski Wiese Mazgaj Staszek in Cracow. He earned his PhD in corporate law in 2013 from the Jagiellonian University in Cracow, Faculty of Law and Administration. His expertise and research interests are in the fields of company law, capital market law, and contract law.

Nasir Muftić is a Teaching and Research Assistant and a PhD student at the University of Sarajevo, Faculty of Law. He graduated from the University of Sarajevo, Faculty of Law in 2016 and obtained an LL.M. degree in International Business Law from the Central European University in 2017. He completed traineeships at the Constitutional Court of Federation of Bosnia and Herzegovina and the Supreme Court of Bosnia and Herzegovina. Before the commencement of his doctoral studies, he worked as a legal assistant at BH Telecom JSC. His research interests include the intersection between technology and law with a focus on private law.

Zvonimir Slakoper is a Full Professor of Civil Law and the Head of the Department of Civil Law at the University of Rijeka, Faculty of Law, and a Full Professor of Commercial Law at the University of Zagreb, Faculty of Economics and Business. His expertise covers the law of obligations, especially banking contracts, and company law, and he has written, co-authored, and edited several books, including university textbooks, and many journal articles in these fields.

Radosław Strugała is an Assistant Professor of Civil and Private International Law at the University of Wrocław, Faculty of Law, Administration, and Economics. His expertise and research interests are in the fields of contract law and tort law, and he has written several monographs and numerous papers in these fields. He was a member of a working group of the Polish Civil Law Codification Commission (2013–2015).

Ivan Tot is an Assistant Professor of Commercial Law at the University of Zagreb, Faculty of Economics and Business. His research mainly focuses on the law of obligations, banking law, and European contract law. He is a Co-Chair of the ELI Croatian Hub.

Christian A Witting is a Professor of Law at the National University of Singapore, Faculty of Law. His previous roles include Professor of Private Law at Queen Mary University of London, Associate Professor at the University of Melbourne, and Solicitor in the Commonwealth Attorney-General's Department (Australia). Professor Witting is author of *Liability of Corporate Groups and Networks* (CUP 2018), *Liability for Negligent Misstatements* (OUP 2004), and the textbook *Street on Torts* (OUP, several editions). He was consultant editor for *Halsbury's Laws of England: Torts* (5th edn, Butterworths 2015). His current research interests concern corporate groups, enterprise liability, and the nature of obligations in tort law.

1 Contract and tort law in the digital age

Contemporary challenges to the law of obligations

Zvonimir Slakoper and Ivan Tot

1. Introduction

In the last two decades, the ongoing 'digital revolution' has profoundly and rapidly transformed the analogue world into a digital one. The most recent phase of the digital revolution was mainly initiated with the technological improvements that have significantly increased and eased access to the internet, including through the development of smartphones. The internet itself has evolved into what is described in the jargon as Web 2.0:[1] a participative, interactive, and social web that runs on user-generated content. The evolved internet has facilitated the rise of online platforms diverse in their functions and structure: from social networks and video-sharing platforms to online marketplaces and app stores. The emergence of transaction platforms as two-sided (or multi-sided) markets,[2] which connect interdependent groups of users and facilitate transactions between them, has led to the expansion of the collaborative economy.[3]

1 The term 'Web 2.0' is commonly employed to contrast the present-day interactive and collaborative web to static websites of the first generation, and not to point to any substantive differences in the underlying technology. The coining of the term is usually attributed to Darci DiNucci, who used it designate the use of the internet on a variety of devices in: Darci DiNucci, 'Fragmented Future' (1999) 53 (4) *Print* 32. The term was brought into the mainstream after the Web 2.0 Conference held in San Francisco in October 2004, where John Battelle and Tim O'Reilly used it to describe the business models focused on harnessing the user-generated content (eg Google and Wikipedia) in contrast to the business models focused on creating software for the end users (eg Netscape and Encyclopaedia Britannica Online). See Tim O'Reilly, 'What is Web 2.0: Design Patterns and Business Models for the Next Generation of Software' (O'Reilly Media, 30 September 2005) <www.oreilly.com/pub/a/web2/archive/what-is-web-20.html> accessed 9 July 2020.

2 See the seminal work on a model of platform competition with two-sided markets: Jean-Charles Rochet and Jean Tirole, 'Platform Competition in Two-Sided Markets' (2003) 1 *J Eur Econ Assoc* 990.

3 The terms 'collaborative economy' and 'sharing economy', among others, are usually used interchangeably and the same is true regarding the use of these concepts in the contributions to this volume. However, the term 'sharing economy' is narrower in its scope than the term 'collaborative economy' since many of the online platforms do not focus solely on the outright sharing of assets. See Vassilis Hatzopoulos, *The Collaborative Economy and EU Law* (Hart Publishing 2018) 4–6.

DOI: 10.4324/9781003080596-1

While the collaborative economy model is in most cases dependent on online platforms to act as intermediaries and matchmakers, the other significant development of the digital revolution is the emergence of a new technology that does not rely on an intermediary to facilitate transactions: distributed ledger technology (DLT).[4] A prime example of DLT is the blockchain technology[5] which was given prominence after 2009 when the first blockchain was created to provide the technical infrastructure for the Bitcoin cryptocurrency.[6] Later on, other blockchains were developed, the most important probably being the Ethereum[7] which was developed to enable blockchain-based smart contracts,[8] and their combination into autonomously operating decentralized structures, known as decentralized autonomous organizations (DAOs).[9]

4 There is no consensus on a definition of a distributed ledger, but it can be understood as an online list of records distributed across multiple devices on a peer-to-peer network that offers a transaction-management system maintained by a consensus protocol rather than by a central authority. For an introduction to DLT and its variants, see eg Carla L Reyes, 'Conceptualizing Cryptolaw' (2017) 96 *Neb L Rev* 384, 390–99; Primavera De Filippi and Aaron Wright, *Blockchain and the Law: The Rule of Code* (HUP 2018) 11–58; Michèle Finck, *Blockchain Regulation and Governance in Europe* (CUP 2018) 6–33.

5 Blockchain is a distributed ledger where the ledger consists of a chain of interconnected blocks with each block containing a list of aggregated transactions. Every blockchain is a distributed ledger, but not all distributed ledgers are blockchains as there are distributed ledgers that do not store data in interconnected blocks. See eg Finck (n 4) 6–9; Eliza Mik, 'Blockchains: A Technology for Decentralized Marketplaces' in Larry A DiMatteo, Michel Cannarsa, and Cristina Poncibò (eds), *The Cambridge Handbook of Smart Contracts, Blockchain Technology and Digital Platforms* (CUP 2019) 162–64; Kelvin FK Low and Eliza Mik, 'Pause the Blockchain Legal Revolution' (2020) 69 *ICLQ* 135, 137–38.

6 Bitcoin was developed by Satoshi Nakamoto who created the first blockchain database as part of the implementation of bitcoin. Satoshi Nakamoto is a pseudonym for a person (or a group) who authored the bitcoin white paper and whose real identity is yet unknown: Satoshi Nakamoto, 'Bitcoin: A Peer-to-Peer Electronic Cash System' (*Bitcoin Project: Introduction: White Paper*, 31 October 2008) <https://bitcoin.org/en/bitcoin-paper> accessed 9 July 2020.

7 Ethereum was introduced in 2013 in the white paper by Vitalik Buterin. See Vitalik Buterin, 'A Next-Generation Smart Contract and Decentralized Application Platform' (Ethereum: White Paper, 2013) <https://ethereum.org/en/whitepaper> accessed 9 July 2020.

8 The term 'smart contract' was coined by Nick Szabo in 1994 who defined it as 'a computerized transaction protocol that executes the terms of a contract': see Nick Szabo, 'Smart Contracts' (1994) <www.fon.hum.uva.nl/rob/Courses/InformationInSpeech/CDROM/Literature/LOTwinterschool2006/szabo.best.vwh.net/smart.contracts.html> accessed 16 July 2020. The notion of a 'blockchain-based smart contract' is a narrower notion which can be understood as a computer code that runs on blockchain and is designed to automatically execute a transaction upon the occurrence of a trigger event, although a myriad of different definitions exists in the literature. For an overview of the various definitions, see eg Riccardo de Caria, 'Definitions of Smart Contracts: Between Law and Code' in Larry A DiMatteo, Michel Cannarsa, and Cristina Poncibò (eds), *The Cambridge Handbook of Smart Contracts, Blockchain Technology and Digital Platforms* (CUP 2019) 21–24, who refers to blockchain-based smart contracts as 'decentralized smart contracts'.

9 DAO is a corporate-type organization where the rules of management are encoded on blockchain in the form of smart contracts. See eg Finck (n 4) 22–23; De Filippi and Wright (n 4) 146–55; Wulf A Kaal, 'Blockchain-Based Corporate Governance' (2021) 4 *Stanford J Blockchain L & Pol'y* 1 <https://ssrn.com/abstract=3441904> accessed 16 July 2020.

While the digital revolution, also dubbed the 'third industrial revolution', is still in progress, a 'fourth industrial revolution' has already arrived and is evolving exponentially.[10] With increased automation without the need for human intervention as a common characteristic, the list of the emerging digital technologies that are part of the fourth industrial revolution keeps expanding and so far includes, among others, artificial intelligence (AI), robotics, machine-to-machine communication, big data analytics, the internet of things (IoT), the industrial internet of things (IIoT), 3D printing, augmented reality, fifth-generation wireless technologies, and fully autonomous vehicles.

The new and emerging digital technologies of the overlapping third and fourth industrial revolutions are frequently described as 'disruptive technologies' due to their disruptive effect on the established traditional market models.[11] Digital technologies and their disruptive effects present significant regulatory challenges,[12] and can also have a disruptive effect on the law 'once it is no longer possible to apply existing legal rules to new circumstances, or to modify the scope of existing legal rules to ensure that these address new issues brought about by technological changes'.[13]

Apart from presenting challenges to regulation in general, the new technological, economic, and sociocultural phenomena are raising challenging questions in various fields of public and private law. This book deals with the challenges they pose to the traditional law of obligations and discusses whether the existing contract and tort law rules and doctrines are well equipped to meet these new challenges or whether an appropriate modification, reinterpretation, or creation of entirely new legal solutions is needed to that purpose. The book is mainly concerned with the following topics: liability of internet intermediaries for illegal third-party content, liability of collaborative economy platforms to their users, liability for artificial intelligence and other emerging digital technologies, and contract law challenges posed by blockchain-based smart contracts. The book aims to contribute to the current debate on private law challenges of the digital technologies and their significant impact on the private law relationships as a supplement to an increasingly growing body of legal literature on the subject.[14]

10 The phrase 'fourth industrial revolution' was first introduced by Klaus Schwab in: 'The Fourth Industrial Revolution: What It Means and How to Respond' *Foreign Affairs* (Online, 12 December 2015) <www.foreignaffairs.com/articles/2015-12-12/fourth-industrial-revolution> accessed 9 July 2020.

11 The terminology on 'disruptive technologies' and 'disruptive innovation' originated in the seminal article: Joseph L Bower and Clayton M Christensen, 'Disruptive Technologies: Catching the Wave' [1995] (1) *Harv Bus Rev* 43.

12 See eg Wulf A Kaal and Erik PM Vermeulen, 'How to Regulate Disruptive Innovation – From Facts to Data' (2017) 57 *Jurimetrics* 169.

13 Christian Twigg-Flesner, 'Disruptive Technology – Disrupted Law? How the Digital Revolution Affects (Contract) Law' in Alberto De Franceschi (ed), *European Contract Law and the Digital Single Market: The Implications of the Digital Revolution* (Intersentia 2016) 27.

14 See especially the following important contributions of the mostly European legal scholarship: Alberto De Franceschi (ed), *European Contract Law and the Digital Single Market: The*

This introductory chapter aims to provide context for the chapters that follow. Since most of the contributions to this volume are approaching the central theme of contemporary challenges to the law of obligations from the perspective of the EU law and the law of the EU Member States, this chapter first presents the main contract and tort law issues dealt with in this book with a focus on the current state of affairs and the recent debates and initiatives within the EU regulatory framework (Section 2) and then continues to introduce the book structure and contributions to this volume (Section 3).

2. Main topics and the overview of the EU legal framework

2.1 Liability of internet intermediaries for third-party content

Online content uploaded on the internet can breach copyright, trademarks, patents, trade secrets, personality rights, and various other private rights, causing damage or loss and thus giving rise to claims for compensation. Since the wrongdoer often cannot be identified, the question arises whether the persons whose legitimate interests were harmed can act against the internet

---

Implications of the Digital Revolution (Intersentia 2016); Reiner Schulze and Dirk Staudenmayer (eds), *Digital Revolution: Challenges for Contract Law in Practice* (Hart Publishing – Nomos 2016); Reiner Schulze, Dirk Staudenmayer, and Sebastian Lohsee (eds), *Contracts for the Supply of Digital Content: Regulatory Challenges and Gaps: Münster Colloquia on EU Law and the Digital Economy II* (Hart Publishing – Nomos 2017); Sebastian Lohsee, Reiner Schulze, and Dirk Staudenmayer (eds), *Trading Data in the Digital Economy: Legal Concepts and Tools: Münster Colloquia on EU Law and the Digital Economy III* (Hart Publishing – Nomos 2017); Tatiana-Eleni Synodinou and others (eds), *EU Internet Law: Regulation and Enforcement* (Springer 2017); Marcelo Corrales, Mark Fenwick, and Nikolaus Forgó (eds), *Robotics, AI and the Future of Law* (Springer 2018); Stefan Grundmann (ed), *European Contract Law in the Digital Age* (Intersentia 2018); Vanessa Mak, Eric Tjong Tjin Tai, and Anne Berlee (eds), *Research Handbook in Data Science and Law* (Edward Elgar 2018); Nikita Aggarwal and others (eds), *Autonomous Systems and the Law* (CH Beck – Nomos 2019); Alberto de Franceschi and Reiner Schulze (eds), *Digital Revolution – New Challenges for Law: Data Protection, Artificial Intelligence, Smart Products, Blockchain Technology and Virtual Currencies* (CH Beck – Nomos 2019); Larry A DiMatteo, Michel Cannarsa, and Cristina Poncibò (eds), *The Cambridge Handbook of Smart Contracts, Blockchain Technology and Digital Platforms* (CUP 2019); Philipp Hacker and others (eds), *Regulating Blockchain: Techno-Social and Legal Challenges* (OUP 2019); Sebastian Lohsee, Reiner Schulze, and Dirk Staudenmayer (eds), *Liability for Artificial Intelligence and the Internet of Things: Münster Colloquia on EU Law and the Digital Economy IV* (Hart Publishing – Nomos 2019); Woodrow Barfield (ed), *The Cambridge Handbook of the Law of Algorithms* (CUP 2020); Christoph Busch and Alberto De Franceschi (eds), *Algorithmic Regulation and Personalized Law: A Handbook* (Hart Publishing – CH Beck – Nomos 2020); Martin Ebers and Susana Navas (ed), *Algorithms and Law* (CUP 2020); Michael Furmston (ed), *The Future of the Law of Contract* (Routledge 2020); Sebastian Lohsee, Reiner Schulze, and Dirk Staudenmayer (eds), *Data as Counter-Performance – Contract Law 2.0? Münster Colloquia on EU Law and the Digital Economy V* (Hart Publishing – Nomos 2020); Tatiana-Eleni Synodinou and others (eds), *EU Internet Law in the Digital Era: Regulation and Enforcement* (Springer 2020).

intermediaries who host or transmit the online content.[15] In the United States, the Digital Millennium Copyright Act (DMCA) set forth safe harbours which limit the liability of internet intermediaries arising from copyright infringements.[16] In the European Union, similar safe harbour regime was introduced with the E-Commerce Directive.[17]

Unlike the DMCA, the E-Commerce Directive employed a horizontal approach covering any liability, both civil and criminal, for any kind of illegal content or activities.[18] The E-Commerce Directive differentiates three types of intermediary activities (mere conduit, caching, and hosting) and specifies the requirements under which the internet intermediaries may be exempted from liability for illegal content uploaded by their users.[19] In addition to the several regulatory gaps that existed already at the time the E-Commerce Directive was adopted,[20] the subsequent development of Web 2.0 has raised new legal issues that were not initially addressed by the E-Commerce Directive. The E-Commerce Directive essentially shields the internet intermediaries from the liability for illegal content as long as their activities are of a mere technical, automatic, and passive nature. The emergence of new types of internet intermediaries (e.g. social networking sites, online marketplaces, online video platforms, and similar) that facilitate publication of user-generated content has led to legal uncertainty regarding their liability for illegal content: because of their more active role, it was questionable whether they can benefit from the liability exemptions set out in the E-Commerce Directive. The Court of Justice (ECJ) has played and continues to play a crucial rule in resolving legal uncertainty created by both the regulatory gaps and the new market developments.[21]

15 For a detailed taxonomy of internet intermediaries, see Jaani Riordan, *The Liability of Internet Intermediaries* (OUP 2016) 26ff. For analysis and discussion of the different internet intermediary liability regimes, see eg Graeme B Dinwoodie (ed), *Secondary Liability of Internet Service Providers* (Springer 2017); Giancarlo Frosio (ed), *The Oxford Handbook of Online Intermediary Liability* (OUP 2020).

16 Codified in 17 USC § 512.

17 Directive 2000/31/EC of the European Parliament and of the Council of 8 June 2000 on certain legal aspects of information society services, in particular electronic commerce, in the Internal Market ('Directive on electronic commerce') [2000] *OJ* L178/1 (E-Commerce Directive).

18 For differences between the DMCA and E-Commerce Directive safe harbour regimes, see Miquel Peguera, 'The DMCA Safe Harbors and Their European Counterparts: A Comparative Analysis of Some Common Problems' (2009) 32 *Colum JL & Arts* 481. For an analysis of the DMCA safe harbour regime in the context of the Web 2.0 environment, see eg Brandon Brown, 'Fortifying the Safe Harbors: Reevaluating the DMCA in a Web 2.0 World' (2008) 23 *Berkeley Tech LJ* 437.

19 E-Commerce Directive, Arts 12–14.

20 For instance, unlike the DMCA, the E-Commerce Directive does not contain specific provisions for search engines or detailed rules on the applicable notice-and-takedown procedure.

21 Especially with the following judgments related to conditions for the liability exemptions: Joined Cases C-236/08 to C-238/08 *Google France SARL and Google Inc v Louis Vuitton Malletier SA, Google France SARL v Viaticum SA and Luteciel SARL, and Google France SARL*

The E-Commerce Directive has not always been interpreted consistently by the national courts of the Member States.[22] The way the E-Commerce Directive has been transposed in the Member States varies greatly and the national law of Member States keeps evolving.[23] In recent years, sector-specific legislation dealing with specific obligations of internet intermediaries has been adopted at the EU level.[24] A significant development was the adoption of the Directive on Copyright in the Digital Single Market,[25] following which the online content-sharing service providers can be held responsible for copyright infringements caused by their users since the enabling of public access to copyright-protected works uploaded by their users now qualifies as an act of communication to the public by the service providers themselves.[26] Additionally, soft law instruments have been introduced to encour-

---

v Centre national de recherche en relations humaines (CNRRH) SARL and Others [2010] *ECR* I-2417, ECLI:EU:C:2010:159; Case C-324/09 *L'Oréal SA and Others v eBay International AG and Others* [2011] *ECR* I-6011, ECLI:EU:C:2011:474; Case C-70/10 *Scarlet Extended SA v Société belge des auteurs, compositeurs et éditeurs SCRL (SABAM)* [2011] *ECR* I-11959, ECLI:EU:C:2011:771; Case C-360/10 *Belgische Vereniging van Auteurs, Componisten en Uitgevers CVBA (SABAM) v Netlog NV* [2012] ECLI:EU:C:2012:85; Case C-484/14 *Tobias Mc Fadden v Sony Music Entertainment Germany GmbH* [2016] ECLI:EU:C:2016:689; Case C-18/18 *Eva Glawischnig-Piesczek v Facebook Ireland Limited* [2019] ECLI:EU:C:2019:821.

22 See eg Sophie Stalla-Bourdillon, 'Internet Intermediaries as Responsible Actors? Why It Is Time to Rethink the E-Commerce Directive as Well' in Mariarosaria Taddeo and Luciano Floridi (eds), *The Responsibilities of Online Service Providers* (Springer 2017) 279–82.

23 For instance, in Germany specific obligations related to removing illegal content and 'fake news' were imposed upon social networks with the Network Enforcement Act (*Netzwerkdurchsetzungsgesetz* of 1 September 2017, *BGBl* I 3352). See eg Gerald Spindler, 'Internet Intermediary Liability Reloaded: The New German Act on Responsibility of Social Networks and its (In-) Compatibility with European Law' (2017) 8 *JIPITEC* 166 <www.jipitec.eu/issues/jipitec-8-2-2017/4567> accessed 16 July 2020.

24 Eg Directive 2010/13/EU of the European Parliament and of the Council of 10 March 2010 on the coordination of certain provisions laid down by law, regulation or administrative action in Member States concerning the provision of audiovisual media services (Audiovisual Media Services Directive) [2010] *OJ* L95/1, as amended by Directive (EU) 2018/1808 of the European Parliament and of the Council of 14 November 2018 amending Audiovisual Media Services Directive in view of changing market realities [2018] *OJ* L303/69; Directive 2011/93/EU of the European Parliament and of the Council of 13 December 2011 on combating the sexual abuse and sexual exploitation of children and child pornography, and replacing Council Framework Decision 2004/68/JHA [2011] *OJ* L335/1; Directive (EU) 2017/541 of the European Parliament and of the Council of 15 March 2017 on combating terrorism and replacing Council Framework Decision 2002/475/JHA and amending Council Decision 2005/671/JHA [2017] *OJ* L88/6; Regulation (EU) 2019/1148 of the European Parliament and of the Council of 20 June 2019 on the marketing and use of explosives precursors, amending Regulation (EC) No 1907/2006 and repealing Regulation (EU) No 98/2013 [2019] *OJ* L186/1.

25 Directive (EU) 2019/790 of the European Parliament and of the Council of 17 April 2019 on copyright and related rights in the Digital Single Market and amending Directives 96/9/EC and 2001/29/EC [2019] *OJ* L130/92.

26 See eg Gerald Spindler, 'Copyright Law and Internet Intermediaries Liability' in Tatiana-Eleni Synodinou and others (eds), *EU Internet Law in the Digital Era: Regulation and Enforcement* (Springer 2020) 3–26.

age self-regulatory efforts by hosting service providers.[27] The result of these developments is a significant legal fragmentation[28] that is expected to be dealt with through an update of the liability regime for the internet intermediaries which is a part of the recently published Digital Services Act package.[29]

2.2 Liability of collaborative economy platforms

Apart from the recent P2B Regulation,[30] which aims to protect professional users against unfair terms and practices applied by online platforms,[31] currently, there is no legislation in force at the EU level that would be specifically tailored to regulate online platforms or, more narrowly, collaborative economy platforms.[32] In the regulatory framework of the EU, one of the

27 Eg Commission Recommendation (EU) 2018/334 of 1 March 2018 on measures to effectively tackle illegal content online [2018] *OJ* L63/50.

28 For a discussion of the weaknesses of the current legal framework and of a potential reform, see Georgios N Yannopoulos, 'The Immunity of Internet Intermediaries Reconsidered?' in Mariarosaria Taddeo and Luciano Floridi (eds), *The Responsibilities of Online Service Providers* (Springer 2017) 43–60; Stalla-Bourdillon (n 22) 275–93; Gerald Spindler, 'Responsibility and Liability of Internet Intermediaries: Status Quo in the EU and Potential Reforms' in Tatiana-Eleni Synodinou and others (eds), *EU Internet Law: Regulation and Enforcement* (Springer 2017) 289–314; Anja Hoffman and Alessandro Gasparotti, 'Liability for Illegal Content Online: Weakness of the EU Legal Framework and Possible Plans of the EU Commission to Address Them in a "Digital Services Act"' (Centre for European Policy 2020) <www.cep.eu/en/eu-topics/details/cep/liability-for-illegal-content-online-cepstudy.html> accessed 16 July 2020; Tambiama Madiega, *Reform of the EU Liability Regime for Online Intermediaries: Background on the Forthcoming Digital Services Act* (European Parliamentary Research Service 2020). In this volume, see contribution by Matija Damjan in Chapter 2.

29 Shortly after the final manuscript of this volume was submitted to the publisher, in December 2020 the European Commission proposed two legislative initiatives jointly known as the 'Digital Services Act package': 'Proposal for a regulation of the European Parliament and of the Council on a Single Market For Digital Services (Digital Services Act) and amending Directive 2000/31/EC' COM (2020) 825 final (DSA), which includes the proposal of the new rules on the liability of providers of intermediary services in Arts 3–9 DSA, and 'Proposal for a regulation of the European Parliament and of the Council on contestable and fair markets in the digital sector (Digital Markets Act)' COM (2020) 842 final (DMA).

30 Regulation (EU) 2019/1150 of the European Parliament and of the Council of 20 June 2019 on promoting fairness and transparency for business users of online intermediation services [2019] *OJ* L186/57 (P2B Regulation).

31 For an assessment of the P2B Regulation, see Christoph Busch, 'Towards Fairness and Transparency in the Platform Economy? A First Look at the P2B Regulation' in Alberto De Franceschi and Reiner Schulze (eds), *Digital Revolution – New Challenges for Law* (CH Beck – Nomos 2020) 57–74.

32 However, the recently proposed DMA builds on the existing regime established with the P2B Regulation. The DMA is concerned with economic imbalances, unfair business practices by gatekeepers, and their negative consequences, such as the weakened contestability of digital platform markets.

key issues related to collaborative economy platforms[33] is whether their services can be qualified as 'information society services', as defined by the Information Society Services Directive,[34] and thus be subject to the legal regime established by the E-Commerce Directive, with a consequence that they cannot be subject to prior authorization or other equivalent market access requirements under the national law of EU Member States. Also, where service falls within that qualification, collaborative economy platforms that provide hosting services can benefit from safe harbours established by the E-Commerce Directive. Dealing with two of the most prominent examples of collaborative economy platforms – Uber and Airbnb – the ECJ famously decided that the intermediation service provided by Uber is inherently linked to a transport service and must be classified as 'a service in the field of transport' and not as an 'information society service',[35] whereas the intermediation service provided by Airbnb must be classified as an 'information society service' under E-Commerce Directive.[36]

In the absence of specific private law legislation at the supranational and national level, contract and tort law aspects of the triangular relationship between collaborative economy platform operators, service providers, and users are governed by the contractual framework established by the parties and the general rules of the applicable national law of obligations. One of the challenges to national legislators and courts is the issue of whether service providers should be construed as employees of the platform operator, rendering the platform operator vicariously liable for acts of service providers – for example, for an Uber driver's negligently caused accidents.[37]

33 For a definition of 'collaborative economy' as triangular business model enabling the exchange of services between service providers (whether private individuals acting as peers, or professional service providers) and users on an online platform, see European Commission, 'A European Agenda for the Collaborative Economy' (Communication) COM (2016) 356 final, 3 (EC Agenda for the Collaborative Economy); Hatzopoulos (n 3) 6–8; Marco Inglese, *Regulating the Collaborative Economy in the European Union Digital Single Market* (Springer 2019) 7ff.

34 Directive (EU) 2015/1535 of the European Parliament and of the Council of 9 September 2015 laying down a procedure for the provision of information in the field of technical regulations and of rules on Information Society services [2015] *OJ* L241/1 (Information Society Services Directive).

35 Case C-434/15 *Asociación Profesional Elite Taxi v Uber Systems Spain, SL* [2017] ECLI:EU:C:2017:981. See eg Philipp Hacker, 'UberPop, UberBlack, and the Regulation of Digital Platforms after the *Asociación Profesional Elite Taxi* Judgment of the CJEU' (2018) 14 *ERCL* 80.

36 Case C-390/18 *Criminal proceedings against X* [2019] ECLI:EU:C:2019:1112 (*Airbnb Ireland*). For more details on the *Airbnb Ireland* judgment, in this volume see contribution by Kosjenka Dumančić in Chapter 12.

37 For application of the vicarious liability concepts and the other tort law principles in common law in the context of collaborative economy, see eg Agnieszka A McPeak, 'Sharing Tort Liability in the New Sharing Economy' (2016) 49 *Conn L Rev* 171. On the inadequacy of traditional tort classifications to define liability in collaborative economy in light of the recent case law in the United States, see Cecilia G Vasquez, 'The Sharing

Platform operators usually present themselves as mere intermediaries between service providers and users, yet they are often directly involved in the relationship between the service provider and the user.[38] The role of the platform operator in the triangular relationship, especially where the platform appears from the user's perspective as the actual party to the service contract with the user, begs the question of whether the service provider's liability for non-performance should be supplemented, and to what extent, with a secondary liability of the platform operator towards the user.[39] Recently, a significant contribution to the debate on the relationship between platform operators and platform users was made with the publication of the ELI Model Rules on Online Platforms,[40] which *inter alia* include provisions on the liability of the platform operator for the non-performance of the contract concluded between the service provider and the user where the user can reasonably rely on the platform operator having a predominant influence over the supplier.[41]

2.3 *Liability for artificial intelligence and other emerging digital technologies*

Issues related to liability for artificial intelligence (AI) have raised a lot of scholarly attention in recent years.[42] The introduction of specific rules

---

Revolution: Changing Times Call for Clarifying Tort Liability' (2020) 80 *La L Rev* 623. For an analysis of the labour relations in the context of collaborative economy, see Hatzopoulos (n 3) 148ff. In this volume, for a view according to which intermediary platforms should be vicariously liable for wrongful acts committed by service providers, see contribution by Radosław Strugała in Chapter 3.

38 See eg the analysis of the private law relationships between Airbnb and its users by Vanessa Mak, 'Regulating Online Platforms – The Case of Airbnb' in Stefan Grundmann (ed), *European Contract Law in the Digital Age* (Intersentia 2018) 90–96.

39 See, especially, Christoph Busch and others, 'The Rise of the Platform Economy: A New Challenge for EU Consumer Law?' (2016) 5 *EuCML* 3, 7–9. See also Irina Domurath, 'Platforms as Contract Partners: *Uber* and Beyond' (2018) 25 *MJ* 565; Felix Maultzsch, 'Contractual Liability of Online Operators: European Proposals and Established Principles' (2018) 14 *ERCL* 209; Alberto De Franceschi, '*Uber Spain* and the "Identity Crisis" of Online Platforms' (2018) 7 *EuCML* 1; Piotr Tereszkiewicz, 'Digital Platforms: Regulation and Liability in EU Law' in Larry A DiMatteo, Michel Cannarsa, and Cristina Poncibò (eds), *The Cambridge Handbook of Smart Contracts, Blockchain Technology and Digital Platforms* (CUP 2019) 143–59.

40 European Law Institute, *Report of the European Law Institute: Model Rules on Online Platforms* (European Law Institute 2019) <www.europeanlawinstitute.eu/projects-publications/completed-projects-old/online-platforms> accessed 16 July 2020 (ELI Model Rules on Online Platforms). The ELI project is a continuation of the earlier work of the Research Group on the Law of Digital Services on a Discussion Draft of a Directive on Online Intermediary Platforms; see Research Group on the Law of Digital Services, 'Discussion Draft of a Directive on Online Intermediary Platforms' (2016) 5 *EuCML* 164.

41 See ELI Model Rules on Online Platforms, Art 20.

42 See, especially, contributions collected in Lohsee, Schulze, and Staudenmayer (eds), *Liability for Artificial Intelligence and the Internet of Things* (n 14). See also Ugo Pagallo, *The Laws of Robots: Crimes, Contracts, and Torts* (Springer 2013) 115–45; Ioannis Revolidis and Alan

on liability for AI and other emerging digital technologies is also heavily discussed in the EU. In 2017, in its 'Building a European Data Economy' Communication,[43] the European Commission stressed that its objective is to enhance legal certainty regarding liability in the context of emerging technologies. Soon after, the European Parliament adopted a resolution on 'Civil Law Rules on Robotics',[44] inviting the European Commission to propose a legislative instrument that would address the civil liability for damage caused by robots and AI. In 2018, in its 'Artificial Intelligence for Europe' Communication,[45] the Commission announced setting up an expert group to carry out an assessment of the current liability frameworks in light of AI and emerging technologies. An Expert Group on Liability and New Technologies was established in 2018 and divided into two formations: Product Liability Directive Formation (PLDF), tasked with the evaluation of the Product Liability Directive[46] in light of the new digital technologies, and New Technologies Formation (NTF), tasked with the assessment of the existing liability schemes.

NTF published its report in 2019,[47] which included its key findings (KF) on how liability regimes should be designed and changed to address the challenges presented by emerging digital technologies. NTF found, *inter alia*, that fault liability should continue to coexist with the strict liability for risks and defective products,[48] that for the purposes of liability it is not necessary to give autonomous systems a legal personality,[49] and that strict liability should

Dahi, 'The Peculiar Case of the Mushroom Picking Robot: Extra-contractual Liability in Robotics' in Marcelo Corrales, Mark Fenwick, and Nikolaus Forgó (eds), *Robotics, AI and the Future of Law* (Springer 2018) 57–79.

43 European Commission, 'Building a European Data Economy' (Communication) COM (2017) 9 final.

44 European Parliament, Resolution of 16 February 2017 with recommendations to the Commission on Civil Law Rules on Robotics (2015/2103(INL)) [2018] *OJ* C252/239.

45 European Commission, 'Artificial Intelligence for Europe' (Communication) COM (2018) 237 final.

46 Council Directive 85/374/EEC of 25 July 1985 on the approximation of the laws, regulations and administrative provisions of the Member States concerning liability for defective products [1985] *OJ* L210/29, as amended by Directive 1999/34/EC of the European Parliament and of the Council of 10 May 1999 [1999] *OJ* L141/20.

47 Expert Group on Liability and New Technologies – New Technologies Formation, *Liability for Artificial Intelligence and Other Emerging Digital Technologies* (European Commission 2019) (NTF Report). Key findings of the NTF Report are extensively discussed in articles published in a special issue of *JETL* devoted to the liability for emerging digital technologies: Bernhard A Koch, 'Liability for Emerging Digital Technologies: An Overview' (2020) 11 *JETL* 115; Piotr Machnikowski, 'Producers' Liability in the EC Expert Group Report on Liability for AI' (2020) 11 *JETL* 137; Christiane Wendehorst, 'Strict Liability for AI and Other Emerging Technologies' (2020) 11 *JETL* 150. In this volume, liability for AI is discussed in Chapter 6, by Nasir Muftić, where the key findings of the NTF Report are also examined.

48 NTF Report (n 47), KF 6.

49 NTF Report (n 47), KF 8.

lie with the person who is in control of the risk connected with the operation of emerging digital technologies and who benefits from their operation.[50]

In 2020, the European Commission published a package of documents on AI,[51] setting out policy options on how to achieve the objectives of promoting the uptake of AI and of addressing the risks associated with certain uses of AI. In October 2020, the European Parliament passed a resolution with recommendations to the Commission on a civil liability regime for AI,[52] requesting the Commission to submit a 'Proposal for a regulation of the European Parliament and of the Council on liability for the operation of Artificial Intelligence-systems'.[53] Most recently, the European Commission proposed the so-called Artificial Intelligence Act.[54]

2.4 Blockchain technology and blockchain-based smart contracts

The use of DLTs, including blockchain technology as its prime example, is currently not subject to any particular EU rules on the potential liability of DLT participants.[55] Yet DLTs also pose specific challenges to liability regimes. For example, a security breach or an error in code may cause damage

50 NTF Report (n 47), KF 10.

51 European Commission, 'Report on the Safety and Liability Implications of Artificial Intelligence, the Internet of Things and Robotics' COM (2020) 64 final; European Commission, 'White Paper on Artificial Intelligence – A European Approach to Excellence and Trust' COM (2020) 65 final; European Commission, 'A European Strategy for Data' (Communication) COM (2020) 66 final; European Commission, 'Shaping Europe's Digital Future' (Communication) COM (2020) 67 final.

52 European Parliament, Resolution of 20 October 2020 with recommendations to the Commission on a civil liability regime for artificial intelligence (2020/2014(INL)) (EP Proposal).

53 The EP Proposal, *inter alia*, includes a strict liability regime for 'high-risk' AI systems (Arts 4 to 7) and a fault-based liability regime for other AI systems (Arts 8 and 9). See Wendehorst (n 47).

54 European Commission, 'Proposal for a regulation of the European Parliament and of the Council laying down harmonised rules on artificial intelligence (Artificial Intelligence Act) and amending certain Union legislative acts' COM (2021) 206 final (AIA). The AIA was published in April 2021, after the final manuscript of this volume was submitted to the publisher.

55 However, recently, as part of the so-called 'Digital Finance Package', the European Commission issued proposals of two regulations related to DLTs: 'Proposal for a regulation of the European Parliament and of the Council on Markets in Crypto-assets, and amending Directive (EU) 2019/1937' COM (2020) 593 final (MiCA Regulation), which deals with crypto-assets that do not qualify as financial instruments, and 'Proposal for a regulation of the European Parliament and of the Council on a pilot regime for market infrastructures based on distributed ledger technology' COM (2020) 594 final, which deals with financial instruments in crypto-asset form. The proposed MiCA Regulation includes specific rules on liability of issuers of crypto-assets, asset-referenced tokens, and e-money tokens for damages caused to a holder of crypto-assets, asset-referenced tokens, and e-money tokens due to issuer's provision of incomplete, unfair, unclear, or misleading information in its crypto-asset white paper; see MiCA Regulation, Arts 14, 22, and 47.

or loss to users of blockchain system or third parties, raising the questions of whether operators and other participants in blockchain are liable, who among them should bear the liability, and whether such liability is a contractual liability or liability in tort.[56]

Whereas in the EU legal framework there is yet no specific regulation relating to validity and enforceability of the blockchain-based smart contracts,[57] in some EU Member States enforceability of smart contracts was recently secured with the introduction of special legislation under which smart contracts are deemed to be equivalent to traditional written contracts under certain conditions.[58]

In recent years, much of the academic debate relating to contract law issues of smart contracts concerned the questions of what smart contracts are, whether they are legally enforceable agreements, how they fit in the existing contract law framework, and whether the traditional contract law is adequate to address the challenges posed by them, or whether it needs to be modified and adapted to that purpose.[59] The literature on the subject ranges from announcing 'the end of classic contract law'[60] to concluding that 'properly decrypted, the promised blockchain legal revolution appears to be a damp, and regrettably widely distributed, squib',[61] and that 'contrary to popular

56 For a comprehensive analysis of the potential liability of DLT participants, see especially Dirk A Zetzsche, Ross P Buckley, and Douglas W Arner, 'The Distributed Liability of Distributed Ledgers: Legal Risks of Blockchain' [2018] *U Ill L Rev* 1361. In this volume, liability for malfunctions of blockchain-base share registers and share trading platforms is discussed in Chapter 5 by Marcin Mazgaj.

57 However, the European Parliament has recently adopted two resolutions asking the European Commission to assess the development and use of DLTs, to provide guidance regarding the questions of validity and enforcement of smart contracts, and to take legislative initiatives if concrete gaps are identified: European Parliament, Resolution of 20 October 2020 with recommendations to the Commission on the Digital Services Act: Improving the functioning of the Single Market (2020/2018(INL)); European Parliament, Resolution of 20 October 2020 with recommendations to the Commission on a Digital Services Act: adapting commercial and civil law rules for commercial entities operating online (2020/2019(INL)).

58 See eg in Italy: Law Decree 135, 'Urgent provisions on support and simplification for businesses and the public administration' (*Decreto-legge* 135, '*Disposizioni urgenti in materia di sostegno e semplificazione per le imprese e per la pubblica amministrazione*') *GU* 290 of 14 December 2018, converted into statute with, and as amended by *Legge* 12 of 11 February 2019, *GU* 36 of 12 February 2019.

59 In this volume, these issues are discussed in Chapter 7, by Mateja Durovic, and in Chapter 10, by Dino Gliha and Sandra Marković, while Chapter 9, by Andrea Faraci and Luigi Lonardo, aims to show that contract law challenges of smart contracts can be resolved through millenary concept of fairness. A comprehensive analysis of the existing common law doctrines is given in Chapter 8, by Nicholas Liu, which deals with the 'contracting problem': uncertainty as to the doctrinal explanation of how algorithmic contracts are formed.

60 See Alexander Savelyev, 'Contract Law 2.0: "Smart" Contracts as the Beginning of the End of Classic Contract Law' (2017) 26 *I & CTL* 116.

61 Low and Mik (n 5) 175.

claims, "smart contracts" do not create new legal problems and that questions regarding their enforceability or validity are inherently misplaced'.[62,63] A consensus seems to be reached that the term 'smart contracts', from the contract law point of view, is a misnomer, as smart contracts are rather a form of a computer code designed to automatically execute a transaction upon the occurrence of a trigger event, and that they are not necessarily legally binding. To avoid problems with the use of the term 'smart contract', the term 'algorithmic contract' was proposed in the literature to describe legally enforceable agreements formed by an algorithm.[64]

62 Eliza Mik, 'Smart Contracts: A Requiem' (2019) 36 *JCL* 70.

63 The most relevant legal literature includes: Joshua AT Fairfield, 'Smart Contracts, Bitcoin Bots, and Consumer Protection' (2014) 71 *Wash & Lee L Rev Online* 35 <https://scholarlycommons.law.wlu.edu/wlulr-online/vol71/iss2/3/> accessed 16 July 2020; Aaron Wright and Primavera De Filippi, 'Decentralized Blockchain Technology and the Rise of *Lex Cryptographia*' (10 March 2015) <https://ssrn.com/abstract=2580664> accessed 16 July 2020; Eliza Mik, 'Smart Contracts: Terminology, Technical Limitations and Real World Complexity' (2017) 9 *Law Innov Technol* 269; Philipp Paech, 'The Governance of Blockchain Financial Networks' (2017) 80 *MLR* 1073; Max Raskin, 'The Law and Legality of Smart Contracts' (2017) 1 *Geo L Tech Rev* 305; Reyes (n 4); Kevin Werbach and Nicolas Cornell, 'Contracts *ex machina*' (2017) 67 *Duke LJ* 313; Kevin Werbach, *The Blockchain and the New Architecture of Trust* (MIT Press 2018) 63–67; De Filippi and Wright (n 4); Mateja Durovic and André Janssen, 'Formation of Smart Contracts under Contract Law' in Larry A DiMatteo, Michel Cannarsa, and Cristina Poncibò (eds), *The Cambridge Handbook of Smart Contracts, Blockchain Technology and Digital Platforms* (CUP 2019) 61–79; Finck (n 4); James Grimmelmann, 'All Smart Contracts are Ambiguous' (2019) 2 *JL & Innovation* 1; Jeffrey M Lipshaw, 'The Persistence of "Dumb" Contracts' (2019) 2 (1) *Stanford J Blockchain L & Pol'y* 1; Mik, 'Blockchains' (n 5); Mik, 'Smart Contracts' (n 62); Florian Möslein, 'Legal Boundaries of Blockchain Technologies: Smart Contracts as Self-Help?' in Alberto De Franceschi and Reiner Schulze (eds), *Digital Revolution – New Challenges for Law: Data Protection, Artificial Intelligence, Smart Products, Blockchain Technology and Virtual Currencies* (CH Beck – Nomos 2019); Eric Tjong Tin Tai, 'Challenges of Smart Contracts: Implementing Excuses' in Larry A DiMatteo, Michel Cannarsa, and Cristina Poncibò (eds), *The Cambridge Handbook of Smart Contracts, Blockchain Technology and Digital Platforms* (CUP 2019) 80–101; Rolf H Weber, 'Smart Contracts: Do We Need New Legal Rules?' in Alberto De Franceschi and Reiner Schulze (eds), *Digital Revolution – New Challenges for Law: Data Protection, Artificial Intelligence, Smart Products, Blockchain Technology and Virtual Currencies* (CH Beck – Nomos 2019); Low and Mik (n 5); Eliza Mik, 'The Resilience of Contract Law in Light of Technological Change' in Furmston M (ed), *The Future of the Law of Contract* (Routledge 2020); Pietro Sirena and Francesco Paolo Patti, 'Smart Contract and Automation of Private Relationships' (2020) *Bocconi Legal Studies Research Paper* 3662402 <https://ssrn.com/abstract=3662402> accessed 1 September 2020.

64 The term was coined by Lauren Henry Scholz who considers algorithmic contracts as contracts in which an algorithm determines the rights and responsibilities of a party by acting as either a gap-filler or a negotiator in the process of contract formation: Lauren Henry Scholz, 'Algorithmic Contracts' (2017) 20 *Stan Tech L Rev* 128. See also Lauren Henry Scholz, 'Algorithmic Contracts and Consumer Privacy' in Larry A DiMatteo, Michel Cannarsa, and Cristina Poncibò (eds), *The Cambridge Handbook of Smart Contracts, Blockchain Technology and Digital Platforms* (CUP 2019) 251–68. For a proposal that smart contracts are better thought of as 'bot' or 'automated' agreements, see Deborah R Gerhardt and David Thaw, 'Bot Contracts' (2020) 62 *Ariz L Rev* 877. Although it is not related to

3. Structure and contributions

The book is structured into three parts. The first part, consisting of five chapters, deals with the challenges the digital technologies pose to tort law. The second part, consisting of four chapters, is concerned with the contract law challenges of smart contracts. The third part, consisting of two chapters, addresses digital contracts as contracts of adhesion. Each of the chapters addresses different aspects of the above-presented themes and issues.

3.1 Digital technologies and other contemporary challenges in tort law

Chapter 2, by Matija Damjan, focuses in more detail on the regime of the internet intermediaries' liability for illegal online content in the EU. The requirements of the E-Commerce Directive under which the internet intermediaries may be exempted from liability are analyzed in light of the several landmark judgments rendered by the ECJ. The chapter particularly discusses the requirement of expeditious action upon receiving a takedown request, the form of a takedown request, and dealing with unfounded takedown requests. Relating to the question of whether the internet intermediary's liability is fault-based or strict, which is to be answered in the national laws of Member States, Damjan argues that the E-Commerce Directive is hinting at fault-based liability although not mandating it. His analysis of Slovenian and Croatian law shows that legislation in these Member States cannot be interpreted as stipulating strict liability of the internet intermediaries. The chapter also addresses the issue of liability for hyperlinks which was not resolved by the E-Commerce Directive, as well as the new regime of civil liability of online content-sharing service providers under the Directive on Copyright in the Digital Single Market.

Chapter 3, by Radosław Strugała, promotes the view according to which collaborative economy platforms should be vicariously liable for wrongful acts committed by service providers. Strugała illustrates his point with the example of Uber, referring to civil law cases, especially in the United States, where plaintiffs argued that Uber should be held liable for vehicular accidents caused by Uber drivers, or for the harms caused to passengers who were assaulted or sexually harassed by Uber drivers. The traditional view on vicarious liability is presented, particularly the requirement of the wrongdoer's act occurring in the course of ordinary employment. The chapter continues to analyze new approaches to vicarious liability in recent case law, both in

---

the blockchain-based smart contracts, see also the concept of 'self-driving contract' as an agreement where the parties set general *ex ante* objectives that are then translated through use of machine-driven analytics and artificial intelligence into specific terms at the time of performance which are based on information gathered after the parties execute the initial agreement: Anthony Casey and Anthony Niblett, 'Self-Driving Contracts' (2017) 43 *J Corp L* 1.

common law and civil law jurisdictions, where a tendency exists to relax the scope of employment requirement, as well as to extend the scope of vicarious liability to relationships with independent contractors. Strugała argues that the new approaches to vicarious liability fit well in the sharing economy context.

Chapter 4, by Christian A Witting, deals with tort law issues in the corporate group context and addresses how the law on extended liability should be reformed. The chapter first considers the ways in which a corporate group might engage in the practice of judgment-proofing or the structuring of group companies in order to protect major assets while avoiding payment of tort liability costs. As the interactions between corporate group companies are becoming automated in nature with the use of smart contracts and blockchain technology, it becomes more difficult to identify fault and allocate blame under traditional tort law rules and doctrines. The chapter examines the responses of common law courts to the problems of corporate groups, including their efforts at judgment-proofing, and explores why common law rules have been inadequate for extending liability by utilization of veil-piercing, the tort of negligence, and the doctrine of joint tortfeasance. The chapter then turns to the analysis of the significant attempts made by legislatures to deal with the judgment-proofing problem, such as the United States' Oil Pollution Act 1990. The chapter suggests how the existing common law liability regime might be developed to deal with the problems of corporate groups, judgment-proofing, and unsatisfied liability claims. Witting argues for a greater role of directed, strict liability doctrines and their application both vertically between parent and subsidiary companies and horizontally between group subsidiaries.

Chapter 5, by Marcin Mazgaj, is aimed at the legal analysis of benefits and risks involved in blockchain-based registration and trade of shares. The chapter identifies several problems related to share registration and share trading that could be solved with the application of DLT, namely the non-traceability of shares and the lack of transparency in trade of shares. The chapter points out the key features of DLT that make it a convenient instrument to solve the identified problems. Addressing the law of obligations aspects of the blockchain-based share registration and share trading, a reassessment of the general rules on the consequences of invalidity of a contract with respect to agreements concluded or registered within distributed ledgers is suggested as in blockchain-based ledgers it is practically impossible to restore the previous state of the ledger. Another key issue is the liability for malfunctions of the code governing the blockchain-based stock ledgers which is so far not regulated in the jurisdictions where specific legislation related to blockchain-based stock ledgers has been adopted (e.g. Delaware, Vermont, France, and Poland). Mazgaj argues that strict liability of the operators of blockchain-based platforms for false entries in the stock ledger should be introduced through legislative interventions, as well as that the possibilities of limiting operator's liability should be reduced or even excluded.

Chapter 6, by Nasir Muftić, presents the state of affairs in the EU concerning the liability of AI. First, the chapter examines the current legal framework in the EU, where tort law is not in principle harmonized, except in the field of product liability. The classic bases of liability (fault-based liability, strict liability, vicarious liability, product liability) that exist in the national laws of Member States are compared in light of the challenges the functional characteristics of AI pose to the current liability regimes. The chapter especially addresses the issues of the identification of the most appropriate actor to be held liable for activities of AI, the appropriate basis of liability, the level and scope of possible regulation, and the inadequacy of the Product Liability Directive to deal with the challenges of AI. The possible solutions to the issues raised and the current proposals made in the recent NTF Report are examined in the last part of the chapter.

3.2 Contract law challenges posed by smart contracts

Chapter 7, by Mateja Durovic, discusses whether traditional contract law has been challenged by the rise of smart contracts. Durovic argues that smart contracts are 'neither smart', as they can only be used for straightforward transactions where simple 'if' and 'then' parameters are used, 'nor they are contracts in the legal sense', as they are only a form of new technology used to secure the execution of promises established through a legal contract. The chapter examines the notion of smart contracts, their history, and relevance from the standpoint of contract law and points out the main differences between smart contracts and legal contracts.

Chapter 8, by Nicholas Liu, deals with the 'contracting problem' – uncertainty as to the doctrinal explanation of how algorithmic contracts are formed. The chapter begins with a discussion of the notion and types of algorithmic contracts. Liu explains that the contracting problem arises only concerning 'active contract forming mechanisms' which execute transactions without human intervention and that his analysis is focused on those algorithmic contracts where the algorithm is 'deterministic' in the sense that, once programmed, it will always produce the same output given the same input. The chapter shows that the existing conventional and statutory framework in the common law world, outside the United States and Canada, does not solve the contracting problem, and continues to examine the nature and the scope of the contracting problem as a matter of common law doctrine. Liu argues that the requirement of the agreement is the core of the contracting problem and undertakes a comprehensive analysis of the existing common law doctrines which proves that the contracting problem is solvable with the existing tools of contract law: the solution requires some reinterpretation of authorities, but no true extension of the law.

Chapter 9, by Andrea Faraci and Luigi Lonardo, aims to show that contract law problems related to smart contracts are not new in their nature and that the millenary concept of fairness as understood by Aristotle can be successfully applied to at least some of them. The chapter discusses the concepts of *epieikeia* and *aequitas* and provides an overview of the contemporary perspectives on equity. The issues of classification, formation, and execution of smart contracts are singled out to illustrate the applications of equity and justice to contract law.

Chapter 10, by Dino Gliha and Sandra Marković, presents the concept, main features, and areas of application of smart contracts. The authors argue that the existing contract law in civil law jurisdictions is well equipped to deal with the issues related to smart contracts and that thus there is no need for special regulation of smart contracts. However, a soft law document providing for uniform terminology and definitions of general concept and processes involved in smart contracting is perceived as most welcome. Authors also point to the human rights dimension of smart contracts which they consider to be neglected in the debate so far.

3.3 Digital contracts, accounts, and services

Chapter 11, by Dubravka Klasiček, deals with the terms of service (TOS) agreements concluded with online service providers as digital contracts of adhesion. The chapter starts with a discussion on contracts of adhesion in general and an examination of the Croatian contract law rules relating to contracts of adhesion. As TOS agreements are regularly concluded as wrap contracts, the chapter continues to discuss the various contracting forms of wrap contracts and addresses the no-reading problem. Klasiček specifically discusses the issue of inheritability of digital accounts, commonly prohibited in the TOS of various online service providers, and also examines the nature of the rights users have over digital content under the TOS agreements.

Chapter 12, by Kosjenka Dumančić, addresses TOS agreements based on the example of Airbnb. The chapter discusses regulatory issues related to the collaborative economy and examines the Airbnb business model. The chapter points to the issues of qualification of services provided by digital platforms as 'information society services' within the meaning of the Information Society Services Directive and the E-Commerce Directive, and also highlights the main points of the ECJ judgment in the *Airbnb Ireland* case.

Bibliography

Aggarwal N and others (eds), *Autonomous Systems and the Law* (CH Beck – Nomos 2019)

Barfield W (ed), *The Cambridge Handbook of the Law of Algorithms* (CUP 2020) [DOI: https://doi.org/10.1017/9781108680844]

Bower JL and Christensen CM, 'Disruptive Technologies: Catching the Wave' [1995] (1) *Harv Bus Rev* 43

Brown B, 'Fortifying the Safe Harbors: Reevaluating the DMCA in a Web 2.0 World' (2008) 23 *Berkeley Tech LJ* 437 [DOI: https://doi.org/10.15779/Z38K68G]

Busch C, 'Towards Fairness and Transparency in the Platform Economy? A First Look at the P2B Regulation' in De Franceschi A and Schulze R (eds), *Digital Revolution – New Challenges for Law* (CH Beck – Nomos 2020) [DOI: https://doi.org/10.17104/9783406759048-57]

——— and others, 'The Rise of the Platform Economy: A New Challenge for EU Consumer Law?' (2016) 5 *EuCML* 3

——— and De Franceschi A (eds), *Algorithmic Regulation and Personalized Law: A Handbook* (Hart Publishing – CH Beck – Nomos 2020)

Buterin V, 'A Next-Generation Smart Contract and Decentralized Application Platform' (Ethereum: White Paper, 2013) <https://ethereum.org/en/whitepaper> accessed 9 July 2020

Casey A and Niblett A, 'Self-Driving Contracts' (2017) 43 *J Corp L* 1

Corrales M, Fenwick M, and Forgó N (eds), *Robotics, AI and the Future of Law* (Springer 2018) [DOI: https://doi.org/10.1007/978-981-13-2874-9]

De Caria R, 'Definitions of Smart Contracts: Between Law and Code' in DiMatteo LA, Cannarsa M, and Poncibò C (eds), *The Cambridge Handbook of Smart Contracts, Blockchain Technology and Digital Platforms* (CUP 2019) [DOI: https://doi.org/10.1017/9781108592239.002]

De Filippi P and Wright A, *Blockchain and the Law: The Rule of Code* (HUP 2018) [DOI: https://doi.org/10.2307/j.ctv2867sp]

De Franceschi A (ed), *European Contract Law and the Digital Single Market: The Implications of the Digital Revolution* (Intersentia 2016) [DOI: https://doi.org/10.1017/9781780685212]

——— '*Uber Spain* and the "Identity Crisis" of Online Platforms' (2018) 7 *EuCML* 1

——— and Schulze R (eds), *Digital Revolution – New Challenges for Law: Data Protection, Artificial Intelligence, Smart Products, Blockchain Technology and Virtual Currencies* (CH Beck – Nomos 2019) [DOI: https://doi.org/10.17104/9783406759048]

DiMatteo LA, Cannarsa M, and Poncibò C (eds), *The Cambridge Handbook of Smart Contracts, Blockchain Technology and Digital Platforms* (CUP 2019) [DOI: https://doi.org/10.1017/9781108592239]

DiNucci D, 'Fragmented Future' (1999) 53 (4) *Print* 32

Dinwoodie GB (ed), *Secondary Liability of Internet Service Providers* (Springer 2017) [DOI: https://doi.org/10.1007/978-3-319-55030-5]

Domurath I, 'Platforms as Contract Partners: *Uber* and Beyond' (2018) 25 *MJ* 565 [DOI: https://doi.org/10.1177/1023263X18806485]

Durovic M and Janssen A, 'Formation of Smart Contracts under Contract Law' in DiMatteo LA, Cannarsa M, and Poncibò C (eds), *The Cambridge Handbook of Smart Contracts, Blockchain Technology and Digital Platforms* (CUP 2019) [DOI: https://doi.org/10.1017/9781108592239.004]

Ebers M and Navas S (ed), *Algorithms and Law* (CUP 2020) [DOI: https://doi.org/10.1017/9781108347846]

European Commission, 'A European Agenda for the Collaborative Economy' (Communication) COM (2016) 356 final

——— 'Building a European Data Economy' (Communication) COM (2017) 9 final

——— 'Artificial Intelligence for Europe' (Communication) COM (2018) 237 final

——— 'Report on the Safety and Liability Implications of Artificial Intelligence, the Internet of Things and Robotics' COM (2020) 64 final

——— 'White Paper on Artificial Intelligence – A European Approach to Excellence and Trust' COM (2020) 65 final

——— 'A European Strategy for Data' (Communication) COM (2020) 66 final
——— 'Shaping Europe's Digital Future' (Communication) COM (2020) 67 final
——— 'Proposal for a regulation of the European Parliament and of the Council on Markets in Crypto-assets, and amending Directive (EU) 2019/1937' COM (2020) 593 final
——— 'Proposal for a regulation of the European Parliament and of the Council on a pilot regime for market infrastructures based on distributed ledger technology' COM (2020) 594 final
——— 'Proposal for a regulation of the European Parliament and of the Council on a Single Market For Digital Services (Digital Services Act) and amending Directive 2000/31/EC' COM (2020) 825 final
——— 'Proposal for a regulation of the European Parliament and of the Council on contestable and fair markets in the digital sector (Digital Markets Act)' COM (2020) 842 final
——— 'Proposal for a regulation of the European Parliament and of the Council laying down harmonised rules on artificial intelligence (Artificial Intelligence Act) and amending certain Union legislative acts' COM (2021) 206 final
European Law Institute, *Report of the European Law Institute: Model Rules on Online Platforms* (European Law Institute 2019) <www.europeanlawinstitute.eu/projects-publications/completed-projects-old/online-platforms> accessed 16 July 2020
European Parliament, Resolution of 16 February 2017 with recommendations to the Commission on Civil Law Rules on Robotics (2015/2103(INL)) [2018] *OJ* C252/239
——— Resolution of 20 October 2020 with recommendations to the Commission on a civil liability regime for artificial intelligence (2020/2014(INL))
——— Resolution of 20 October 2020 with recommendations to the Commission on the Digital Services Act: Improving the functioning of the Single Market (2020/2018(INL))
——— Resolution of 20 October 2020 with recommendations to the Commission on a Digital Services Act: adapting commercial and civil law rules for commercial entities operating online (2020/2019(INL))
Expert Group on Liability and New Technologies – New Technologies Formation, *Liability for Artificial Intelligence and Other Emerging Digital Technologies* (European Commission 2019) [DOI: https://doi.org/10.2838/25362]
Fairfield JAT, 'Smart Contracts, Bitcoin Bots, and Consumer Protection' (2014) 71 *Wash & Lee L Rev Online* 35 <https://scholarlycommons.law.wlu.edu/wlulr-online/vol71/iss2/3> accessed 16 July 2020
Finck M, *Blockchain Regulation and Governance in Europe* (CUP 2018) [DOI: https://doi.org/10.1017/9781108609708]
Frosio G (ed), *The Oxford Handbook of Online Intermediary Liability* (OUP 2020)
Furmston M (ed), *The Future of the Law of Contract* (Routledge 2020) [DOI: https://doi.org/10.4324/9780429056550]
Gerhardt DR and Thaw D, 'Bot Contracts' (2020) 62 *Ariz L Rev* 877
Grimmelmann J, 'All Smart Contracts are Ambiguous' (2019) 2 *JL & Innovation* 1
Grundmann S (ed), *European Contract Law in the Digital Age* (Intersentia 2018) [DOI: https://doi.org/10.1017/9781780686431]
Hacker P, 'UberPop, UberBlack, and the Regulation of Digital Platforms after the *Asociación Profesional Elite Taxi* Judgment of the CJEU' (2018) 14 *ERCL* 80 [DOI: https://doi.org/10.1515/ercl-2018-1005]

——— and others (eds), *Regulating Blockchain: Techno-Social and Legal Challenges* (OUP 2019)

Hatzopoulos V, *The Collaborative Economy and EU Law* (Hart Publishing 2018) [DOI: https://doi.org/10.5040/9781509917167]

Hoffman A and Gasparotti A, 'Liability for Illegal Content Online: Weakness of the EU Legal Framework and Possible Plans of the EU Commission to Address Them in a "Digital Services Act"' (Centre for European Policy 2020) <www.cep.eu/en/eu-topics/details/cep/liability-for-illegal-content-online-cepstudy.html> accessed 16 July 2020

Inglese M, *Regulating the Collaborative Economy in the European Union Digital Single Market* (Springer 2019) [DOI: https://doi.org/10.1007/978-3-030-30040-1]

Lipshaw JM, 'The Persistence of "Dumb" Contracts' (2019) 2 (1) *Stanford J Blockchain L & Pol'y* 1

Kaal WA, 'Blockchain-Based Corporate Governance' (2021) 4 *Stanford J Blockchain L & Pol'y* 1 <https://ssrn.com/abstract=3441904> accessed 16 July 2020

——— and Vermeulen EPM, 'How to Regulate Disruptive Innovation – From Facts to Data' (2017) 57 *Jurimetrics* 169 [DOI: https://doi.org/10.2139/ssrn.2808044]

Koch BA, 'Liability for Emerging Digital Technologies: An Overview' (2020) 11 *JETL* 115 [DOI: https://doi.org/10.1515/jetl-2020-0137]

Lohsee S, Schulze R, and Staudenmayer D (eds), *Trading Data in the Digital Economy: Legal Concepts and Tools: Münster Colloquia on EU Law and the Digital Economy III* (Hart Publishing – Nomos 2017) [DOI: https://doi.org/10.5771/9783845288185]

——— Schulze R, and Staudenmayer D (eds), *Liability for Artificial Intelligence and the Internet of Things: Münster Colloquia on EU Law and the Digital Economy IV* (Hart Publishing – Nomos 2019) [DOI: https://doi.org/10.5771/9783845294797]

——— Schulze R, and Staudenmayer D (eds), *Data as Counter-Performance – Contract Law 2.0? Münster Colloquia on EU Law and the Digital Economy V* (Hart Publishing – Nomos 2020) [DOI: https://doi.org/10.5771/9783748908531]

Low KFK and Mik E, 'Pause the Blockchain Legal Revolution' (2020) 69 *ICLQ* 135 [DOI: https://doi.org/10.1017/S0020589319000502]

Machnikowski P, 'Producers' Liability in the EC Expert Group Report on Liability for AI' (2020) 11 *JETL* 137 [DOI: https://doi.org/10.1515/jetl-2020-0138]

Madiega T, *Reform of the EU Liability Regime for Online Intermediaries: Background on the Forthcoming Digital Services Act* (European Parliamentary Research Service 2020) [DOI: https://doi.org/10.2861/08522]

Mak V, 'Regulating Online Platforms – The Case of Airbnb' in Grundmann S (ed), *European Contract Law in the Digital Age* (Intersentia 2018) [DOI: https://doi.org/10.1017/9781780686431.003]

——— Tjong Tjin Tai E, and Berlee A (eds), *Research Handbook in Data Science and Law* (Edward Elgar 2018) [DOI: https://doi.org/10.4337/9781788111300]

Maultzsch F, 'Contractual Liability of Online Operators: European Proposals and Established Principles' (2018) 14 *ERCL* 209 [DOI: https://doi.org/10.1515/ercl-2018-1013]

McPeak AA, 'Sharing Tort Liability in the New Sharing Economy' (2016) 49 *Conn L Rev* 171

Mik E, 'Smart Contracts: Terminology, Technical Limitations and Real World Complexity' (2017) 9 *Law Innov Technol* 269 [DOI: https://doi.org/10.1080/17579961.2017.1378468]

——— 'Blockchains: A Technology for Decentralized Marketplaces' in DiMatteo LA, Cannarsa M, and Poncibò C (eds), *The Cambridge Handbook of Smart Contracts, Blockchain Technology and Digital Platforms* (CUP 2019) [DOI: https://doi.org/10.1017/9781108592239.009]

——— 'Smart Contracts: A Requiem' (2019) 36 *JCL* 70

——— 'The Resilience of Contract Law in Light of Technological Change' in Furmston M (ed), *The Future of the Law of Contract* (Routledge 2020) [DOI: https://doi.org/10.4324/9780429056550-7]

Möslein F, 'Legal Boundaries of Blockchain Technologies: Smart Contracts as Self-Help?' in De Franceschi A and Schulze R (eds), *Digital Revolution – New Challenges for Law: Data Protection, Artificial Intelligence, Smart Products, Blockchain Technology and Virtual Currencies* (CH Beck – Nomos 2019) [DOI: https://doi.org/10.17104/9783406759048-313]

Nakamoto S, 'Bitcoin: A Peer-to-Peer Electronic Cash System' (*Bitcoin Project: Introduction: White Paper*, 31 October 2008) <https://bitcoin.org/en/bitcoin-paper> accessed 9 July 2020

O'Reilly T, 'What is Web 2.0: Design Patterns and Business Models for the Next Generation of Software' (O'Reilly Media, 30 September 2005) <www.oreilly.com/pub/a/web2/archive/what-is-web-20.html> accessed 9 July 2020

Paech P, 'The Governance of Blockchain Financial Networks' (2017) 80 *MLR* 1073 [DOI: https://doi.org/10.1111/1468-2230.12303]

Pagallo U, *The Laws of Robots: Crimes, Contracts, and Torts* (Springer 2013) [DOI: https://doi.org/10.1007/978-94-007-6564-1]

Peguera M, 'The DMCA Safe Harbors and Their European Counterparts: A Comparative Analysis of Some Common Problems' (2009) 32 *Colum JL & Arts* 481

Raskin M, 'The Law and Legality of Smart Contracts' (2017) 1 *Geo L Tech Rev* 305

Research Group on the Law of Digital Services, 'Discussion Draft of a Directive on Online Intermediary Platforms' (2016) 5 *EuCML* 164

Revolidis I and Dahi A, 'The Peculiar Case of the Mushroom Picking Robot: Extra-contractual Liability in Robotics' in Corrales M, Fenwick M, and Forgó N (eds), *Robotics, AI and the Future of Law* (Springer 2018) [DOI: https://doi.org/10.1007/978-981-13-2874-9_3]

Reyes CL, 'Conceptualizing Cryptolaw' (2017) 96 *Neb L Rev* 384 [DOI: https://doi.org/10.2139/ssrn.2914103]

Riordan J, *The Liability of Internet Intermediaries* (OUP 2016)

Rochet JC and Tirole J, 'Platform Competition in Two-Sided Markets' (2003) 1 *J Eur Econ Assoc* 990 [DOI: https://doi.org/10.1162/154247603322493212]

Savelyev A, 'Contract Law 2.0: "Smart" Contracts as the Beginning of the End of Classic Contract Law' (2017) 26 *I & CTL* 116 [DOI: https://doi.org/10.1080/13600834.2017.1301036]

Scholz LH, 'Algorithmic Contracts' (2017) 20 *Stan Tech L Rev* 128

——— 'Algorithmic Contracts and Consumer Privacy' in DiMatteo LA, Cannarsa M, and Poncibò C (eds), *The Cambridge Handbook of Smart Contracts, Blockchain Technology and Digital Platforms* (CUP 2019) [DOI: https://doi.org/10.1017/9781108592239.014]

Schulze R and Staudenmayer D (eds), *Digital Revolution: Challenges for Contract Law in Practice* (Hart Publishing – Nomos 2016) [DOI: https://doi.org/10.5771/9783845273488]

——— Staudenmayer D, and Lohsee S (eds), *Contracts for the Supply of Digital Content: Regulatory Challenges and Gaps: Münster Colloquia on EU Law and the Digital Economy II* (Hart Publishing – Nomos 2017) [DOI: https://doi.org/10.5771/9783845281391]

Schwab K, 'The Fourth Industrial Revolution: What It Means and How to Respond' *Foreign Affairs* (Online, 12 December 2015) <www.foreignaffairs.com/articles/2015-12-12/fourth-industrial-revolution> accessed 9 July 2020

Sirena P and Patti FP, 'Smart Contract and Automation of Private Relationships' (2020) *Bocconi Legal Studies Research Paper* 3662402 <https://ssrn.com/abstract=3662402> accessed 1 September 2020

Spindler G, 'Internet Intermediary Liability Reloaded: The New German Act on Responsibility of Social Networks and its (In-) Compatibility with European Law' (2017) 8 *JIPITEC* 166 <www.jipitec.eu/issues/jipitec-8-2-2017/4567> accessed 16 July 2020

——— 'Responsibility and Liability of Internet Intermediaries: Status Quo in the EU and Potential Reforms' in Synodinou TE and others (eds), *EU Internet Law: Regulation and Enforcement* (Springer 2017) [DOI: https://doi.org/10.1007/978-3-319-64955-9_12]

——— 'Copyright Law and Internet Intermediaries Liability' in Synodinou TE and others (eds), *EU Internet Law in the Digital Era: Regulation and Enforcement* (Springer 2020) [DOI: https://doi.org/10.1007/978-3-030-25579-4_1]

Stalla-Bourdillon S, 'Internet Intermediaries as Responsible Actors? Why It Is Time to Rethink the E-Commerce Directive as Well' in Taddeo M and Floridi L (eds), *The Responsibilities of Online Service Providers* (Springer 2017) [DOI: https://doi.org/10.1007/978-3-319-47852-4_15]

Synodinou TE and others (eds), *EU Internet Law: Regulation and Enforcement* (Springer 2017) [DOI: https://doi.org/10.1007/978-3-319-64955-9]

——— and others (eds), *EU Internet Law in the Digital Era: Regulation and Enforcement* (Springer 2020) [DOI: https://doi.org/10.1007/978-3-030-25579-4]

Szabo N, 'Smart Contracts' (1994) <www.fon.hum.uva.nl/rob/Courses/InformationInSpeech/CDROM/Literature/LOTwinterschool2006/szabo.best.vwh.net/smart.contracts.html> accessed 16 July 2020

Tereszkiewicz P, 'Digital Platforms: Regulation and Liability in EU Law' in DiMatteo LA, Cannarsa M, and Poncibò C (eds), *The Cambridge Handbook of Smart Contracts, Blockchain Technology and Digital Platforms* (CUP 2019) [DOI: https://doi.org/10.1017/9781108592239.008]

Tjong Tin Tai E, 'Challenges of Smart Contracts: Implementing Excuses' in DiMatteo LA, Cannarsa M, and Poncibò C (eds), *The Cambridge Handbook of Smart Contracts, Blockchain Technology and Digital Platforms* (CUP 2019) [DOI: https://doi.org/10.1017/9781108592239.005]

Twigg-Flesner C, 'Disruptive Technology – Disrupted Law? How the Digital Revolution Affects (Contract) Law' in De Franceschi A (ed), *European Contract Law and the Digital Single Market: The Implications of the Digital Revolution* (Intersentia 2016) [DOI: https://doi.org/10.1017/9781780685212.003]

Vasquez CG, 'The Sharing Revolution: Changing Times Call for Clarifying Tort Liability' (2020) 80 *La L Rev* 623

Weber RH, 'Smart Contracts: Do We Need New Legal Rules?' in De Franceschi A and Schulze R (eds), *Digital Revolution – New Challenges for Law: Data Protection, Artificial Intelligence, Smart Products, Blockchain Technology and Virtual Currencies* (CH Beck – Nomos 2019) [DOI: https://doi.org/10.17104/9783406759048-299]

Wendehorst C, 'Strict Liability for AI and Other Emerging Technologies' (2020) 11 *JETL* 150 [DOI: https://doi.org/10.1515/jetl-2020-0140]

Werbach K, *The Blockchain and the New Architecture of Trust* (MIT Press 2018) [DOI: https://doi.org/10.7551/mitpress/11449.001.0001]

——— and Cornell N, 'Contracts *ex machina*' (2017) 67 *Duke LJ* 313

Wright A and De Filippi P, 'Decentralized Blockchain Technology and the Rise of *Lex Cryptographia*' (10 March 2015) <https://ssrn.com/abstract=2580664> accessed 16 July 2020

Yannopoulos GN, 'The Immunity of Internet Intermediaries Reconsidered?' in Taddeo M and Floridi L (eds), *The Responsibilities of Online Service Providers* (Springer 2017) [DOI: https://doi.org/10.1007/978-3-319-47852-4_3]

Zetzsche DA, Buckley RP, and Arner DW, 'The Distributed Liability of Distributed Ledgers: Legal Risks of Blockchain' [2018] *U Ill L Rev* 1361

Part I

Digital technologies and other contemporary challenges in tort law

2 Civil liability of internet intermediaries for illegal online content

Matija Damjan

1. Introduction: illegal online content

Information posted on the internet can breach various private rights. Copyright, for example, can be breached by the unauthorized online publication of videos and music, or by an unlicensed digital distribution of software or e-books. The sale of counterfeit goods through online markets can violate producers' trademarks, design rights, or patents. Celebrities' right to privacy is often breached by leaks of their private photos and videos in online media, whereas the publication of insulting or derogatory comments in online forums or on social networks can violate the personality rights of the persons referred to. Posting of a company's documentation containing confidential information in an online repository can constitute unlawful disclosure of a trade secret. The spreading of computer viruses, worms, and other malicious computer code through a website can damage a computer or give malicious users access to the system. Any such illegal activity can cause damage or loss and gives rise to claims for compensation or other forms of judicial redress.[1]

The person who uploaded the illegal content often cannot be identified, since they are anonymous, are hiding under a fake name, or might be located in a hard-to-reach jurisdiction. Hence, rather than dealing with the direct perpetrator, the persons affected by the unlawful activity may be tempted in such a situation to act against one of the internet intermediaries who host or transmit the objectionable content. Due to their technical role in the transmission and storage of information, internet access providers, operators of hosting services, social networks, online forums, web aggregators, and search engines have a certain degree of control over third parties' content. Being mainly commercial entities, who are easily identifiable and (typically) have deeper pockets than the actual wrongdoers, they are an ideal target of the injured parties' claims for damages.[2]

1 Andrew Murray, *Information Technology Law: The Law and Society* (OUP 2010) 47–48.
2 Diane Rowland, Uta Kohl, and Andrew Charlesworth, *Information Technology Law* (4th edn, Routledge 2012) 72–73.

DOI: 10.4324/9781003080596-3

The basic conditions under which internet intermediaries may be held liable for the loss or injury caused by the illegal content uploaded by their users were laid down twenty years ago in the E-Commerce Directive.[3] However, the internet keeps evolving and now looks very different to how it did in the year 2000.[4] The business models of new online services, particularly social networks, blur the distinction between users and service providers and do not fall neatly into the categories set out in the directive. Thus, intermediary liability rules remain contentious and keep being refined by the courts. Additionally, new legislative attempts are on the rise to introduce new stricter rules of intermediary liability in specific fields, such as online media and copyright law. This chapter will discuss the recent developments of the intermediary liability regime in the EU and some of the outstanding issues of the current system.

2. Safe haven under the E-Commerce Directive

2.1 General

Internet intermediaries act as gatekeepers to online publications, so their cooperation is essential to ensure effective control over online content. However, shifting the responsibility for preventing online access to illegal third-party content to intermediaries would penalize the messenger rather than the sender. Increased business risks might reduce investment in information infrastructure and hinder the development of information technology.[5] Additionally, if internet intermediaries were required to verify all online content, this would mandate gross interference with internet users' privacy and business confidentiality.[6] The legislators, therefore, tried to strike a balance between efficiency and the fairness of control by formulating a compromise under which intermediaries are not responsible for third-party content

3 Directive 2000/31/EC of the European Parliament and of the Council of 8 June 2000 on certain legal aspects of information society services, in particular electronic commerce, in the Internal Market ('Directive on electronic commerce') [2000] *OJ* L178/1 (E-Commerce Directive).

4 Many of today's ubiquitous online services emerged after the adoption of the E-Commerce Directive in 2000: Wikipedia has existed since 2001, YouTube since 2005, Facebook and Twitter since 2006, Instagram since 2010.

5 Rowland, Kohl, and Charlesworth (n 2) 73; Gerald Spindler, 'Copyright Law and Internet Intermediaries Liability' in Tatiana-Eleni Synodinou and others (eds), *EU Internet Law in the Digital Era: Regulation and Enforcement* (Springer 2020) 3–4.

6 Harper points out that the quantum, detail, and breadth of information that internet intermediaries carry are significantly greater than what traditional telephone companies carry. And since the information is in digital form, it is relatively easy to collect, copy, and interpret. Therefore, the need for privacy protection in internet communications is even greater than in telephone communications, where it is uncontentious in law that telephone operators may not arbitrarily eavesdrop and record user calls. Jim Harper, 'Against ISP Liability: do ISPs have a duty to protect the world?' (2005) 28 *Regulation* 30, 31.

if they are prepared to remove or prevent access to unlawful user content at the request of the affected parties.[7]

In the USA, for historical and political reasons, separate liability regimes were established for infringement of intellectual property rights and other types of civil and criminal liability.[8] Conversely, the EU established a single liability regime for all types of unlawful online content.[9] The E-Commerce Directive created a safe haven for all intermediary service providers which exempts them from liability for illegal content uploaded by their users as long as they act in line with the requirements laid down in Arts 12 to 15 of the Directive. An information society service means any service that is usually provided for payment, remotely, by electronic means and at the individual request of the recipient of the services.[10] However, the ECJ held in cases *Papasavvas*[11] and *Mc Fadden*[12] that intermediaries can rely on the safe haven provisions even when their service is not provided against remuneration, but only in connection with some other commercial activity.

The E-Commerce Directive does not grant internet intermediaries a blanket immunity from liability for the content provided by recipients of their service but defines the criteria by distinguishing between three types of intermediary activities: mere conduit, caching, and hosting. The categories are based on the role that the intermediary plays in the online communication chain and its level of involvement in the contentious activity, which can range from being an entirely passive middleman to taking an active facilitatory role.[13]

As a basic principle, intermediary service providers are not obliged to monitor the information that they transmit or store, nor actively to seek facts or circumstances indicating illegal activity. Article 15 of the E-Commerce Directive expressly prohibits the Member States from imposing such a general monitoring obligation on intermediary service providers. However, this principle does not prevent national authorities from ordering monitoring obligations in a specific case and in accordance with national legislation (recital 47). The law may also stipulate that a service provider must promptly inform

7 ibid 30–33; Lilian Edwards, 'The Fall and Rise of Intermediary Liability Online' in Lilian Edwards and Charlotte Waelde (eds), *Law and the Internet* (3rd edn, Hart Publishing 2009) 59–61.

8 The former is governed by the Digital Millennium Copyright Act (DMCA), 17 USC § 512, the latter by the Communications Decency Act (CDA), 47 USC § 230(C).

9 Edwards (n 7) 50.

10 Directive (EU) 2015/1535 of the European Parliament and of the Council of 9 September 2015 laying down a procedure for the provision of information in the field of technical regulations and of rules on Information Society services [2015] *OJ* L241/1, Art 1(1)(b).

11 Case C-291/13 *Sotiris Papasavvas v O Fileleftheros Dimosia Etaireia Ltd, Takisu Kounnafiju, Giorgiosu Sertisu* [2014] ECLI:EU:C:2014:2209, para 30.

12 Case C-484/14 *Tobias Mc Fadden v Sony Music Entertainment Germany GmbH* [2016] ECLI:EU:C:2016:689.

13 Rowland, Kohl, and Charlesworth (n 2) 71.

the competent public authorities of alleged illegal activities undertaken, or of information provided by recipients of their service, or to provide at the competent authorities' request information enabling the identification of these recipients.[14]

2.2 Mere conduit and caching

The first two immunities under the E-Commerce Directive apply to information society services of mere conduit and caching of information, which can be compared to the traditional immunity of telephone companies or the postal service.[15]

Mere conduit consists of data transmission in a communication network or the provision of access to a communication network. This includes the automatic, intermediate, and transient storage of the information transmitted in so far as this serves the sole purpose of carrying out the transmission. Internet service providers (ISPs) and Wi-Fi operators are typical providers of mere conduit services. Under Art 12 of the E-Commerce Directive, a mere conduit provider is not liable for the information transmitted, as long as it does not initiate the transmission, select the receiver of the transmission, and select or modify the information contained in the transmission.

Caching, on the other hand, is a ubiquitous technical process on the internet, in which data that is likely to be reused is automatically temporarily stored to increase the efficiency of information's onward transmission to other recipients of the service. Under Art 13 of the E-Commerce Directive, a caching provider is not liable for the illegal content of such information, as long as it:

(a) does not modify the information
(b) complies with conditions on access to the information (e.g. passwords, age verification)
(c) updates the information in compliance with the recognized industry standards
(d) does not interfere with the lawful use of technology, widely recognized and used by industry, to obtain data on the use of the information, and
(e) acts expeditiously to remove or to disable access to the stored information upon obtaining actual knowledge of the fact that the information at the initial source of the transmission has been removed from the network, or access to it has been disabled, or that a court or an administrative authority has ordered such removal or disablement.

14 Klemen Tičar and Boštjan Makarovič, 'Udeleženci internetne komunikacije' in Boštjan Makarovič and Janez Toplišek (eds), *Pravni vodnik po internetu* (GV Založba 2007) 263–64.
15 Rowland, Kohl, and Charlesworth (n 2) 75.

Recitals 42 to 44 of the E-Commerce Directive explain that the exemptions from liability cover only cases where the activity of the information society service provider is of a mere technical, automatic, and passive nature, which implies that the information society service provider has neither knowledge of nor control over the information that is transmitted or stored and is in no way involved with the information transmitted. Where a service provider deliberately collaborates with one of the recipients of the service in order to undertake illegal acts, it cannot benefit from the liability exemptions established for mere conduit and caching.

2.3 Hosting

While the services of mere conduit and caching are relatively uncontroversial and rarely lead to disputes, the liability of web hosting providers is much more contentious. Hosting consists of the storage of information provided by the recipient of the service and, typically, making this information available to third parties. Hosting is usually provided under a contract between the provider and the recipient of the service under which the recipient essentially leases disk space on the host's server – for example, for hosting of their website. With many modern hosting services, such as social networks, online forums, and blog hosting sites, hosting is provided for free and the service contract is concluded in the form of online click-through acceptance of the service's terms and conditions. The hosted information can be controlled by both the service recipient and the service provider but hosting providers generally restrict themselves to the administration of server infrastructure and do not interfere with their users' content. Nevertheless, the service provider has a greater role in the publishing process and firmer control over the service recipients' information. Hence, a hosting provider's liability is more strictly defined.[16]

Under Art 14 of the E-Commerce Directive, a hosting service provider is not liable for the information stored at the request of a recipient of the service, on condition that the provider does not have actual knowledge of illegal activity or information and, as regards claims for damages, is not aware of facts or circumstances from which the illegal activity or information is apparent. This means that hosting service providers cannot be held criminally liable in the absence of actual knowledge of illegal activity or information; however, it is immune from civil liability if it is also unaware of facts or circumstances from which the illegal activity or information is apparent.[17] As soon as a hosting provider learns of illegal activity or information or becomes aware of facts or circumstances from which the illegal activity or information is apparent,

16 Edwards (n 7) 65.
17 ibid; Tičar and Makarovič (n 14) 269–70.

however, it can escape liability only if it acts expeditiously to remove or to disable access to the information.

These provisions set up a notice-and-takedown system under which hosting service providers are not obliged to seek unlawful content on their own, but must quickly remove such content as soon as they learn of the infringement – for example, when notified by the right holder or the injured party.[18] The E-Commerce Directive does not list the circumstances under which service providers should be aware of unlawful activity or information even when it is not expressly reported to them. This creates some uncertainty as to the required diligence of the hosting provider. Article 15 of the Directive excludes the obligation of service providers to actively search for and eliminate potentially illegal content. However, recital 48 of the Directive allows the Member States to require hosting service providers to apply duties of care, which can reasonably be expected from them in order to detect and prevent certain types of illegal activities.[19]

Of course, a court can also order the service provider to stop or prevent the violation. The Directive specifically mentions the possibility for a court or administrative authority, in accordance with Member States' legal systems, to require the service provider to terminate or prevent an infringement. Typical reasons for which the law may authorize the court to order such action are crime detection and prevention, the protection of privacy, and the protection of classified information and trade secrets. The ECJ recently expanded the potential scope of such court orders in the case *Glawischnig-Piesczek*[20] where it held that the E-Commerce Directive does not preclude a court from ordering a hosting provider to remove or block content which is identical or equivalent to the content previously declared unlawful irrespective of who requested the storage of that information. It also confirmed that an injunction can compel the provider to remove or block such content worldwide.

3. Technical neutrality of service providers

The E-Commerce Directive provides immunity from liability for service users' unlawful content only to intermediaries whose activity is 'of a mere technical, automatic and passive nature, which implies that the information society service provider has neither knowledge of nor control over the information which is transmitted or stored'.[21] However, such a technically neutral role could be called into doubt in the case of social networks, online marketplaces, video-sharing platforms, and other interactive online platforms whose operators actively encourage users to publish and share their content, which generates high web traffic and leads to increased advertising revenue

18 Rowland, Kohl, and Charlesworth (n 2) 85.

19 Giuseppe Mazziotti, *EU Digital Copyright Law and the End-User* (Springer 2008) 168.

20 Case C-18/18 *Eva Glawischnig-Piesczek v Facebook Ireland Limited* [2019] ECLI:EU:C:2019:821.

21 E-Commerce Directive, recital 42.

for the operator. Providing access to user-generated content is an essential part of the platform operator's business model regardless of the legality of the content in question: the operator also benefits from the hosting of unlawful content (such as copyrighted videos) uploaded by the platform's users.[22] Since it is clear in advance that a certain share of user-generated content on such mass platforms will always be illegal, the question arises whether the hosting service provider should be considered to have been aware of facts or circumstances from which the illegal activity or information is apparent in the sense of Art 14(1)(a) of the E-Commerce Directive.[23]

The ECJ first ruled on the liability of an information society service provider in such a situation in the *Google AdWords* case.[24] In its paid referencing service 'AdWords', Google permitted advertisers offering to internet users imitations of Louis Vuitton's goods to select keywords corresponding to Louis Vuitton's trademarks, in combination with keywords such as 'imitation' and 'copy'. Louis Vuitton filed a lawsuit alleging that Google, by hosting adverts that infringed their trademark, should also be liable for the infringement. Referring to recital 42 of the E-Commerce Directive, the court held that in examining whether the service provider's role is neutral, the mere facts that the referencing service is subject to payment, that Google sets the payment terms, or that it provides general information to its clients were not decisive. Likewise, concordance between the keyword selected and the search term entered by an internet user was not sufficient of itself to justify the view that Google had knowledge of, or control over, the data entered into its system by advertisers and stored in memory on its server. Of crucial importance, however, was the role played by Google in the drafting of the commercial message which accompanied the advertising link or in the establishment or selection of keywords.[25] If Google had been actively cooperating with advertisers in the creation of the content of their ads, it would no longer have had a technically neutral role and could be held liable for the unlawful ads. However, since Google had set up an automated process for the selection of keywords and the creation of ads, it was able to avoid the liability.[26]

22 Carlisle George and Jackie Scerri, 'Web 2.0 and User-Generated Content: legal challenges in the new frontier' [2007] (2) *JILT* 3–5 <http://go.warwick.ac.uk/jilt/2007_2/george_scerri> accessed 20 February 2020; Murray (n 1) 107–10; Rowland, Kohl, and Charlesworth (n 2) 89.

23 Edwards (n 7) 67.

24 Joined cases C-236/08 to C-238/08 *Google France SARL and Google Inc v Louis Vuitton Malletier SA*, *Google France SARL v Viaticum SA and Luteciel SARL* and *Google France SARL v Centre national de recherche en relations humaines (CNRRH) SARL and Others* [2010] *ECR* I-2417, ECLI:EU:C:2010:159 (*Google Adwords*).

25 ibid, paras 113–18.

26 Rowland, Kohl, and Charlesworth (n 2) 88.

This view was confirmed in *L'Oréal v eBay*[27] in relation to the operator of an online marketplace through which users were selling counterfeit goods bearing L'Oréal trademarks. The ECJ held that merely because eBay stored sales offers on its servers, set out the terms of its service, received payment for it, and provided general information to customers, it could not be denied the possibility of invoking liability exemptions. If, on the contrary, the operator provides assistance to its users – in particular, the optimization of the presentation of sales offers or of their promotion – the operator is no longer in a neutral position between the seller and potential buyers but plays an active role in which it can have knowledge and control over the content of these offers. Therefore, such a service provider cannot rely on the intermediary liability exception.[28] Additionally, the exemption cannot be invoked by a service provider who does not play such an active role but is aware of facts or circumstances on the basis of which a diligent economic operator should have identified the illegality in question and acted accordingly.[29] The information society service provider is therefore required to exercise due care in verifying the legality of the third-party data it stores. This is in line with recital 48 of the E-Commerce Directive, which mentions the possibility for Member States of requiring hosting service providers to apply duties of care, which can reasonably be expected from them and which are specified by national law, in order to detect and prevent certain types of illegal activities. What activities this duty of care entails, however, depends on the circumstances of each case.

The E-Commerce Directive prohibits Member States from imposing on service providers any general obligation to monitor the legality of information that they transmit or store or to actively seek facts or circumstances indicating illegal activity (Article 15). Taking this provision into account, the duty of care cannot be interpreted in such a way as to require service providers to set up an automated (software-based) system of filtering of any potentially illegal information uploaded or transmitted by their users. The Article 14 requirement of the intermediary's actual knowledge or awareness of the unlawful information does not encompass any knowledge that the intermediary could obtain upon monitoring the hosted contents.[30] This does not prevent court-ordered monitoring obligations in specific cases, but the ECJ has repeatedly held (in cases *Scarlet Extended*,[31] *Sabam v Netlog*,[32] and

27 Case C-324/09 *L'Oréal SA and Others v eBay International AG and Others* [2011] *ECR* I-6011, ECLI:EU:C:2011:474.

28 ibid, paras 115–16.

29 ibid, paras 120–22.

30 Rowland, Kohl, and Charlesworth (n 2) 87.

31 Case C-70/10 *Scarlet Extended SA v Société belge des auteurs, compositeurs et éditeurs SCRL (SABAM)* [2011] *ECR* I-11959, ECLI:EU:C:2011:771.

32 Case C-360/10 *Belgische Vereniging van Auteurs, Componisten en Uitgevers CVBA (SABAM) v Netlog NV* [2012] ECLI:EU:C:2012:85.

UPC Telekabel[33]) that an injunction may not compel internet intermediaries to establish a permanent system of preventive filtering of user data to protect themselves from civil liability. The guiding principle remains that the intermediary is free from liability as long as it retains a technically neutral role with regard to illegal content.

4. Reaction time

The E-Commerce Directive requires service providers to 'act expeditiously' upon receiving a takedown notice to remove or to disable access to the illegal information. The meaning of the word 'expeditiously' is not defined, so it is not clear whether the service provider must disable access to the disputed information immediately, as soon as it receives such a request from the alleged injured party or, for instance, within twenty-four hours thereafter, or whether the service provider may take a reasonable time to verify the facts of the case and to obtain legal advice on the illegality of the content at stake before it decides whether to disable access to it.

On one hand, prompt action to prevent access to unlawful content is necessary to ensure effective protection against interference with personal or property rights of the affected parties. On the other hand, the requirement for immediate removal of any contentious information in respect of which the service provider received a takedown request potentially allows the abuse of such requests to remove any unwelcome information. A very short deadline for the takedown can also present a practical problem for service providers, as it can take some time for the matter to reach a competent staff member and for the content in question to be located (e.g. if it appears in several places on a complex website). Hence, the requirement for expeditious action should not be interpreted in terms of a short, fixed deadline for the takedown of the contentious information. It is more appropriate to require service providers to act with due care after having received a takedown request and to do whatever is necessary to prevent the disputed content from being further disseminated as soon as this is reasonably and practically possible. The length of time reasonably necessary to take such action must be judged by taking into account the circumstances of each case.[34] This interpretation is supported by recital 46 of the E-Commerce Directive, which states that the removal or disabling of access has to be undertaken in the observance of the principle of freedom of expression and of procedures established for this purpose at the national level. It further notes that the Directive does not affect the possibility of Member States establishing specific requirements which must be fulfilled expeditiously prior to the removal or disabling of information.

33 Case C-314/12 *UPC Telekabel Wien GmbH v Constantin Film Verleih GmbH and Wega Filmproduktionsgesellschaft mbH* [2014] ECLI:EU:C:2014:192.

34 Edwards (n 7) 66–67.

5. Unfounded takedown requests

The E-Commerce Directive does not define the form in which an information society service provider must be informed of the unlawfulness of information in order to be obliged to take it down. Is an email sufficient? What about a phone call or a text message? Must the service provider act even upon an anonymous notice or should the sender identify themselves and specify the rights that the information in question is alleged to have infringed? Is the service provider entitled to assess the merits of the takedown request?

Requiring the service provider to act upon each takedown request regardless of its form and without performing even a perfunctory test of its validity would make it easy to abuse the notice-and-takedown system to take offline any unwanted content, regardless of its (un)lawfulness. This would push hosting service providers into performing private censorship, potentially for political or business purposes, which is particularly problematic because it would take place without the involvement of the courts. Even when liability rules are unclear, the intermediaries are likely to play safe and remove any material upon any request, which has been exploited by competitors relying on the unlikelihood of litigation to establish the invalidity of their takedown requests.[35] According to some reports, at least one-third of the takedown requests received by service providers are in practice unfounded.[36] Several studies have shown that service providers often automatically block disputed content after receiving a takedown request, without verifying the accuracy of the claims, even when they are manifestly unfounded (e.g. because the copyright has long since expired).[37] The removal of legally published information is also problematic because the information society service provider may thereby breach the contract with the recipient of services – that is, the provider of the content that the service provider has removed or blocked (unless such liability is specifically excluded in the service contract).[38]

As already mentioned, recital 46 of the E-Commerce Directive notes that the Member States may establish specific requirements which must be fulfilled prior to the removal or disabling of information. National law could therefore prescribe the conditions and procedures that must be fulfilled by the requesting party and by the information society service provider in the

35 Rowland, Kohl, and Charlesworth (n 2) 86.

36 Jennifer M Urban and Laura Quilter, 'Efficient Process or Chilling Effects – Takedown Notices under Section 512 of the Digital Millennium Copyright Act' (2006) 22 *Santa Clara High Tech LJ* 621, 666.

37 See Lumen research project of the Berkman Klein Center for Internet & Society at Harvard University, which has created a database containing millions of takedown notices: <https://lumendatabase.org> accessed 20 February 2020.

38 In contrast, in the USA, DMCA specifically grants ISPs immunity from claims of the recipients of their services if the ISP blocks or removes the content in good faith. It also penalizes frivolous and illegitimate takedown demands. Rowland, Kohl, and Charlesworth (n 2) 86.

event of a request for removal or blocking of certain contents. However, it seems that the Member States have generally not made use of this option. A brief analysis of the relevant e-commerce legislation in Slovenia, Croatia, Germany, and Austria shows that their national laws just repeat, almost verbatim, the phrasing used in the Directive, without providing any additional procedural safeguards.[39] In the absence of explicit regulation, such conditions could also be adopted by service providers themselves through self-regulation. Taking into account the Directive's recitals, the courts could accept that service providers can avoid liability even if they refuse to block or remove infringing content upon request unless the complaining party followed the service provider's reasonable procedural and formal requirements, and demonstrated with a certain likelihood that the information in question indeed infringed their exclusive rights.[40]

In *L'Oréal v eBay*, the ECJ hinted that an intermediary service provider may escape liability where the notifications of allegedly illegal activities or information turn out to be insufficiently precise or inadequately substantiated to enable a diligent economic operator to identify the illegality.[41] Accordingly, the European Commission recommended in its 2017 Communication on Tackling Illegal Content Online[42] that online platforms should put in place effective mechanisms to facilitate the submission of notices that are sufficiently precise and adequately substantiated to enable the platforms to take a swift and informed decision about the follow-up. This should facilitate the provision of notices that contain an explanation of the reasons why the notice provider considers the content illegal and a clear indication of the location of the potentially illegal content (e.g. the URL address). Users should normally not be obliged to identify themselves when reporting what they consider illegal content unless this information is required to determine the legality of the content (e.g. asserting ownership for intellectual property (IP) rights). Some further room for such reasoning is provided by the Directive on Copyright in the Digital Single Market[43] in relation to the liability of

39 By way of comparison, 17 USC § 512 specifies that a notification of claimed infringement must be in writing and must include a physical or electronic signature of a person authorized to act on behalf of the owner of an exclusive right that is allegedly infringed; identification of the copyrighted work(s) claimed to have been infringed; identification of the infringing material, including its location; contact information of the complaining party; a statement that the complaining party has a good faith belief that use of the material in the manner complained of is not authorized by the copyright owner, its agent, or the law, and that the information in the notification is accurate.

40 cf Tičar and Makarovič (n 14) 271.

41 *L'Oréal v eBay* (n 27), para 122.

42 European Commission, 'Tackling Illegal Content Online: Towards an enhanced responsibility of online platforms' (Communication) COM (2017) 555 final.

43 Directive (EU) 2019/790 of the European Parliament and of the Council of 17 April 2019 on copyright and related rights in the Digital Single Market and amending Directives 96/9/EC and 2001/29/EC [2019] *OJ* L130/92 (Directive on Copyright in the Digital Single Market).

online content-sharing service providers for violations of copyright and related rights: under Article 17(4) they are obliged to act only upon receiving 'a sufficiently substantiated notice from the rightholder'.

6. Type of liability

Chapter II, Section 4 of the E-Commerce Directive lays down exemptions from liability of intermediary service providers for the information transmitted or stored. However, it does not specify what form of liability is involved if the service provider does not comply with the provisions of Arts 12 to 14 of the Directive, but merely lists the conditions upon which the service provider's liability is excluded. The precise conditions of liability are settled by the Member States' laws.

Since the unlawful information is provided by recipients (users) of the service provider's service and not by the provider itself, the first issue to be resolved is whether the service provider is responsible for its own conduct or its users' conduct. The answer to this should be straightforward. The intermediary is not empowered to act as its users' legal guardian. On the other hand, the users of intermediary services are not the service provider's employees, agents, or proxies and cannot act on its behalf of or in its interest. Hence, their misconduct relating to uploading of unlawful content cannot be attributed to the service provider. Only the intermediary's own knowledge and conduct when dealing with the user's unlawful content are decisive in determining its liability. If the intermediary fails to act as required after it has learned of the illegality of certain content, then the public availability of such content on its servers is the result of its own omission and this may be the basis of its own liability.

The next issue is whether the intermediary's liability is fault-based or strict. Recital 48 of the E-Commerce Directive states that the Member States may require hosting service providers to apply duties of care, which can reasonably be expected from them and which are specified by national law, to detect and prevent certain types of illegal activities. Liability arising out of a violation of such a duty of care will normally be based on the violator's fault. A ental element, hinting at fault-based liability although not mandating it, is also contained in the Directive's exemptions from liability where an intermediary can only rely on the immunity when it does not know or is unaware of the activity in question.[44]

From the perspectives of Slovenian and Croatian law, information society services cannot, in general, be considered an activity that gives rise to an increased risk of damage in the surroundings, which is the main instance of strict liability in these two legal systems. Any other case of strict liability

44 Rowland, Kohl, and Charlesworth (n 2) 87.

must be laid down in law specifically.[45] Hence, the mere absence of reference to the intermediary's intent or negligence in the provisions on their liability cannot be interpreted as stipulating strict liability. Intermediaries' liability must therefore be judged by the general rules of fault-based civil liability for damages, taking into account the general rules on compensation for specific types of infringement (property rights, personality rights, IP rights) in combination with the specific rules on the exclusion of liability arising out of the E-Commerce Directive. Since internet intermediaries perform their services as a professional activity, their duty of care is set out higher than for regular individuals: they must act with high diligence, according to the rules and custom of the profession (the diligence of a good expert).[46] This seems to correspond to the standard of a diligent economic operator which the ECJ established in *L'Oréal v eBay* with regard to the intermediary's duties in identifying the illegal content. The Directive on Copyright in the Digital Single Market, on the other hand, speaks of 'high industry standards of professional diligence'.

7. New liability regime for content-sharing service providers

When the E-Commerce Directive was being drafted, the distinction between a hosting service provider and a content provider seemed clear. But the further development of the internet has placed increasing emphasis on interactive capabilities of the network as a platform on which users can run software application through the browser (Web 2.0). Users are no longer mere consumers of information supplied by the content provider, but active uploaders of user-generated content. Content-sharing sites such as Facebook, Instagram, Twitter, or YouTube have generated tremendous advertising revenue while still benefiting from the provisions of the E-Commerce Directive protecting them from liability for illegal third-party content.[47] This situation was met with increasing dissatisfaction by copyright holders.

The issue was addressed by the EU's legislators in the Directive on Copyright in the Digital Single Market adopted in April 2019 after two years of tumultuous debate. Article 17 of the Directive turns on its head the existing safe haven system for a new category of internet intermediaries: online content-sharing service providers. Such an intermediary is defined as a provider of an information society service of which the main or one of the main purposes is to store and give the public access to a large amount of copyright-protected works or other protected subject-matter uploaded by its users, which it

45 Slovenian Obligations Code (*Obligacijski zakonik*, OZ), *UL RS* 97/2007, 64/2016, 20/2018, Art 131; Croatian Obligations Act (*Zakon o obveznim odnosima*, ZOO) *NN* 35/2005, 41/2008, 125/2011, 78/2015, 29/2018, Art 1045.

46 See Art 6(2) OZ and Art 10 ZOO. cf Rowland, Kohl, and Charlesworth (n 2) 86.

47 George and Scerri (n 22) 3–5; Murray (n 1) 107–10.

organizes and promotes for profit-making purposes. When a content-sharing service provider gives the public access to copyright-protected works or other protected subject-matter uploaded by its users, this now qualifies an act of communication to the public by the service provider itself. For such use of copyrighted works, the service provider must obtain permission from the right holders – for example, by entering into a licence agreement with a collecting society. Without proper authorization, content-sharing platforms will be held liable for copyright infringements committed by their users and will no longer be able to avoid liability by relying solely on takedown notices. The new arrangement is expected to force online platforms to negotiate with copyright holders the terms of use of their works and thus close the value gap alleged particularly by the music industry. Critics of the new directive warn that online platforms will not actually be able to obtain licences for all users' content, as collecting societies do not represent all copyrighted works distributed on the internet, and therefore expect that a lot of content will have to be removed.[48]

However, the new obligations do not fully apply to new content-sharing service providers whose services have been available to the public for less than three years and whose annual turnover is less than 10 million euros. Non-profit online encyclopaedias (e.g. Wikipedia), non-profit educational and scientific repositories, open-source software development and sharing platforms (e.g. SourceForge and GitHub), electronic communications service providers, online marketplaces, business-to-business cloud services, and cloud services that allow users to upload content for their own use are completely excluded from the concept of a content-sharing service provider.

Where no authorization has been granted, online content-sharing service providers will be able to escape liability if they can demonstrate that they have:

(a) made best efforts to obtain an authorization, and
(b) made, in accordance with high industry standards of professional diligence, best efforts to ensure the unavailability of specific works and other subject-matter for which the right holders have provided the service providers with the relevant and necessary information, and in any event
(c) acted expeditiously, upon receiving a sufficiently substantiated notice from the right holders, to disable access to, or to remove from their websites, the notified works or other subject-matter, and made best efforts to prevent their future uploads in accordance with point (b).[49]

The Directive on Copyright in the Digital Single Market states that the application of Article 17 should not lead to any general monitoring obligation,

48 Spindler (n 5) 13.
49 See ibid.

but due to the enormous amount of users' posts on content-sharing platforms, it is hardly conceivable how the removal of all illegal content and the prevention of its future uploads (an additional requirement not contained in the E-Commerce Directive) could be achieved otherwise than by using automated filtering tools.[50] These, however, are a dangerous step towards private censorship of user content.[51] It seems that 'high industry standards of professional diligence' referred to in Article 17(4) will represent the benchmark for the requirement of applying upload filters. In accordance with Article 17(10), these standards should be defined in consultation with all relevant stakeholders. In the end, however, the courts will have to assess whether they strike a balance between the fundamental rights laid down in the Charter of Fundamental Rights of the European Union, in particular the freedom of expression and the freedom of the arts, and the right to property, including intellectual property, as referred to in recital 70 of the Directive.[52]

8. Liability for hyperlinks

Hyperlinks to other websites or to specific content located thereon are an essential feature of the modern internet. Aggregator websites and social networks combine content from various other sites so that a user can read only the title and a few lines from the selected page or compare prices. The provider posting a hyperlink merely directs its users to various third-party content, over which it has no technical or substantive control.[53] While the US DMCA specifically grants internet service providers immunity from liability for hyperlinks under certain conditions, the EU's legal regime leaves this issue unresolved. Linking to other websites clearly does not constitute a hosting service, since the content in question is not located on the provider's server. The exception for mere conduit does not fit providers of hyperlinks, since they select the information contained in the transmission, although they do not modify it. The caching exception also cannot apply since the transmitted information is not provided by the person clicking the hyperlink as the recipient of the service.[54]

Article 21(2) of the E-Commerce Directive requires the European Commission, when reporting on the implementation of the Directive, to specifically analyze the need for proposals regarding the liability of hyperlink providers. However, no such proposal has been brought forward yet. Consequently, the development of rules concerning liability for hyperlinks is left to

50 ibid 16.

51 See Swiss Institute of Comparative Law, 'Comparative Study on Blocking, Filtering and Takedown of Illegal Internet Content' (Council of Europe 2017) 17–22.

52 cf Spindler (n 5) 14.

53 Edwards (n 7) 77–78.

54 Rowland, Kohl, and Charlesworth (n 2) 79–80.

the courts, which must take into account the specific circumstances of each case. The ECJ expounded such rules particularly in the field of copyright law.

In case *Svensson v Retriever Sverige*,[55] the ECJ held that hyperlinking can be a form of making available copyrighted works since it allows the public to access such works, irrespective of whether they avail themselves of that opportunity. However, in order to be covered by the concept of 'communication to the public', a hyperlink must also be directed at a new public that was not taken into account by the copyright holders when they authorized the initial communication to the public. The ECJ then held that all internet users constitute the same public if access to the works on the originating website is not restricted. Hence, the provision on a website of clickable links to works freely available on another website does not constitute an 'act of communication to the public'.[56] In *GS Media v Sanoma Media*,[57] the ECJ imposed an additional criterion of knowledge of the illegality of the content freely available on the linked-to website. When the posting of hyperlinks is carried out for profit, however, such knowledge must be presumed, since the person who posts such links for profit should carry out the necessary checks to ensure that the work concerned is not illegally published.[58]

In case *Spiegel Online*,[59] the ECJ further held that a reference made by means of a hyperlink to a file which has been made available to the public on the internet and can be downloaded independently can be covered by the copyright concept of quotation as an exception to the exclusive rights of reproduction and of communication to the public, as long as the hyperlink is used for the purposes of illustrating an assertion, of defending an opinion, or of allowing an intellectual comparison between that work and the assertions of that user. The court also reiterated the underlying position that hyperlinks contribute to the sound operation of the internet, which is of particular importance to freedom of expression and of information, enshrined in Article 11 of the Charter, as well as to the exchange of opinions and information in that network characterized by the availability of incalculable amounts of information.

The Directive on Copyright in the Digital Single Market contains a provision that has been dubbed 'hyperlink tax' by its opponents but is officially referred to as 'protection of press publications concerning online uses'. Under Article 15, press publishers are entitled to compensation for the posting of links to their online publications where these links contain snippets of

55 Case C-466/12 *Nils Svensson and Others v Retriever Sverige AB* [2014] ECLI:EU:C:2014:76.

56 Jane C Ginsburg and Luke Ali Budiardjo, 'Liability for Providing Hyperlinks to Copyright-Infringing Content: International and Comparative Law Perspectives' (2018) 41 *Colum JL & Arts* 153, 161–62.

57 Case C-160/15 *GS Media BV v Sanoma Media Netherlands BV and Others* [2016] ECLI:EU:C:2016:644.

58 Ginsburg and Budiardjo (n 56) 162.

59 Case C-516/17 *Spiegel Online GmbH v Volker Beck* [2019] ECLI:EU:C:2019:625.

their journalistic content, such as automatic link previews generated by social networks showing the article headline, a thumbnail picture, and a short excerpt.[60] Strictly speaking, the new press publishers' right is not a limitation on hyperlinking, since it does not cover the posing of bare hyperlinks without snippets of the articles linked to. However, using extracts of targeted content as part of hyperlinks is important in practice, since readers want to know where the link leads before they click on it. The Directive states that the publishers' right does not apply in respect of the use of individual words or very short extracts of a press publication. Yet it will be difficult to draw a clear line between a 'very short extract' not covered by the new right and a short extract, for the use of which compensation should be paid to the media outlet. Despite the explicit provision in the Directive that the publisher's right does not prevent the insertion of hyperlinks, the new solution can significantly impair their practical functionality. The publisher's right does not apply to the private or non-commercial use of press publications by individual users, but it is not entirely clear when an internet user ceases to be an individua – for example, in the case of online influencers with thousands of followers on social networks who receive significant advertising revenue from this activity.

9. Conclusion

Clearly, the current EU regime of information society service providers' liability does not answer all the questions concerning the responsibility of various internet intermediaries for third parties' information and does not regulate all such situations in a satisfactory manner. This is understandable since the internet is still developing relatively quickly, so the legislation cannot foresee all future online services. The regulation will have to adapt to the emphasized interactivity and convergence of different online services, either through changes in legislation or case law. The content industry, in particular, has exerted considerable pressure to move the basic model from *ex post* control based on the notice-and-takedown system to *ex ante* detection of illegal content carried out by the internet intermediaries. The Directive on Copyright in the Digital Single Market has indicated a move in this direction, but Article 15 of the E-Commerce Directive still prevents service providers from establishing a general obligation to control the content of service recipients. The rules of civil liability of internet intermediaries are likely to evolve in parallel with the development of rules on tackling other forms of illegal content, such as child sexual abuse, terrorist propaganda, online gambling, as signalled in the Commission Recommendation on measures to

60 Maria-Daphne Papadopoulou and Evanthia-Maria Moustaka, 'Copyright and the Press Publishers Right on the Internet: Evolutions and Perspectives' in Tatiana-Eleni Synodinou and others (eds), *EU Internet Law in the Digital Era: Regulation and Enforcement* (Springer 2020) 112.

effectively tackle illegal content online.[61] In any case, when interpreting any such rules, the courts will have the important task of balancing the interest for removing unlawful online content on one hand with fundamental rights, particularly the freedom of expression on the other.

Bibliography

Edwards L, 'The Fall and Rise of Intermediary Liability Online' in Edwards L and Waelde C (eds), *Law and the Internet* (3rd edn, Hart Publishing 2009)

European Commission, 'Tackling Illegal Content Online: Towards an enhanced responsibility of online platforms' (Communication) COM (2017) 555 final

George C and Scerri J, 'Web 2.0 and User-Generated Content: legal challenges in the new frontier' [2007] (2) *JILT* <http://go.warwick.ac.uk/jilt/2007_2/george_scerri> accessed 20 February 2020

Ginsburg JC and Budiardjo LA, 'Liability for Providing Hyperlinks to Copyright-Infringing Content: International and Comparative Law Perspectives' (2018) 41 *Colum JL & Arts* 153

Harper J, 'Against ISP Liability: do ISPs have a duty to protect the world?' (2005) 28 *Regulation* 30

Mazziotti G, *EU Digital Copyright Law and the End-User* (Springer 2008) [DOI: https://doi.org/10.1007/978-3-540-76985-0]

Murray A, *Information Technology Law: The Law and Society* (OUP 2010)

Papadopoulou MD and Moustaka EM, 'Copyright and the Press Publishers Right on the Internet: Evolutions and Perspectives' in Synodinou TE and others (eds), *EU Internet Law in the Digital Era: Regulation and Enforcement* (Springer 2020) [DOI: https://doi.org/10.1007/978-3-030-25579-4_5]

Rowland D, Kohl U, and Charlesworth A, *Information Technology Law* (4th edn, Routledge 2012)

Spindler G, 'Copyright Law and Internet Intermediaries Liability' in Synodinou TE and others (eds), *EU Internet Law in the Digital Era: Regulation and Enforcement* (Springer 2020) [DOI: https://doi.org/10.1007/978-3-030-25579-4_1]

Swiss Institute of Comparative Law, 'Comparative Study on Blocking, Filtering and Takedown of Illegal Internet Content' (Council of Europe 2017)

Tičar K and Makarovič B, 'Udeleženci internetne komunikacije' in Makarovič B and Toplišek J (eds), *Pravni vodnik po internetu* (GV Založba 2007)

Urban JM and Quilter L, 'Efficient Process or Chilling Effects – Takedown Notices under Section 512 of the Digital Millennium Copyright Act' (2006) 22 *Santa Clara High Tech LJ* 621 [DOI: https://doi.org/10.31235/osf.io/pyzua]

61 Commission Recommendation (EU) 2018/334 of 1 March 2018 on measures to effectively tackle illegal content online [2018] *OJ* L63/50.

3 The sharing economy as the contemporary challenge for the law of torts

Radosław Strugała

1. Introduction: the sharing economy – not only pros[1]

When the phenomenon of the sharing economy appeared some years ago, there was a lot of enthusiasm about it and most commonly the focus was on the benefits that this model would bring to society at large. Ever since huge companies like Uber and Airbnb got involved and started to build their business based on the sharing economy framework, there has been a strong tendency to draw public attention not only to the pros but also to the cons of this model. It is underlined that the big firms' involvement may create a risk of market distortion and exploitation. Uber, for example, is constantly accused of undermining competition and taking advantage of the drivers. The former is due to the fact that Uber may enable the provision of services typically rendered by taxi drivers without complying with the regulations applicable for the taxi industry – namely, without an occupational licence which is usually required from taxi drivers and without adhering to the fixed taxi fares that are in place in many countries.[2] The position of drivers, on the other hand, is of concern because they are left outside the scope of the legal protection measures that employees normally enjoy, despite the fact that the conditions they work in are quite similar to employment.

2. Private law measures as a remedy

Where there is a risk of market distortion and exploitation, there is usually law stepping in to punish the subjects that create that risk or at least to protect the weaker party of a transaction. Private law is familiar with the second perspective. Bearing in mind that it is public law (mostly competition law

1 The work was supported by the National Science Centre, Poland, under research project 'Sprawiedliwość prawa deliktów w XXI w. Funkcje odpowiedzialności deliktowej w świecie nowych technologii', no UMO-2017/27/B/HS5/0089.

2 See Kristóf Gyódi, 'Uber vs Licensed Taxi Drivers: A War Between Technological Standards' (2017) *Working Paper DELab UW* 2, 3 <www.delab.uw.edu.pl/wp-content/uploads/2020/07/WP_2_2017_K.Gyodi_.pdf> accessed 28 February 2020.

DOI: 10.4324/9781003080596-4

and labour law) that deals with potential questions that the sharing economy poses, it is interesting to take a closer look at how private law may approach them and whether it protects the subjects involved in a sufficient manner. There is a huge debate going on about whether Uber drivers should be treated as employees in the legal sense of the word and thus enjoy the same level of legal protection that employees normally do.[3] However, to think of Uber, there are yet other subjects involved who deserve legal protection – namely clients (passengers). What deserves special attention is the question of whether they are granted enough protection from harms and losses that they may incur while using the service rendered by Uber drivers. The question is, obviously, valid beyond the context of Uber. It could well be asked in respect of any business structured so that clients to whom some kind of tangible services are rendered use an app provided by the intermediary platform which limits its activity to matching (via this app) the tangible service providers and clients. Uber, as probably the best known intermediary platform, is a good example.

3. Does tort law has a say?

The most obvious instance of harms that an Uber client can incur during the ride are losses caused by a car accident. But there is more. Case law provides us with other examples – for example, harms caused to a client who was sexually abused by an Uber driver.[4] In such scenarios, throughout Europe victims are normally protected by the law of torts. The passenger harmed in a car accident caused by an Uber driver can usually recover not only *vis-à-vis* the driver himself but also against the insurer as personal injury protection insurance is compulsory in most of the countries.[5] The same is true for particular damages, like those incurred by the client (passenger) who was assaulted or sexually harassed by the driver. The law of torts covers such harms, and the driver would obviously be held liable for his own illegal acts. The only difference in car accident cases is that the duty to compensate for this kind of damage would be imposed only by tort law. In the car accident cases, as the contracts concluded between the passenger and the driver oblige (at least impliedly) the driver to abide by the standard of safety, the accident typically constitutes a breach of contract. Thus, in such instances the duty to compensate may be additionally imposed on the driver by the law of contract

3 Marco Inglese, *Regulating the Collaborative Economy in the European Union Digital Single Market* (Springer 2019) 133.

4 See eg *Doe v Uber Technologies, Inc et al*, Case 1:19-CV-00903 (DDC); *Doe v Uber Techs*, Case 19-cv-03310-JSC (ND Cal, 22 November 2019).

5 See Attila Fenyves and others (eds), *Compulsory Liability Insurance from a European Perspective* (De Gruyter 2016).

which operates alongside the law of torts and gives rise to the victim's right of election – that is, to choose between tort law and contract law remedies.[6]

4. The sharing economy and reasons underlying vicarious liability

At this point, however, one could ask whether the sole liability of the Uber driver is enough. In my view, it is doubtful whether this remedy on its own is sufficient to address the problem of losses caused within the context of the sharing economy. There seem to be quite a lot of reasons that justify the imposition of a duty to compensate for these harms on Uber or any other platform of this kind. In an attempt to list such reasons, one should take into account the drivers' possible inability to pay damages. The sharing economy is often described as the gig economy. It is labelled in this way for a reason. The notion actually serves to stress the link between the new economic framework and the phenomenon of precarious work and precarious workers,[7] the latter being the subjects rendering tangible services in connection to intermediary platforms. In the world of the precariat, the scenario in which these subjects become insolvent and incapable of paying damages to victims who thus remain uncompensated is quite likely. The intermediary platforms – usually big and wealthy companies – do not face similar problems. Consequently, their liability would definitely strengthen the position of victims. Moreover, the business organized by the platform and around the platform increases the probability of harms. In other words, if a given platform had not existed, some of such harms would not have happened or would have happened with lower probability. This increase in the probability of harms seems to speak in favour of the imposition of liability on platforms. Another reason to make platforms liable for losses is that platforms are aimed at making a profit from the activity of subjects rendering tangible services within the business that they organize. It seems fair that they internalize the risks created in the course of economic activity by allocating the burden of compensation (at least to a certain extent) on the platforms.

6 This right of election is familiar to many legal systems (there are, however, notable exceptions, such as French, Belgian, or Hungarian law). It appears where the same act giving rise to damage that is to be compensated for constitutes both a breach of contract subsequently concluded by the author of the damage and the victim and a tort. See Jane Swanton, 'The Convergence of Tort and Contract' (1989) 12 *Syd LR* 71; Christian von Bar and Ulrich Drobnig, *The Interaction of Contract Law and Tort and Property Law in Europe: A Comparative Study* (De Gruyter 2009) 198; Yihan Goh and Man Yip, 'Concurrent Liability in Tort and Contract: An Analysis of Interplay, Intersection and Independence' (2017) 24 *TLJ* 148.

7 See Carles Muntaner, 'Digital Platforms, Gig Economy, Precarious Employment, and the Invisible Hand of Social Class' (2018) 48 *Int J Health Serv* 597.

5. Vicarious liability: the traditional view

The above-mentioned reasons that justify the liability of platforms are familiar to lawyers who deal with tort law. In fact, they are commonly identified as the idea underlying vicarious liability – the strict liability of the so-called principal (or master) for losses caused directly by the so-called agent.[8] However, this generic and loose idea which constitutes the *ratio* of vicarious liability is reflected in some formal, fixed conditions that, as a matter of law, need to be met for vicarious liability to arise in a given case. The common denominator, similar in the majority of legal systems, is the requirement that for the master's liability to arise the activity of the agent that caused harm must fall within the so-called scope of employment.[9] As this term suggests, according to the traditional view, to trigger vicarious liability it is necessary that the agent be an employee in the strict, legal sense of the word. These prerequisites of vicarious liability were traditionally present in common law jurisdictions. The classic test of vicarious liability was set forth in an 1834 English case, *Joel v Morison*.[10] Respective prerequisites reflecting the scope of the employment requirement are present in the majority of continental civil law legal systems,[11] such as in French, German,[12] or Polish law.[13]

Historically, it was widely accepted that a principal cannot be responsible for every act of an agent. It was a common view that vicarious liability is justified only where an employee causes harms to a third person while following the principal's instructions. Conversely, the latter was traditionally exempted from liability if an agent deviated from these instructions or acted beyond the sphere of the principal's consent. While ascertaining whether a given act falls within the scope of employment, usually the criterion of 'principal's interest' is used. To trigger vicarious liability the act of the agent that caused harm must serve the purposes of the master, which in a traditional view means that it must be authorized (at least impliedly) by the master. On the other hand, the liability cannot arise if the agent acts with an objective to accomplish his

8 See Paula Giliker, *Vicarious Liability in Tort: A Comparative Perspective* (CUP 2010) 21.

9 Cees van Dam, *European Tort Law* (2nd edn, OUP 2013) 510; Giliker (n 8) 145.

10 *Joel v Morison* [1834] EWHC KB J39. See Arthur Best and David W Barnes, *Basic Tort Law: Cases, Statutes, and Problems* (Aspen Publishers 2007) 404.

11 However, there are also exceptions. For example, under Italian law vicarious liability is traditionally said to arise even where the agent acts outside the scope of employment provided that the position of agent provides for an occasion to cause damage – the so-called nesso di occasionalità. See Francesco Caringella, *Responsabilità civile e assicurazioni: Normativa e giurisprudenza ragionata* (Giuffrè Editore 2008) 203; Massimo Franzoni, *L'illecito* (2nd edn, Giuffrè Editore 2010) 821.

12 Giliker (n 8) 150–57.

13 Adam Szpunar, 'Czyny niedozwolone w kodeksie cywilnym' (1970) 15 *Stud Cywilis* 67; Piotr Machnikowski, 'Odpowiedzialność za wykonawcę powierzonej czynności' in Adam Olejniczak (ed), *System Prawa Prywatnego: Prawo zobowiązan' – część ogólna*, vol 6 (3rd edn, CH Beck 2018) 471.

own purposes, even where the act is performed when using the opportunity created by special tasks or place of employment.[14]

6. Vicarious liability: a new approach

If the traditional view on vicarious liability was accepted, the intermediary platforms could easily escape liability. As long as Uber drivers or similar persons are not treated as employees in the legal sense of the word, the liability of a platform cannot arise. Even if they were included into the category of employees, the liability of platforms would be limited and some harms would still remain beyond its scope. This is true for cases of sexual harassment or other assaults as they are never authorized by the platform.

However, in recent case law courts more and more often reject the traditional view on vicarious liability. The law of vicarious liability is even said to be 'on the move'.[15] The direction of this move is to broaden the boundaries of the vicarious liability scheme and is followed in both common law and civil law jurisdictions.

First, there is a strong tendency to relax the 'scope of employment' requirement. In common law, for instance, the criterion of sufficiently close connection tends to replace the authorization criterion. By using this criterion, vicarious liability is imposed on principals for losses caused by acts of agents that are sufficiently connected with the principal (its business), even if not authorized by the principal. As a result, vicarious liability is likely to cover instances of harms caused by agents intentionally, including harms consequent upon assaults or sexual harassment. The case that is said to constitute a breakthrough for the traditional view on vicarious liability is *Lister v Hesley Hall Ltd*.[16] The House of Lords held that vicarious liability can arise for unauthorized, intentional wrongdoings committed by an employee acting for his own benefit, in so far as there exists a connection between the wrongdoings and the work for which he was employed. On the facts of the case, the wrongdoings at stake were acts of sexual abuse committed on regular basis by a warden who was employed at a boarding school for boys and the sufficient connection between his work the acts of abuse that rendered the

14 See Paula Giliker, 'Analysing Institutional Liability for Child Sexual Abuse in England and Wales and Australia: Vicarious Liability, Non-Delegable Duties and Statutory Intervention' (2018) 77 *CLJ* 506, 515; Giliker (n 8) 157. See also Clair McIvor, 'The Use and Abuse of the Doctrine of Vicarious Liability' (2006) 35 *CLWR* 268; Anthony Gray, *Vicarious Liability: Critique and Reform* (Hart Publishing 2018) 13; Catherine M Sharkey, 'Institutional Liability for Employees' Intentional Torts: Vicarious Liability as a Quasi-Substitute for Punitive Damages' (2018) 53 *Val U L Rev* 1. For Polish law, see also Wojciech Dubis in Edward Gniewek and Piotr Machnikowski (eds), *Kodeks cywilny: Komentarz* (9th edn, CH Beck 2019) 944.

15 See Mohamud v WM Morrison *Supermarkets plc* [2016] UKSC 11; *The* Catholic Child Welfare Society *& Ors v Various claimants & Ors* [2012] UKSC 56.

16 See *Lister v Hesley Hall Ltd* [2002] 1 AC 215.

boarding school liable was found in the fact that the abuse was committed at the time, premises, and during the course of the warden's care of the boys. Other examples of common law judgments taking this relaxed approach are *Armes v Nottinghamshire County Council*[17] and *Mohamud v Morrison.*[18] The former concerns the abuse of a foster child abuse by foster parents that triggered the vicarious liability of local authorities that selected persons to be appointed foster parents. In the latter, a company running a petrol station was held vicariously liable *vis-à-vis* Mohamud who had used a petrol station kiosk and approached a member of staff for the acts of an employee who responded in an aggressive manner and assaulted him.

The same line of reasoning is reflected in continental case law. Taking the Polish examples, one can mention the judgment of the Court of Appeal in Poznan[19] and the judgment of the Supreme Court of 25 November 2015.[20] In the first, the court dismissed the appeal against the judgment granting damages under Article 430 of the Civil Code (based on the vicarious liability framework) in respect of harm suffered as a result of sexual abuse committed by a priest who is a member of the defendant convent. In the second judgment, the Supreme Court held a bank vicariously liable for a theft committed by a cashier – a bank employee who embezzled money from the claimant's account.

Second, in contemporary case law, there is no requirement for agents necessarily to be employees. In common law, the relationship 'akin to employment' is said to suffice. This means in practical terms that independent contractors may fall into the scope of vicarious liability as approached in current case law. In *Armes v Nottinghamshire County Council* and *Cox v Ministry of Justice*[21] this requirement was even more relaxed. In the latter case, the Supreme Court took the view that an employment relationship is to be ascertained between the Ministry of Justice and a prisoner who negligently caused injury to another prison employee.

7. Future of vicarious liability and the platforms: fairness, justice, and trust

The reasons underlying the evolution of vicarious liability are quite different from the traditional idea behind this liability scheme. They seem to be shared in both common law and civil law; however, they are easier to grasp while analyzing case law within common law jurisdictions. In *Lister v Hesley Hall*

17 See *Armes v Nottinghamshire County Council* [2017] UKSC 60.
18 See *Mohamud v WM Morrison Supermarkets plc* [2016] UKSC 11.
19 Poznań Court of Appeal (*Sąd Apelacyjny w Poznaniu*) judgment of 2 October 2018, I ACa 539/18.
20 Supreme Court of the Republic of Poland (*Sąd Najwyższy*) judgment of 25 November 2015, II CSK 683/14, LEX 1962511.
21 See *Cox v Ministry of Justice* [2016] UKSC 10.

Ltd, it was held that the 'scope of employment' condition is met if the acts of the abuser were 'so closely connected with his employment that it would be fair and just to hold the employers vicariously liable'. This view was later supported in *Mohamud v WM Morrison Supermarkets plc* where a connection between the position of the agent and his wrongful conduct was said to be sufficient to give rise to vicarious liability, where it makes it right for the principal to be held liable for reasons of social justice. Vicarious liability is predominantly used to 'sue into deeper pockets'. Another reason that renders the imposition of vicarious liability fair seems to be a particular feature of the situation in which loss has been caused – for instance, trust that is extended to the principal institution by the victim and which is abused by the acts of the agent who caused harm.[22] It appears that the liberalization of the traditional view on the prerequisites of vicarious liability and a gradual widening of its scope of application is motivated largely by public policy considerations. Originally, the new approach to vicarious liability evolved in a very particular context of vulnerable victims of wrongful acts of sexual harassment (very often acts committed by clergy), where these policy considerations played the primary role. In such cases, there is serious social pressure on ascribing liability to the master (principal institutions) and the need for fairness in calls for liability. The new approach, however, appears to stretch to all areas and thus develops into the modern theory of vicarious liability. An apt example is the *Morrisons* data leak case.[23]

The judgment concerning the case was issued in the UK before the General Data Protection Regulation (GDPR) was in place and thus decided on the Data Protection Act from 1998. The Morrisons supermarket chain was found (both by the High Court and the Court of Appeal) liable for a personal data breach carried out by an employee, a senior internal auditor at the supermarket, who deliberately leaked the details of staff members (information about staff salaries, bank details, and national insurance numbers) to take revenge on the employer for disciplinary punishment. The High Court dismissed the primary claims as Morrisons had not authorized misuse of information and had appropriate measures in place that were intended to prevent misuse of personal data by Morrisons employees. Despite this, Morrisons was held vicariously liable.

8. The sharing economy and vicarious liability: conclusions

The new approach to vicarious liability seems to fit the sharing economy context. An average client (average intermediary platform user) does not

22 See the so-called 'occasion test' proposed in the Australian case *Prince Alfred College Incorporated v ADC* [2016] HCA 37, and the Canadian case *Bazley v Curry* [1999] 2 SCR 534. See also Mohamud v WM Morrison *Supermarkets plc* [2016] UKSC 11; Gray (n 13) 83.

23 *WM Morrison Supermarkets plc v Various Claimants* [2018] EWCA Civ 2339.

realize that a driver who gives them a lift is not legally linked to the platform and that the platform is not liable for acts of the driver. For an average client, it is not clear that the contract for a ride is made only with the driver and not with Uber. It is the label of Uber that seems to be decisive when choosing to use the service.[24] The freelancer driver who is not connected to Uber would not be approached by an average client. In other words, it is trust towards Uber that attracts clients. This brings us back to the traditional approach to vicarious liability as the condition of enterprise causation underpinning vicarious liability seems to be met. What is more, the scenario at hand seems to reflect the logic behind the new approach – since it is special trust, enhanced by the intermediary platforms, that enables the provision of a tangible service, it seems to be fair and just to impose on the platform liability for the acts of agents (drivers) who abuse this trust, be it acts of negligent driving or intentional assaults.

Bibliography

Bar C von and Drobnig U, *The Interaction of Contract Law and Tort and Property Law in Europe: A Comparative Study* (De Gruyter 2009)

Best A and Barnes DW, *Basic Tort Law: Cases, Statutes, and Problems* (Aspen Publishers 2007)

Caringella F, *Responsabilità civile e assicurazioni: Normativa e giurisprudenza ragionata* (Giuffrè Editore 2008)

Fenyves A and others (eds), *Compulsory Liability Insurance from a European Perspective* (De Gruyter 2016) [DOI: https://doi.org/10.1515/9783110486179]

Franzoni M, *L'illecito* (2nd edn, Giuffrè Editore 2010)

Giliker P, *Vicarious Liability in Tort: A Comparative Perspective* (CUP 2010) [DOI: https://doi.org/10.1017/cbo9780511779008]

——— 'Analysing Institutional Liability for Child Sexual Abuse in England and Wales and Australia: Vicarious Liability, Non-Delegable Duties and Statutory Intervention' (2018) 77 *CLJ* 506 [DOI: https://doi.org/10.1017/S0008197318000685]

Gniewek E and Machnikowski P (eds), *Kodeks cywilny: Komentarz* (9th edn, CH Beck 2019)

Goh Y and Yip M, 'Concurrent Liability in Tort and Contract: An Analysis of Interplay, Intersection and Independence' (2017) 24 *TLJ* 148

Gray A, *Vicarious Liability: Critique and Reform* (Hart Publishing 2018) [DOI: http://dx.doi.org/10.5040/9781509920266]

Gyódi K, 'Uber vs Licensed Taxi Drivers: A War Between Technological Standards' (2017) *Working Paper DELab UW* 2 <www.delab.uw.edu.pl/wp-content/uploads/2020/07/WP_2_2017_K.Gyodi_.pdf> accessed 28 May 2021

Inglese M, *Regulating the Collaborative Economy in the European Union Digital Single Market* (Springer 2019) [DOI: https://doi.org/10.1007/978-3-030-30040-1]

24 It is emblematic that starting from 2020 in Poland the cars are literally labelled as Uber cars, because the drivers are under a legal duty to sign their cars.

Machnikowski P, 'Odpowiedzialność za wykonawcę powierzonej czynności' in Olejniczak A (ed), *System Prawa Prywatnego: Prawo zobowiązań – część ogólna*, vol 6 (3rd edn, CH Beck 2018)
McIvor C, 'The Use and Abuse of the Doctrine of Vicarious Liability' (2006) 35 *CLWR* 268 [DOI: https://doi.org/10.1350%2Fclwr.2006.35.4.268]
Muntaner C, 'Digital Platforms, Gig Economy, Precarious Employment, and the Invisible Hand of Social Class' (2018) 48 *Int J Health Serv* 597 [DOI: https://doi.org/10.1177%2F0020731418801413]
Sharkey CM, 'Institutional Liability for Employees' Intentional Torts: Vicarious Liability as a Quasi-Substitute for Punitive Damages' (2018) 53 *Val U L Rev* 1
Swanton J, 'The Convergence of Tort and Contract' (1989) 12 *Syd LR* 71
Szpunar A, 'Czyny niedozwolone w kodeksie cywilnym' (1970) 15 *Stud Cywilis* 67
Van Dam C, *European Tort Law* (2nd edn, OUP 2013)

4 Rethinking tort law in the corporate group situation

Christian A Witting[1]

1. Introduction

Modern tort law must deal with disputes that are far removed from the individual contests over personal liberty and the possession of property that characterized the common law well up to the nineteenth century. Although these individual contests continue to be at the heart of philosophical discussion of the subject, the discussion misses an important point. Many torts committed today arise on a mass scale and are subject to tort liability regimes – sometimes statutory in nature, sometimes not – that attempt to respond to important social, commercial, and legal challenges. The passage of the Product Liability Directive[2] is an example of a modern tort liability regime that attempts to fix responsibility for product defects upon manufacturers and/or suppliers[3] – although it has several critical flaws, including a wide development risks defence and a relatively restrictive limitation period that make it inapplicable to most of the corporate group liability problems discussed in this chapter.

This chapter concerns itself with the rise of the corporate group and its place in tort law. Ever since the 1920s or 1930s, companies that are constituents of corporate groups have undertaken the bulk of industrial and commercial activity.[4] This is reflected, for example, in the fact that some 40% of the international trans-shipment of goods actually involves intra-group sales.[5] The contention is that liability rules in the common law world have not

1 The paper on which this chapter was based was presented at the Zagreb International Conference on the Law of Obligations while the author was Professor of Private Law at Queen Mary University of London (QMUL), which institution funded the author's travel to and subsistence in Zagreb. The author gratefully acknowledges QMUL's funding.

2 Council Directive 85/374/EC of 25 July 1985 on the approximation of laws, regulations and administrative provisions of the Member States concerning liability for defective products [1985] *OJ* L210/29 (Product Liability Directive).

3 Product Liability Directive, Arts 1, 3(1), and 3(3).

4 Jose Antunes, *Liability of Corporate Groups: Autonomy and Control in Parent-Subsidiary Relationships in US, German and EU Law* (Kluwer 1994) 37.

5 Geoffrey Jones, *Multinationals and Global Capitalism: From the Nineteenth to the Twenty-First Century* (OUP 2005) 40.

DOI: 10.4324/9781003080596-5

responded adequately to the rise and dominance of corporate groups. This has been evident especially in the long and drawn-out wake of the asbestos contamination tragedy. The failure of common law legislatures and courts to devise an appropriate system of extended liability rules (applicable when a group subsidiary is unable to meet its tort debts) has been a result, in part, of law-makers not understanding fully the modern corporate group and the way in which it operates. It is a result also of the fact that those same law-makers have not appreciated fully that existing legal tools are very unsatisfactory in dealing with the challenges. From this it is not hard to see that – just like tech companies operating in the digital commerce space – corporate groups frequently operate in a kind of legal 'Wild West' that fails to hold them responsible, when it is appropriate to do so, for injuries that they cause. The aim of this chapter is to survey the subject matter and to offer guidance about the best way forward.

The chapter is structured as follows. First, consideration is given to the ways in which a corporate group might engage in judgment-proofing – or the structuring of group companies in order to protect major assets while avoiding payment of tort liability costs. Second, the chapter will examine the responses of common law courts to the problems of corporate groups, including their efforts at judgment-proofing. Courts have entertained claims for extensions of liability from insolvent subsidiaries to parent companies in cases involving veil-piercing, the tort of negligence, and the doctrine of joint tortfeasance. Some observations are made as to why common law rules have been inadequate to the task of extending liability by utilization of these torts and doctrines. Third, the chapter turns to consider a very interesting attempt by a legislature to create an appropriate extended liability regime in circumstances where mass torts have the potential to arise on a catastrophic scale – which subsists in the United States' Oil Pollution Act 1990. Despite some obvious shortcomings, the Act has useful provisions on financial responsibility and the deployment of strict liability that hold lessons for the future. Finally, the chapter presents advice about how the existing common law liability regime (such as it is) might be developed so as to deal with the problems of corporate groups, judgment-proofing, and unsatisfied liability claims.

2. Judgment-proofing in corporate groups

One of the reasons for which corporate groups are pervasive in modern, international commerce is that many kinds of industrial and other commercial activity must be carried out on a large scale in order to be profitable. The conduct of commercial activity on a large scale creates, in turn, business pressures to divisionalize operations. Divisionalization involves senior management structuring operations so that corporate headquarters is not overloaded by excessive flows of information and decision-making responsibility (with which it cannot deal effectively) but given a selective role only. The corporate headquarters has responsibility for a limited range of decisions, typically with respect to group/corporate structure, acquisitions and divestments, financing of operations, strategic decision-making, and performance goals.[6] Rarely will corporate headquarters executives in medium- and larger-size businesses have sufficient recent industry expertise and time to make decisions with an operational dimension.[7] Instead, corporate management will divisionalize, so that different kinds of business activity are separated from each other and day-to-day operating decisions are delegated down the management hierarchy to second-tier, third-tier, and even more junior decision-making units.[8]

The decision-making efficacy that accompanies divisionalization of operations – whether done according to geographical markets, product types, or functions – leads inexorably to the adoption by medium- and larger-size businesses of the multidivisional or M-Form corporate group.[9] This is to say that each division and sub-division within the group will be incorporated as separate legal entities, each entity being related to the other entities by way of equity holdings arranged in a vertical alignment. This will facilitate the transmission of decisions from corporate headquarters down to divisional headquarters and from there to the operating companies via a set of operating plans.[10] Each company holding shares in subordinate divisional companies will (likely elect to) take advantage of limited liability so that it is not legally responsible for ordinary trading debts or for losses caused by those subordinates.

Not coincidentally, then, the corporate group presents a substantial problem for tort law and for the enforcement of obligations. The parent company, which (especially in conglomerate groups) might be a mere holding company with limited managerial capability,[11] will want to ensure that group assets are protected and that liabilities are incurred only by thinly capitalized subsidiaries.[12] By way of a simple example, we see that the parent company will incorporate Sub-A to hold assets and Sub-B to conduct risky activities. The operating company, Sub-B, will have the use of plant and machinery only through contractual leasehold arrangements.[13] The parent company

6 See eg Alfred Chandler, *Strategy and Structure: Chapters in the History of the Industrial Enterprise* (MIT Press 1962) 13; Henry Mintzberg, *The Structuring of Organizations* (Pearson 1979) 154–56.

7 Chandler, *Strategy and Structure* (n 6) 623; Jones (n 5) 182.

8 Dwarka Chakravarty and others, 'Multinational enterprise regional management centers: Characteristics and performance' (2017) 52 *J World Bus* 296, 298.

9 Alfred Chandler, *Scale and Scope: The Dynamics of Industrial Capitalism* (Belknap Press 1990) 45.

10 ibid 232.

11 Eg *Vedanta Resources plc v Lungowe* [2019] 2 WLR 1051 (nineteen employees in ultimate parent of the group); *Okpabi v Royal Dutch Shell plc* [2017] EWHC 89 (TCC) (Royal Dutch Shell plc, apart from setting overall group business strategy and business principles, was said to be little more than an investment vehicle).

12 See, especially, Lynn M LoPucki, 'The Death of Liability' (1996) 106 *Yale LJ* 1.

13 See ibid 28; Andrew Muscat, *The Liability of the Holding Company for the Debts of Its Insolvent Subsidiaries* (Dartmouth 1996) 90; Antunes (n 4) 6.

will provide capital or loan funds to Sub-B only when convenient to do so.[14] If Sub-B causes injuries, it will be unable to compensate all victims and the parent company will rely upon its own limited liability in order to avoid making contributions to compensation awards. This is the practice of judgment-proofing, which Lynn LoPucki thought would lead to the 'death of liability'.[15]

Consistent with theory, recent empirical work confirms that, especially in jurisdictions where rules extending liability within groups are weak, the conduct of riskier types of business activity with their expected higher liabilities results in corporate groups engaging in more extensive divisionalization, incorporation of subsidiaries, and asset-partitioning.[16]

In a related judgment-proofing scenario, the threat of large tort liabilities might encourage the parent company to move assets from one group company to another in order to protect them. This can be done in a multitude of ways, including by the imposition of management and other fees,[17] the payment of dividends to the parent, the withdrawal of finance support by the parent, the unwarranted extension by the subsidiary of guarantees to other group companies, disadvantageous transfer pricing, and/or the commingling of subsidiary assets with those of other companies.[18] While, in theory, shuttling strategies are vulnerable to reversal under certain statutory provisions and common law doctrines, the point is that operating companies are likely to be inadequately financed when tort liability threatens.[19] In multinational groups, judgment-proofing might involve further strategies.[20] For example, a parent company might incorporate subsidiaries in low-regulation jurisdictions, which permit exclusion in employment contracts of liability for death and personal injuries.[21] Even in the absence of this 'benefit', the parent company might locate risky physical processes in low-regulation jurisdictions, typically developing countries, because of their relaxed safety standards and lower damages awards.[22] In other cases, especially when tort liability

14 Muscat (n 13) 314.

15 LoPucki (n 12). Liability is more likely to be subverted in cases where the parent company is indifferent to the potential hit to its reputation: see Christian Witting, *Liability of Corporate Groups and Networks* (CUP 2018), especially 95.

16 Sharon Belenzon, Niron Hashai, and Andrea Patacconi, 'The architecture of attention: Group structure and subsidiary autonomy' (2019) 40 *Strateg Manag J* 1610, 1614.

17 John Farrar, 'Legal Issues Involving Corporate Groups' (1998) 16 *C&SLJ* 184, 189.

18 Muscat (n 13) 76–83. Note that commingling probably is rare due to the need for companies to keep proper records of their assets and liabilities under company and tax legislation: ibid 291.

19 Eg *Vedanta Resources plc v Lungowe* [2019] 2 WLR 1051.

20 Leading writers have asserted that there are distinct patterns of judgment-proofing behaviour: eg Henry Hansmann and Reinier Kraakman, 'Toward Unlimited Shareholder Liability for Corporate Torts' (1991) 100 *Yale LJ* 1879, 1881.

21 *Newton-Sealy v ArmorGroup Services Ltd* [2008] EWHC 233 (QB), [36].

22 *Sithole v Thor Chemicals Holdings Ltd* 2000 WL 1421183 (English Court of Appeal, 28 September 2000).

threatens, parent companies might deliberately keep valuable assets offshore. While some assets are more mobile than others, it has become commonplace, for example, to transfer intellectual property rights to subsidiaries in low-tax jurisdictions.[23]

In the chemical, asbestos, and tobacco industries,[24] judgment-proofing has been observed as a late-stage strategy utilized in order to protect group assets.[25] A favoured tactic in those contexts is the divestment of subsidiaries that undertake particularly risky physical and related processes and/or the sub-contracting of such processes to independent, thinly capitalized companies.[26] In the asbestos industry,[27] for example, this was evident in:

(1) The United States, where Cape Industries plc[28] sold its asbestos distribution subsidiary to the manager of that company (an individual) and moved its remaining assets out of the jurisdiction. Victims of asbestos sued the subsidiary company successfully in Texas, but enforcement proceedings in the UK failed because the parent company was held not to have been 'present' in the US after divestment.[29]

(2) Australia, where the James Hardie Industries Group[30] tried to divest its asbestos-producing subsidiaries before relocating group headquarters to Amsterdam (and from there to Dublin).[31] While the reasons for re-incorporation outside Australia were said to be related to the greater focus on northern hemisphere (and particularly United States') business activity and to associated tax benefits, the Australian subsidiaries were left with inadequate assets to meet growing numbers of asbestos liability

23 Vanessa Houlder, Katie Carnie, and Caroline Nevitt, 'Tax Reduction Jargon Explained' *Financial Times* (Online, 10 June 2013) <www.ft.com/personal-finance/tax> accessed 7 February 2020.

24 Antunes (n 4) 271; Meredith Dearborn, 'Enterprise Liability: Reviewing and Revitalizing Liability for Corporate Groups' (2009) 97 *CLR* 195, 198; Mark Roe, 'Corporate Strategic Reaction to Mass Tort' (1986) 72 *Va L Rev* 1, 39–40.

25 Jay Lawrence Westbrook, 'Transparency in Corporate Groups' (2018) 13 *Brook J Corp Fin & Com L* 33, 36.

26 See eg Hansmann and Kraakman (n 20) 1881 and 1884 (discussing empirical evidence).

27 See Witting, *Liability of Corporate Groups and Networks* (n 15) ch 4 (Case study I).

28 Andrea Boggio, 'Linking Corporate Power to Corporate Structures: An Empirical Analysis' (2012) 22 *S & LS* 107. See also Jock McCulloch and Geoffrey Tweedale, *Defending the Indefensible* (OUP 2008).

29 *Adams v Cape Industries plc* [1990] Ch 433.

30 See Gideon Haigh, *Asbestos House: The Secret History of James Hardie Industries* (Scribe 2006); David Francis Jackson QC, 'Report of the Special Commission of Inquiry into the Medical Research and Compensation Fund' (NSW Government 2004); Stefan HC Lo, *In Search of Corporate Accountability: Liabilities of Corporate Participants* (Cambridge Scholars 2015), especially ch 2.

31 Ian Verrender, 'Hardie's Legal Marathon Ends with Statement of the Bleeding Obvious' *The Sydney Morning Herald* (Online, 5 May 2012) <www.smh.com.au/business/hardies-legal-marathon-ends-with-statement-of-the-bleeding-obvious-20120504-1y4c5.html> accessed 28 May 2021.

claims. This attempt at separation might well have succeeded had it not inspired the ire of activist trade unions. The New South Wales government threatened to reverse the James Hardie group divestment by way of legislation, which forced it to the negotiating table and to provide eventually the necessary funds for meeting asbestos claims.[32]

Although asbestos has presented the major example of ruinous judgment-proofing activity to date, future problems might well arise from industries contributing to the 'synthetic living' that is pervasive in modern society.[33] 'Synthetic living' involves the use of artificial products, the deployment of new technologies, and scientific discoveries the medium- to long-term risks of which might not become apparent until many years after testing is over and consumption has begun.[34] Moreover, the mass production, storage, and distribution of goods means that catastrophes become large-scale events which have a substantial impact upon persons, property, and the environment.[35] As adumbrated, the European Union Product Liability Directive (and Member State transpositions of relevant rules) might be unable to accommodate resulting liability claims[36] because of the operation of the development risks defence[37] and the limitation of actions under the ten-year long-stop provision.[38]

The pharmaceutical industry is an obvious candidate for *future* judgment-proofing problems.[39] Although there are well-established processes for the testing and certification of new pharmaceutical products, these have inherent limitations.[40] Frequently, it will be impossible to predict all of the medium- to long-term health consequences of the consumption or application of new drugs and other pharmaceutical products. And 'Big Pharma' understands the potential liability problems only too well. The practice for many years has been for pharma groups to rely upon drug discovery companies for researching and developing new molecules. The pharma group will join forces with a drug discovery company when development has reached a satisfac

32 James Hardie Industries NV and New South Wales Government, 'Amended and Restated Final Funding Agreement' (NSW Government, 21 November 2006).

33 *Dalehite v United States*, 346 US 15, 51–2 (1953).

34 Kip Viscusi and Richard Zeckhauser, 'Deterring and Compensating Oil-Spill Catastrophes: The Need for Strict Two-Tier Liability' (2011) 64 *Vand L Rev* 1717, 1726.

35 ibid 1727.

36 David Harland, 'The Influence of European Law on Product Liability in Australia' (1995) 17 *Syd LR* 336, 344.

37 Product Liability Directive, Art 7(e).

38 Product Liability Directive, Art 11. The long-stop is designed to ensure legal certainty, the ability of producers to insure against liability, and continued innovation in industries such as the pharmaceuticals industry: Case C–358/08, *Aventis Pasteur SA v OB* [2009] *ECR* I-11305, ECLI:EU:C:2009:744, 113 BMLR 1, [41]–[42], and [46].

39 Witting, *Liability of Corporate Groups and Networks* (n 15) ch 4 (Case study II).

40 See Ben Goldacre, *Bad Pharma* (Fourth Estate 2013) (expressing grave concerns about these processes).

tory stage perhaps by taking over the smaller entity[41] – or else by entering into a funding, licensing, and/or distribution agreement that eschews equity involvement.[42] The point is that risky physical processes are not undertaken by the large, well-funded pharma group, but by a relative commercial minnow. This method of conducting risky research and development activity is likely to be a feature in other areas as well. Thus, the problem of judgment-proofing and under-funded corporate injurers is a structural one.

Corporate groups are evolving in further ways that might make it difficult to impose liability upon them using traditional rules and doctrines. We find, for example, that interactions between corporate group companies (and even between network partners) are becoming automated in nature. Thus, Sub-A might receive an online order for a drug or other risky product and send the order automatically to Sub-B or to an outside supplier. The order will be received and fulfilled by way of a computer program.[43] The risks of liability between the companies might be determined in advance according to smart contracts, which are computer code instructions triggered automatically upon the happening of specified events. Although today's smart contracts are not very reliable, due to shortcomings in the underlying blockchain technology,[44] the direction of travel in the structuring of corporate group (and network) transactions is clearly towards greater automation of decision-making and a lesser involvement for humans in assessing specific risks and taking precautions. This will make it more difficult to identify fault and allocate blame under traditional tort rules and doctrines. The greater problem for tort law is simply this: that tort law rules would mean nothing if they could be easily and regularly evaded by the corporate groups that undertake the bulk of commercial activity involving physical risk-taking.

3. The judicial response to judgment-proofing

How have courts dealt with the type of responsibility minimization-cum-avoidance evident in judgment-proofing and related corporate group practices? The basic approach of common law courts to judgment-proofing activity is to hold that this is *permissible*, so long as the structuring of relations among group companies does not occur *after* liabilities have started to arise. This was affirmed in the most strident terms in *Adams v Cape Industries plc*, where the English Court of Appeal held that group companies are to be

41 Peter Lee, 'Innovation and the Firm: A New Synthesis' (2018) 70 *Stan L Rev* 1431, detecting a movement back to the group form in the biotech industry.

42 Matthew Jennejohn, 'The Private Order of Innovation Networks' (2016) 68 *Stan L Rev* 281 (analyzing sample of agreements).

43 Jay Galbraith, *Designing Organizations: Strategy, Structure and Process at the Business Unit and Enterprise Levels* (3rd edn, Jossey-Bass 2014), 39–40.

44 Kelvin FK Low and Eliza Mik, 'Pause the Blockchain Legal Revolution' (2020) 69 *ICLQ* 135.

treated as separate entities with their own legal obligations, and that it is impermissible for a court to

> lift the corporate veil as against a defendant company which is the member of a corporate group merely because the corporate structure has been used so as to ensure that the legal liability (if any) in respect of particular future activities of the group [...] will fall on another member of the group rather than the defendant company.[45]

In the United Kingdom, the company law doctrine of veil-piercing is available against a parent company with under-funded or insolvent subsidiaries only where the parent has exercised control over the subsidiaries and specific prior legal obligations have been evaded.[46] 'Legal obligations' refer, in this context, to causes of action already formed at the time of the actions constituting evasion,[47] which is a very restrictive conception of actionability emanating (so it seems) from the old fraud ground for veil-piercing.[48] Given the restrictive nature of the rules, it is unsurprising to find that there have been no successful veil-piercing cases in the UK arising from judgment-proofing in corporate groups.[49] Although veil-piercing law in Australia is wider, there have been no successful actions there either. In the United States, while some successful veil-piercing actions against corporate groups can be found, the doctrine is seen to be in a poor state with inconsistent results.[50]

Other common law rules and doctrines might be invoked in order to extend liability from under-funded or insolvent subsidiaries. The law of negligence has proven slightly more useful than veil-piercing in facilitating extended liability claims in the corporate group context, but the number of successful cases is small, nevertheless. Liability appears to be dependent upon the exercise of operational control by one entity over another, the evidence for which is rarely to be found and expensive to obtain. In the eponymous case of *Chandler v Cape plc*,[51] the English Court of Appeal held that a parent

45 [1990] Ch 433, 544.

46 *Prest v Petrodel Resources plc* [2013] 2 AC 415, [35].

47 But see argument in Stefan HC Lo, 'Piercing of the Corporate Veil for the Evasion of Tort Obligations' (2017) 46 *CLWR* 42.

48 See Christian Witting, 'Piercing the Corporate Veil' in William Day and Sarah Worthington (eds), *Challenging Private Law* (Hart 2020), Ch 17.

49 See, especially, *Adams v Cape Industries plc* [1990] Ch 433 for explanation. Note that, in this chapter, true veil-piercing is considered to be available only against parent companies and does not 'go the other way' so as to allow access to the assets of subsidiary companies: see Edwin Mujih, 'Piercing the corporate veil: where is the reverse gear?' (2017) 133 *LQR* 322 (describing the latter cases as involving reverse veil-piercing). For this reason, *Smith Stone & Knight v Birmingham Corpn* [1939] 4 All ER 116 is not considered herein to be a true veil-piercing case. Even if it had been, it would not be decided the same way were current veil-piercing rules applied to its facts.

50 Kurt Strasser, 'Piercing the Veil in Corporate Groups' (2005) 37 *Conn L Rev* 637, 639.

51 [2012] 1 WLR 3111.

company owed a duty of care to employees of the subsidiary where the parent company itself had intervened in subsidiary company affairs, by making arrangements as to the required health and safety practices in the subsidiary company.[52] Although the case represented a slight liberalization of the law in this area, it should be kept in mind that the facts were (by modern standards) unusual because the parent company was located at the same geographical location as the subsidiary company, the latter undertaking the hazardous manual labour work that impacted upon the claimant.[53] Modern corporate groups are unlikely to operate in this way and larger groups especially are unlikely to exercise operational control over subsidiaries – which could make a difference to the result.

In the more recent negligence case of *Vedanta Resources plc v Lungowe*,[54] the United Kingdom Supreme Court held out the prospect that a parent company might owe duties of care to those affected by subsidiary company activities where the parent company has imposed improper policies upon, or given erroneous advice to, the subsidiary company about hazardous operations *and* where steps have been taken to see that they are implemented.[55] This might be an indication that parent company liability will be extended in the future from cases of direct control by the parent over the activities of the subsidiary to cases where the links to the causation of harm are more indirect in nature.[56]

Another branch of the common law might prove important in the development of an appropriate legal response to the liability problems presented by corporate groups – that being the branch constituted by the rules on joint tortfeasance. Although these rules were of little relevance to the corporate group situation until relatively recently, that changed with the United Kingdom Supreme Court's decision in *Fish & Fish Ltd v Sea Shepherd UK*.[57] The case had the advantage (for us) of having concerned a small-scale 'corporate group'. The court decided that liability could be extended beyond a primary tortfeasor in circumstances where three elements are satisfied: First, D2 must act to assist D1 in the commission of acts amounting to a tort. D2's act must be substantial (more than merely facilitative) in nature.[58] Second, there must be a 'common design' as between D1 and D2 consisting in agreement of some kind (whether explicit or not) that they should work towards a

52 [2012] 1 WLR 3111, 3116–18.
53 [2012] 1 WLR 3111, 3114–15.
54 [2019] 2 WLR 1051.
55 [2019] 2 WLR 1051, [49] and [51]–[53].
56 Having said this, experience tells us that, in contentious cases, courts revert to narrow and legalistic criteria of liability: Virginia Harper Ho, 'Theories of Corporate Groups: Corporate Identity Reconceived' (2012) 42 *Seton Hall L Rev* 879, 932.
57 *Fish & Fish Ltd v Sea Shepherd UK* [2015] AC 1229.
58 [2015] AC 1229, at [21], [23], [37], [49], [57], and [58]. See also Pey Woan Lee, 'Accessory Liability in Tort and Equity' (2015) 27 *S Ac LJ* 853, 861.

common end.[59] Third, the primary wrongdoer must commit the tort regarding which D2's acts of assistance must be a contributing cause.[60] The most difficult aspect of this definition of joint tortfeasance concerns the 'common design'. In *Sea Shepherd*, there were differing opinions on what would suffice. Lord Sumption JSC held that there must be a shared *intention* to commit the acts which prove to be tortious,[61] while Lords Toulson JSC and Neuberger PSC would have accepted knowledge in D2 of D1's intention to commit a tort[62] (which is more consistent with the general law in this area).[63]

In the subsequent case of *Glaxo Wellcome UK Ltd v Sandoz Group*,[64] the rules established in outline in the *Sea Shepherd* case were interpreted in a liberal fashion. The English Court of Appeal accepted that four companies in a group each had the common intention and design of selling a certain product with a chosen design and get-up so as to create confusion about its origins, thereby arguably committing the tort of passing off. This was in circumstances where each company had a role to play in the development, testing, marketing, and sale of the allegedly infringing product. In so holding, Sir Timothy Lloyd stated that 'if the common design is shared between several parties to a combination, it matters not that some relevant acts are done only by one or some parties and other relevant acts are done by others'.[65] But there would be no joint tort in a case where one company merely sold an infringing product to another company in the same group.[66] Still, *Glaxo* is an encouraging follow-up to the Supreme Court decision, which takes a wider rather than a narrower view of the requirements.

Needless to say, the limits of the joint tortfeasance doctrine in the group context are still being worked out, but there is great potential with respect to the doctrine because once a party is declared to be a joint tortfeasor, that party will be liable for all the consequences of a common design even though it has not participated in all relevant acts and 'even though as to some of the incidents [the defendant might] not have anticipated that they would happen'.[67]

What does the developing case law on veil-piercing, negligence, and joint tortfeasance tell us about the common law extended liability regime as it applies to corporate groups? Although small steps have been made which have had the effect of liberalizing substantive liability rules, and although these rules have become more accommodative of liability claims extending from

59 [2015] AC 1229, [23], [37], and [55]. See also *Unilever plc v Gillette (UK) Ltd* [1989] RPC 583, 609; Joachim Dietrich and Pauline Ridge, *Accessories in Private Law* (CUP 2015) 117.
60 Paul S Davies, *Accessory Liability* (Hart 2015) 12–13; Dietrich and Ridge (n 59) 38.
61 [2015] AC 1229, at [44]. See Lee (n 58) 862–64.
62 [2015] AC 1229, at [27] and [60] respectively.
63 Dietrich and Ridge (n 59) 4, 12–13, 29, 43–60, 93–94, 116–17, and 127–30.
64 [2017] FSR 32.
65 [2017] FSR 32, [31].
66 [2017] FSR 32, [32].
67 Dietrich and Ridge (n 59) 133, citing *Schumann v Abbott and Davis* [1961] SASR 149, 155.

insolvent subsidiary companies to their parents, they have not proven to be especially useful yet in practical terms. It is suggested that the following are important lessons about the common law's response (so far).

First, company law rules of separate legal personality and limited liability have prevailed over tort law rules, doctrine, and ideals. While the company law rules on separate legal personality and limited liability are laid out in legislation – and in that sense are primary – there has been little questioning of how far they really extend. Thus, we might note that rules on limited liability were introduced before companies started acquiring shares in other companies and before tort liability presented any threat to the solvency of companies.[68] It appears to be possible, at least, to argue that the legislation was never intended to – and that it does not – apply to situations that were not foreseen and that have not been debated. The counterargument would be that the rules have been re-enacted on several occasions since being introduced so that they and their consequences have been sufficiently well known to the legislature.

Second, courts have been content to leave the burden of obtaining evidence of corporate group operating practices upon claimants who, typically, have little access to group documentation and other types of evidence. Most claims never get off the ground because of the difficulties involved with outside parties trying to prove the existence of control, duties of care, and/or fault in parent companies. Dearborn has presented an argument for a type of enterprise liability that would overcome some of the difficulty by creating a reversed onus of proof upon 'enterprises'. Once a company (the injuring company) has been found to have had a causal connection to the commission of a mass tort which resulted in the claimant's injury, her preferred liability regime would place the onus upon the defendant company (the target company) to rebut the presumption of enterprise.[69] Although this idea has its problems (which are concerned with the defensibility of enterprise liability as a theory of corporate groups),[70] the suggestion about using reversed onuses of proof in order to counter obvious evidential difficulties is an appropriate one.

Third, courts have little understanding of the way in which corporate groups operate. They have assumed (without questioning) that parent companies do exercise control and an onus has been placed upon claimants in

68 Ben Pettet, 'Limited Liability – A Principle for the 21st Century?' (1995) 48 *CLP* 125, 152.

69 Dearborn (n 24) 253. See also Case C-97/08P *Akzo Nobel NV and Others v Commission of the European Communities* [2009] *ECR* I-8237, ECLI:EU:C:2009:536 (rebuttable presumption of parent company exercising decisive influence over (almost) wholly owned subsidiaries as a matter of European competition law so as to result in an 'undertaking' within the terms of the Treaty on the Functioning of the European Union, Art 101. But note that competition laws in this area are acknowledged to be sui generis because of the particular regulatory and policy objectives that inform them).

70 As to which, see Witting, *Liability of Corporate Groups and Networks* (n 15) 177ff.

both veil-piercing[71] and negligence[72] cases to prove control by the parent company. But this rarely is to be found in practice, especially in larger groups which operate along classic M-Form lines. As adumbrated, the M-Form group is decentralized in nature – major operating decisions being made either by second-tier 'divisional headquarters' companies in the product segments or by third-tier operating entities themselves.[73] So courts insist upon the presence of a factual element in the application of liability rules that is likely *not* to be present in the operation of the group, almost ensuring the defeat of liability claims.

4. Special statutory scheme: The Oil Pollution Act 1990

There has been a lot of interest, especially in the European literature on corporate group liability, in the recent developments in the United Kingdom rules on extended liability that have just been described. But it is not only courts that have sought to respond to the judgment-proofing problem. Legislatures in the common law world have made a small number of significant attempts at dealing with this problem as well – although these have been ad hoc and narrowly focused on resolving particular industry-based problems. Two important (and related) attempts have emanated from the United States: the Comprehensive Environmental Response, Compensation and Liability Act 1980 (CERCLA 1980)[74] and the Oil Pollution Act 1990 (OPA 1990).[75] While much has been written on CERCLA 1980 (because it is the pioneering legislation in this area), less has been written on the OPA 1990. This is despite the facts that the OPA 1990 embodies a more developed liability scheme and that it was the legislation that applied to the well-known *Deepwater Horizon* oil spill of 2010. Some important features of this scheme are worthy of our attention in thinking through the ways in which liability rules might be developed.

The OPA 1990 applies to environmental damage cases involving oil spills (and displaces CERCLA 1980 as the relevant legislative scheme in those particular cases). The Act facilitates United States' federal oversight of oil drilling and transportation, and provides important environmental safeguards by setting requirements for oil transportation vessel construction, mandating contingency planning, enhancing US federal disaster response capability,

71 ibid, especially 324.
72 *Vedanta Resources plc v Lungowe* [2019] 2 WLR 1051; *Chandler v Cape plc* [2012] 1 WLR 3111.
73 Chandler, *Scale and Scope* (n 9); Chakravarty and others (n 8) 296.
74 United States Code (USC), Title 42, Comprehensive Environmental Response, Compensation and Liability §§ 9601 to 9675. See also Directive 2004/35/EC of the European Parliament and of the Council of 21 April 2004 on environmental liability with regard to the prevention and remedying of environmental damage [2004] *OJ* L143/56.
75 USC, Title 33, Chapter 40, Oil Pollution §§ 2701 to 2761.

broadening enforcement authority, increasing potential liabilities, and imposing broad financial responsibility requirements.[76] Of interest to us is the fact that the OPA 1990 sets out a framework for making claims for damage from vessel- and facility-caused oil pollution occurring in US navigable waters.[77] The Act imposes strict joint and several liability for damage caused by oil spills. (Moreover, the liability regime is not exclusive in nature; it does not preclude the further imposition of liability under state law.[78]) The intention was to ensure that oil spill costs are internalized within the industry.[79] The US Coast Guard administers the regime insofar as it relates to vessels, operating the National Pollution Funds Center, while the Bureau of Ocean Energy Management administers the regime relating to offshore facilities.[80]

The OPA 1990 requires that operators of offshore facilities and of vessels establish their financial responsibility prior to commencement of operations.[81] For offshore facilities, for example, the OPA 1990 mandates that responsible parties demonstrate the availability of at least US$75 million, subject to increase by the US President up to a maximum of $150 million.[82] Following an oil spill giving rise to response costs and damage, claims can be made against responsible parties and (subject to limited defences) against guarantors that provide evidence of financial responsibility.[83] Ideally, financial responsibility would mandate significant *external* insurance cover, which creates incentives for external monitoring. But many oil industry participants act as self-insurers.[84] 'In this sense, it is fortunate that BP plc, and not a smaller firm, was the responsible party for the *Deepwater Horizon* spill'. 'Many smaller drilling firms would have been unable to cover the multibillion-dollar liability and would have gone bankrupt.'[85]

The OPA 1990 is enlivened where there is an oil discharge or a substantial threat of a discharge into US navigable waters or adjoining shorelines, or

76 US Coast Guard, 'Oil Pollution Act of 1990 (OPA)' (2016). The need for the legislation is evident in the fact that there have been close to 5,000 relevant oil spills between 1990 and 2015: US Coast Guard, 'Oil Pollution Act Liability Limits in 2015: Report to Congress' (October 2015) 5.

77 33 USC § 2702(a).

78 Mark A Cohen and others, 'Deepwater Drilling: Law, Policy, and Economics of Firm Organization and Safety' (2011) 64 *Vand L Rev* 1853, 1889.

79 *Rice v Harken Exploration Co*, 250 F 3d 264, 266 (5th Cir 2001).

80 See Bureau of Ocean Energy Management, 'BOEM Governing Statutes' (Undated); Jeffrey Morgan, 'The Oil Pollution Act of 1990: A Look at its Impact on the Oil Industry' (1994) 6 *Fordham Intl LJ* 1, 13 and 21.

81 33 USC § 2716.

82 33 USC § 2716(c)(1)(C).

83 In the case of external insurers, this reduces the possibility that liability cannot be satisfied because insurers have avoided policies: Morgan (n 80) 25.

84 Cohen and others (n 78) 1900. cf Morgan (n 80) 15 (expressing doubts about the feasibility of self-insurance).

85 Cohen and others (n 78) 1895.

into its exclusive economic zone.[86] In order to achieve simplicity in the regime that it creates, the OPA 'channels' responsibility to predefined parties. This is important, given that oil-drilling operations typically involve several partners and contractors. Channelling 'creates incentives for a responsible party to select and monitor partners and subcontractors with care, since the responsible party is ultimately responsible for damage[s] claims'.[87] In the case of an oil discharge from a vessel, the OPA defines 'responsible party' as encompassing 'any person owning or operating' the vessel.[88] In this, the Act creates 'a default presumption assigning liability to owners and operators of vessels that discharge oil into the navigable waters of the United States'.[89] In the case of an oil discharge from an offshore facility, the 'responsible party' means the holder of the drilling permit.[90] Responsible parties are liable to compensate for the causation of damage regardless of fault; liability is strict in nature.[91] This is seen as appropriate because of the clear understanding that the predefined parties take responsibility for oil operations, and because it reduces litigation costs.[92] Provisions like these have the potential to create liability in parent companies,[93] as well as in relevant network participants. Indeed, while OPA 1990 provisions are intended to facilitate straightforward claims by injured parties, they do not preclude legal actions by responsible parties against industry partners.[94] The legislation simply shifts the burden of establishing fault-based liability to responsible parties, who are provided with incentives to protect their legal position, in part, through ongoing monitoring of activity.[95]

The OPA 1990 provides an affirmative defence for responsible parties that can prove that an oil spill was caused solely by an act or omission of an unrelated third party, and that its own conduct was not negligent. The defence applies only where the responsible parties have no contractual relationships with those third parties.[96]

Under the OPA 1990, responsible parties are liable for the full costs of remediating public land, shorelines, inland waterways, and US coastal waters.[97]

86 33 USC § 2702(a).
87 Cohen and others (n 78) 1889.
88 33 USC § 2701(32)(A).
89 *Bean Dredging LLC* v *United States*, 773 F Supp 2d 63, 86 (DDC 2011).
90 33 USC § 2701(32)(C).
91 Morgan (n 80) 4.
92 Cohen and others (n 78) 1889.
93 See also Morgan (n 80) 9.
94 33 USC §§ 2712 and 2717.
95 Colin McDonell, 'The Gulf Coast Claims Facility and the *Deepwater Horizon* Litigation: Judicial Regulation of Private Compensation Schemes' (2012) 64 *Stan L Rev* 765, 768–69.
96 33 USC § 2703(a)(3). See Alfred Light, 'The Deepwater Horizon Oil Spill Trust and the Gulf Coast Claims Facility: The "Superfund" Myth and the Law of Unintended Consequences' (2011) 5 *Golden Gate U Envtl LJ* 87, 94–95.
97 33 USC § 2702. See Light (n 96) 97.

Claims can be made for the costs of removal of oil spills[98] and for various heads of damages.[99] Damages claims encompass: damage to real and personal property;[100] natural resources losses, including costs of restoring, rehabilitating, or replacing the claimant's natural resources as well as any diminution in the value of those resources pending restoration;[101] and purely financial losses, such as lost profits.[102] Claims for personal injury are precluded,[103] this being the most obvious (and intended) 'gap' in the operation of the regime. Moreover, the total amount of damages payable is subject to various caps, depending on the entity responsible for the spill.[104] However, the caps do not apply in situations of gross negligence, wilful misconduct, or violation of applicable federal regulations pertaining to safety, construction, or operation.[105] The latter exception would appear to be a wide one because of the great number of relevant rules in existence – meaning, in fact, that caps apply rarely.[106]

The OPA 1990 provides financing mechanisms for a trust fund,[107] which is used to cover the costs of oil spill clean-up and to meet uncompensated private claims up to a value of US$1 billion per oil spill incident.[108] The Oil Spill Liability Trust Fund (OSLTF), which is administered by the National

98 33 USC § 2702(a).

99 33 USC § 2702(b).

100 33 USC § 2702(b)(2)(B).

101 33 USC § 2702(b)(2)(A). These are payable to designated 'Natural Resource Trustees' rather than to private parties: see US Coast Guard, 'Oil Spill Liability Trust Fund (OSLTF) Funding for Oil Spills' (January 2006) 11.

102 33 USC § 2702(b)(2)(E). See, generally, McDonell (n 95) 768–69. 'OPA favors restoration and remediation to try to bring the resource back to its pre-spill condition': Viscusi and Zeckhauser (n 34) 1741. The availability of damages for purely financial losses represents a change from pre-existing law: Catherine Sharkey, 'The BP Oil Spill Settlements, Class-wide Punitive Damages, and Societal Deterrence' (2015) 64 *DePaul L Rev* 681, 695.

103 Light (n 96) 90.

104 33 USC § 2704(a). Arguments have been made for abolition of the caps because of their potential to cause 'moral hazard': eg Michael Greenstone, 'Liability and Financial Responsibility for Oil Spills under the Oil Pollution Act of 1990 and Related States' (Testimony before House of Representatives Committee on Transportation and Infrastructure) (9 June 2010).

105 33 USC § 2704(c). See Viscusi and Zeckhauser (n 34) 1739–40.

106 Cohen and others (n 78) 1890; Inho Kim, 'Financial Responsibility Rules under the Oil Pollution Act of 1990' (2002) 42 *Nat Resources J* 565, 566. The caps have been described as 'deceptive': Morgan (n 80) 7. But where caps *are* applicable, so that the Oil Spill Liability Trust Fund must pay, the numbers do add up. Between enactment and 2015, the trust was required to cover US$1.3 billion in removal costs: US Coast Guard, 'Oil Pollution Act Liability Limits in 2015' (n 76) 9.

107 The fund was created prior to passage of the Oil Pollution Act 1990 but was provided with funding only after the *Exxon Valdez* disaster: US Coast Guard, 'Oil Pollution Act Liability Limits in 2015' (n 76) 2.

108 USC, Title 26, Hazardous Substance Superfund, § 9509.

Pollution Funds Center (NPFC),[109] has two components.[110] First, the Emergency Fund, which comprises a sum of money set aside each year[111] for rapid response to oil spills and that requires no appropriation by Congress. It can be used for oil spill containment, countermeasures, clean-up, and disposal activities. Second, there is the Principal Fund, which can be used to pay uncompensated private removal costs and, potentially, could satisfy damages claims where a responsible party is not identified, is unable to pay, or has reached the applicable liability limit.[112] While the OSLTF frequently has been used for discharges from ships, it has been used also for discharges at industrial and onshore oil storage and production facilities.[113] The OSLTF has been used almost exclusively to pay for clean-up costs, rather than damages – it not having received sufficient appropriations for the latter.[114] The Principal Fund derives its revenues from several sources, including a nine-cent-per-barrel excise tax, cost recoveries from responsible parties, and criminal penalties and civil fines.[115]

In an interesting further example of judgment-proofing occurring in the commercial world, we might note that the passage of the OPA 1990 resulted in significant restructuring of parts of the oil industry and insurance provision, reflecting a desire on the part of industry participants to avoid the internalization of oil spill costs that Congress sought to achieve. Two notable effects were: first, there was significant disaggregation in corporate operations, in that parent companies moved towards the holding of subsidiaries with smaller fleets in order to protect group assets,[116] although this does not necessarily defeat the liability of the parent company should it be characterized as a responsible party.[117] Whether this is so or not, subdivision of fleets makes it more difficult to enforce the statutory provisions – especially when the bulk of corporate group assets is held outside the United States.[118] Second, captive insurers refused to provide financial responsibility statements, which would make them liable as guarantors.[119] In this, they demonstrated

109 See National Pollution Funds Center, 'Oil Pollution Act of 1990 (OPA)' (United States Coast Guard) <www.uscg.mil/Mariners/National-Pollution-Funds-Center/About_NPFC/OPA/> accessed 27 May 2021.

110 US Coast Guard, 'OSLTF' (n 101).

111 This sum has been modest and currently stands at US$50 million per year, with the possibility of obtaining a further $100 million advance from the Principal Fund if necessary: US Coast Guard, 'OSLTF' (n 101).

112 USC, Title 33, Chapter 40, Oil Pollution, § 2708.

113 US Coast Guard, 'OSLTF' (n 101).

114 Light (n 96) 90; Lawrence Kiern, 'Liability, Compensation, and Financial Responsibility under the Oil Pollution Act of 1990: A Review of the Second Decade' (2011) 36 *Tul Mar LJ* 1, 55.

115 US Coast Guard, 'OSLTF' (n 101).

116 Morgan (n 80) 8–9.

117 Kim (n 106) 568.

118 ibid 569.

119 Morgan (n 80) 14.

concern about the stability of OPA liability caps, and about the potential for further liability under state laws.[120] This second change in practice has spawned a sub-insurance market for financial responsibility purposes only.[121] Although internalization of costs within the industry has been deficient, the presence of external insurers does introduce a level of independent monitoring of industry practices.

The consequences of the OPA 1990's polluter-pays approach were evident in the aftermath of the *Deepwater Horizon* oil spill, 'given that BP quickly accepted designation as the "responsible party" [...] and committed publicly to pay both for the clean-up and all "legitimate claims"'.[122] BP agreed to waive the $75 million claims limit notionally applicable; indeed, total costs for clean-up, penalties, fines, and damages have exceeded US$55 billion.[123] Although BP has paid the majority of the costs of the oil spill, that event did serve to highlight inadequacies in the liability regime.

> The limited amount of emergency funding available, the low per-incident caps, and the small size of the OSLTF all seem woefully inadequate when compared to the extraordinary costs and potential damages for which it may be responsible in a major oil spill.[124]

Indeed, although *Deepwater Horizon* is the best known, there have been dozens of oil spills in each of which the damages claims have exceeded the liability caps placed on responsible parties, and for which the OSLTF has had to cover the funding deficit.[125] The simple fact is that 'the Fund is the ultimate insurer with respect to oil removal costs and damages when there is a discharge or substantial threat of discharge to navigable waters, adjoining shorelines, or the exclusive economic zone'.[126] It is not surprising that the US Coast Guard believes formal OPA liability caps to be too low for offshore facility incidents.[127] By contrast, drilling firms' exposure to liability is much greater under most state laws.[128] Florida and Texas, for example, permit uncapped liability.[129]

In concluding the brief discussion of this topic, we might say that the polluter-pays legislation in the United States (under both the OPA 1990 and CERCLA 1980) makes significant inroads into the separate legal personality

120 Kim (n 106) 573–74.
121 ibid 577.
122 Kiern (n 114) 5–6.
123 Ed Crooks, 'US Court Signs Off on BP's $20bn Oil Spill Settlement' *Financial Times* (Online, 5 April 2016) <www.ft.com/content/ca842362-faee-11e5-b3f6-11d5706b613b> accessed 28 May 2021.
124 Kiern (n 114) 62.
125 US Coast Guard, 'Oil Pollution Act Liability Limits in 2015' (n 76) 3–8.
126 ibid 12.
127 ibid 13.
128 Cohen and others (n 78) 1891.
129 ibid.

and limited liability principles protective of parent companies in corporate groups in order to create extended liability regimes. It has placed responsibility on the parties most appropriate to the undertaking of potentially harmful activities and placed the onus upon those parties to reduce the prospects of accidents occurring. However, a basic limitation of this kind of legislation is that it singles out particular types of activity for *special* regulation and liability provisions, while then excluding other, analogous types of activity. Moreover, the focus is upon funding environmental clean-up and not upon the costs of physical injury to persons (which in this case would be covered in part by state workers' compensation statutes and in part by personal injury insurance cover). In the corporate group situation, it is arguable that a more comprehensive type of exception to separate legal personality and limited liability is required that applies to all cases of personal injury.

5. The way forward

This chapter seeks, finally, to address how defects in the common law world's responses to the problems of corporate groups can be remedied through both legislative and case law means. Reflection upon the shortcomings in the current law points to several different types of possible development. These are as follow.

First, the law should not attempt to analogize corporate liability rules with rules designed for application to natural persons – which frequently are best justified by reference to fault. These fault-based rules were developed in an earlier and simpler age, when tort law was focused upon individual acts which are amenable to characterization as 'good' or 'bad' in personal, moral terms. The various concepts of fault (clearly present, as noted already, in the law of negligence and also significant in veil-piercing rules based on the presence of control and/or the evasion of prior legal obligations) apply awkwardly to corporate group situations, where decision-making about risks might be devolved to thinly capitalized operating subsidiaries, where interactions between group companies increasingly are automated in nature, and where mistakes made might result in large-scale injuries that groups have a unique capacity to redress in a way that ensures that claimants are not forced back (where applicable) upon protections offered by the welfare state.

Second, if there is a desire to create a clear pathway to parent company liability, it might be best that this be undertaken by way of legislation. This is because the parent company is prima facie protected by the statutory rule of limited liability, which presents a barrier to the making of common law claims against it. This barrier might be overcome by claims of fault-based liability (principally in the tort of negligence), but no strict liability doctrine is likely to be successful against it because such doctrines are 'automatic' in nature and inconsistent with the limited liability regime.[130] Our study of the

130 See Phillip David James Morgan, 'Vicarious Liability for Group Companies: The Final Frontier of Vicarious Liability?' (2015) 31 *J Prof Neglig* 276 (arguing for the vicarious

Oil Pollution Act 1990 provides some indication of how creative statutory rules could be used to help to resolve the problems to which corporate groups give rise. Legislation in this area would be useful in: (a) setting out in clear terms any exception to limited liability, so that courts would accept this as a legitimate choice; (b) specifying what sorts of losses were to be covered – the suggestion of the present writer being that the focus should be on extensions of liability for personal injuries but not for purely financial losses (as discussed below); (c) and specifying whether there should be a fault basis to the extended liability claim or not. The present writer would suggest (for reasons already traversed) that a requirement for proof of fault is inappropriate. The aim should be to ensure that corporate groups absorb all of the relevant costs of their commercial activities. Indeed, a liability regime that ensures this provides a clear incentive to avoiding the causation of accidents and injuries. Taking all of this into account, a statutory provision might be passed that provides something like this:

> Shareholders with control or substantial influence over the direction of a company are liable to lose the benefit of limited liability insofar as it protects them against liability for personal injury where there has been misuse of the corporate form. In determining whether such misuse has occurred, a court shall take into account:
>
> (1) whether the insolvent company was ever capable of conducting operations in a serious and responsible manner, given the capital available to it;
> (2) whether a parent company, other group company, or such shareholders as have been mentioned had the ability to capitalize the company properly for its intended operations;
> (3) whether potentially liable parties have been guilty of material misstatements about the capitalization or operations of the investee company; and
> (4) other factors affecting the merits of the claims against shareholders.

Unfortunately, at the time of writing, the chances of such reform being implemented are low.

Third, and relatedly, the law should concentrate on creating rules that have a forward-looking operation rather than a backward-looking operation. This would acknowledge the fact that tort law comprises more than simple

---

liability of corporate group parents for torts of subsidiaries), now modified by Phillip David James Morgan, 'Judgment-Proofing Voluntary Sector Organisations from Liability in Tort' (2020) 6 *Can J Comp & Contemp L* 220 (accepting that vicarious liability is not part of the present law). See also Vibe Ulfbeck, 'Vicarious Liability in Groups of Companies and in Supply Chains – Is Competition Law Leading the Way?' (2020) 3 *Mkt & Competition L Rev* 107.

remedial doctrines, which permit extensions of liability where injury has been caused. Tort law has a forward-looking 'regulatory' operation which has a real role to play in setting standards of interaction that resolve coordination problems, that are meant to deter substandard actions, and which therefore help to prevent losses from actually occurring.[131] In the present context, this means allowing a greater role for directed, strict-liability doctrines. In an increasingly corporatized and automated world, there is a need for the forward-looking affixation of responsibility upon commercial actors – such as occurs in the United States' Oil Pollution Act 1990 – in circumstances where those commercial parties can bargain among themselves (if they so desire) in order to reallocate risks and costs.

Fourth, tort doctrines need to be flexible in nature and have the potential to operate not only vertically as between parent company and subsidiary, but horizontally as between group subsidiaries and/or external contractors. This is to say that tort doctrines should move from being control- and fault-based to being more responsive to risks arising in the coordination of activities between laterally situated parties.[132] This seems extremely important in a commercial world that is becoming ever more automated, and which might be controlled eventually by artificial intelligence. In such a world, there might be little possibility of finding the exercise by a parent company of control so that what is required, instead, is the ex-ante affixation of responsibility for the causation of losses.

Fifth, the law should prioritize the protection of bodily interests over other interests in creating directed forms of strict liability and liability among coordinating parties. The externalization of purely financial losses might be said to be 'fair game' under companies' legislation creating limited liability.[133] Both incorporated companies and individuals understand that they take a risk of losses when transacting with limited liability companies. Limited liability is an important incentive for investment in risky projects, which might or might not pay off in the long run. Without limited liability, innovation, commercial success, and economic well-being might be stunted.[134] However, the weight of the argument goes the other way when death and personal injury arise. Death and personal injury reduce productive capacity and lead to diminished lives. Moreover, the policies behind limited liability rules become far less attractive and the externalization of costs is not acceptable when falling upon taxpayer-funded health systems.

131 Eg Christian Witting, 'Modelling Organisational Vicarious Liability' (2019) 39 *LS* 694, 700–1.

132 Compare Christian Witting and James Rankin, 'Tortious Liability of Corporate Groups: From Control to Coordination' (2014) 22 *Tort L Rev* 91 (arguing for a recklessness standard in lateral interactions).

133 Eg Insolvency Act 1986 (UK), s 74(2)(d).

134 See Stephen Bainbridge and Todd Henderson, *Limited Liability: A Legal and Economic Analysis* (Edward Elgar 2016) 302–3.

6. Conclusions

This chapter has considered some of the ways in which the formation of corporate groups can be used in order to subvert the operation of the tort system. There have been notable examples of parent companies structuring group relations in order to reduce liability and protect group assets. This is of considerable concern, given the important place that corporate groups have in the conduct of risky commercial activities in the modern business world. It is the reason why scholars are demonstrating much more interest now in this topic. This chapter's survey of common law causes of action pleaded in cases involving claims for the extended liability of corporate groups reveals that although the common law is developing in the right direction, it is moving very slowly and remains far from satisfactory in responding to judgment-proofing. It could be that the only satisfactory solution to the problem will be a legislative one. Any legislative solution must create an exception to the limited liability of parent companies but could go much further. The appropriate liability regime of the future will be much less concerned than at present with establishing fault in the causation of injury, will be more forward-looking, will allocate responsibility to the parties that are in the best position to take precautions and avoid the causation of mass torts and other injuries, and will focus on protection from personal injuries in particular.

Bibliography

Antunes J, *Liability of Corporate Groups: Autonomy and Control in Parent–Subsidiary Relationships in US, German and EU Law* (Kluwer 1994)

Bainbridge S and Henderson T, *Limited Liability: A Legal and Economic Analysis* (Edward Elgar 2016) [DOI: https://doi.org/10.4337/9781783473038]

Belenzon S, Hashai N, and Patacconi A, 'The architecture of attention: Group structure and subsidiary autonomy' (2019) 40 *Strateg Manag J* 1610 [DOI: https://doi.org/10.1002/smj.3059]

Boggio A, 'Linking Corporate Power to Corporate Structures: An Empirical Analysis' (2012) 22 *S & LS* 107 [DOI: https://doi.org/10.1177/0964663912458447]

Bureau of Ocean Energy Management, 'BOEM Governing Statutes' (Undated)

Chakravarty D and others, 'Multinational enterprise regional management centers: Characteristics and performance' (2017) 52 *J World Bus* 296 [DOI: https://doi.org/10.1016/j.jwb.2016.12.011]

Chandler A, *Strategy and Structure: Chapters in the History of the Industrial Enterprise* (MIT Press 1962)

——— *Scale and Scope: The Dynamics of Industrial Capitalism* (Belknap Press 1990)

Cohen MA and others, 'Deepwater Drilling: Law, Policy, and Economics of Firm Organization and Safety' (2011) 64 *Vand L Rev* 1853

Crooks E, 'US Court Signs Off on BP's $20bn Oil Spill Settlement' *Financial Times* (Online, 5 April 2016) <www.ft.com/content/ca842362-faee-11e5-b3f6-11d5706b613b> accessed 28 May 2021

Davies PS, *Accessory Liability* (Hart 2015) [DOI: https://doi.org/10.5040/9781474203081]

Dearborn M, 'Enterprise Liability: Reviewing and Revitalizing Liability for Corporate Groups' (2009) 97 *CLR* 195
Dietrich J and Ridge P, *Accessories in Private Law* (CUP 2015) [DOI: https://doi.org/10.1017/CBO9781107478138]
Farrar J, 'Legal Issues Involving Corporate Groups' (1998) 16 *C&SLJ* 184
Galbraith J, *Designing Organizations: Strategy, Structure and Process at the Business Unit and Enterprise Levels* (3rd edn, Jossey-Bass 2014)
Goldacre B, *Bad Pharma* (Fourth Estate 2013)
Haigh G, *Asbestos House: The Secret History of James Hardie Industries* (Scribe 2006)
Hansmann H and Kraakman R, 'Toward Unlimited Shareholder Liability for Corporate Torts' (1991) 100 *Yale LJ* 1879 [DOI: https://doi.org/10.2307/796812]
Harland D, 'The Influence of European Law on Product Liability in Australia' (1995) 17 *Syd LR* 336
Harper Ho V, 'Theories of Corporate Groups: Corporate Identity Reconceived' (2012) 42 *Seton Hall L Rev* 879
Houlder V, Carnie K, and Nevitt C, 'Tax Reduction Jargon Explained' *Financial Times* (Online, 10 June 2013) <www.ft.com/personal-finance/tax> accessed 7 February 2020
Jackson DF, 'Report of the Special Commission of Inquiry into the Medical Research and Compensation Fund' (NSW Government 2004)
Jennejohn M, 'The Private Order of Innovation Networks' (2016) 68 *Stan L Rev* 281
Jones G, *Multinationals and Global Capitalism: From the Nineteenth to the Twenty-First Century* (OUP 2005)
Kiern L, 'Liability, Compensation, and Financial Responsibility under the Oil Pollution Act of 1990: A Review of the Second Decade' (2011) 36 *Tul Mar LJ* 1
Kim I, 'Financial Responsibility Rules under the Oil Pollution Act of 1990' (2002) 42 *Nat Resources J* 565
Lee P, 'Innovation and the Firm: A New Synthesis' (2018) 70 *Stan L Rev* 1431
Lee PW, 'Accessory Liability in Tort and Equity' (2015) 27 *S Ac LJ* 853
Light A, 'The Deepwater Horizon Oil Spill Trust and the Gulf Coast Claims Facility: The "Superfund" Myth and the Law of Unintended Consequences' (2011) 5 *Golden Gate U Envtl LJ* 87
Lo SHC, *In Search of Corporate Accountability: Liabilities of Corporate Participants* (Cambridge Scholars 2015)
——— 'Piercing of the Corporate Veil for the Evasion of Tort Obligations' (2017) 46 *CLWR* 42 [DOI: https://doi.org/10.1177%2F1473779516682195]
LoPucki LM, 'The Death of Liability' (1996) 106 *Yale LJ* 1 [DOI: https://doi.org/10.2307/797267]
Low KFK and Mik E, 'Pause the Blockchain Legal Revolution' (2020) 69 *ICLQ* 135 [DOI: https://doi.org/10.1017/S0020589319000502]
McCulloch J and Tweedale G, *Defending the Indefensible* (OUP 2008)
McDonell C, 'The Gulf Coast Claims Facility and the *Deepwater Horizon* Litigation: Judicial Regulation of Private Compensation Schemes' (2012) 64 *Stan L Rev* 765
Mintzberg H, *The Structuring of Organizations* (Pearson 1979)
Morgan J, 'The Oil Pollution Act of 1990: A Look at its Impact on the Oil Industry' (1994) 6 *Fordham Intl LJ* 1
Morgan PDJ, 'Vicarious Liability for Group Companies: The Final Frontier of Vicarious Liability?' (2015) 31 *J Prof Neglig* 276

——— 'Judgment-Proofing Voluntary Sector Organisations from Liability in Tort' (2020) 6 *Can J Comp & Contemp L* 220
Mujih E, 'Piercing the corporate veil: where is the reverse gear?' (2017) 133 *LQR* 322
Muscat A, *The Liability of the Holding Company for the Debts of Its Insolvent Subsidiaries* (Dartmouth 1996) [DOI: https://doi.org/10.4324/9781315238692]
National Pollution Funds Center, 'Oil Pollution Act of 1990 (OPA)' (United States Coast Guard) <www.uscg.mil/Mariners/National-Pollution-Funds-Center/About_NPFC/OPA> accessed 27 May 2021
Pettet B, 'Limited Liability – A Principle for the 21st Century?' (1995) 48 *CLP* 125 [DOI: https://doi.org/10.1093/clp/48.Part_2.125]
Roe M, 'Corporate Strategic Reaction to Mass Tort' (1986) 72 *Va L Rev* 1 [DOI: https://doi.org/10.2307/1072990]
Sharkey C, 'The BP Oil Spill Settlements, Classwide Punitive Damages, and Societal Deterrence' (2015) 64 *DePaul L Rev* 681
Strasser K, 'Piercing the Veil in Corporate Groups' (2005) 37 *Conn L Rev* 637
Ulfbeck V, 'Vicarious Liability in Groups of Companies and in Supply Chains – Is Competition Law Leading the Way?' (2020) 3 *Mkt & Competition L Rev* 107 [DOI: https://doi.org/10.7559/mclawreview.2019.2361]
US Coast Guard, 'Oil Spill Liability Trust Fund (OSLTF) Funding for Oil Spills' (January 2006)
——— 'Oil Pollution Act Liability Limits in 2015: Report to Congress' (October 2015)
——— 'Oil Pollution Act of 1990 (OPA)' (2016)
Verrender I, 'Hardie's Legal Marathon Ends with Statement of the Bleeding Obvious' *The Sydney Morning Herald* (Online, 5 May 2012) <www.smh.com.au/business/hardies-legal-marathon-ends-with-statement-of-the-bleeding-obvious-20120504-1y4c5.html> accessed 28 May 2021
Viscusi K and Zeckhauser R, 'Deterring and Compensating Oil-Spill Catastrophes: The Need for Strict Two-Tier Liability' (2011) 64 *Vand L Rev* 1717
Westbrook JL, 'Transparency in Corporate Groups' (2018) 13 *Brook J Corp Fin & Com L* 33
Witting C, *Liability of Corporate Groups and Networks* (CUP 2018) [DOI: https://doi.org/10.1017/9781139626828]
——— 'Modelling Organisational Vicarious Liability' (2019) 39 *LS* 694 [DOI: https://doi.org/10.1017/lst.2019.10]
——— 'Piercing the Corporate Veil' in Day W and Worthington S (eds), *Challenging Private Law* (Hart 2020)
——— and Rankin J, 'Tortious Liability of Corporate Groups: From Control to Coordination' (2014) 22 *Tort L Rev* 91

5 Blockchain-based registration and transfer of shares

Consequences in the area of the law of obligations

Marcin Mazgaj

1. Introduction

The discussion concerning the application of blockchain for corporate purposes has been particularly vivid for the past few years. One reason for it is, certainly, the dynamic development of blockchain technology. The other, at least equally important, is, however, the fact that nowadays corporate laws in many jurisdictions are undergoing significant reforms that, in certain aspects, overturn the legal principles that have been in force for many years. Coexistence of these trends has given rise to interesting concepts, some of them very far-reaching, such as the creation of *quasi*-corporate forms (e.g. the well-known case of The DAO)[1] or the introduction of provisions on blockchain-based companies (e.g. blockchain-based limited liability companies incorporated in Vermont).[2] Despite that, at present there is no evidence that the development of blockchain might lead to the end of traditional corporations. Instead, it seems that it could facilitate certain corporate processes, such as, *inter alia*, share trading and maintenance of corporate records. These aspects of the application of blockchain have so far been analyzed from the

1 For details see eg Wulf A Kaal, 'Blockchain-Based Corporate Governance' (Blockchain and Procedural Law: Law and Justice in the Age of Disintermediation, 2nd Seminar: Automating Legal Instruments, Max Planck Institute Luxembourg, December 2019) 8–15 <https://ssrn.com/abstract=3441904> accessed 14 March 2020; Philipp Hacker, 'Corporate Governance for Complex Cryptocurrencies? A Framework for Stability and Decision Making in Blockchain-Based Organizations' in Philipp Hacker and others (eds), *Regulating Blockchain: Techno-Social and Legal Challenges* (OUP 2019) 145–46.

2 Vermont's blockchain-based limited liability companies are subject to regulation of 11 Vermont Statutes Annotated (VSA) §§ 4171 to 4176. For details see Section 3.2 of this chapter.

DOI: 10.4324/9781003080596-6

legal perspective, but from the point of view of 'core' corporate law.[3] This chapter is aimed at legal analysis (with particular emphasis on the law of obligations) of the benefits and risks involved in blockchain-based registration and trade of shares. This is due to the fact that these two areas seem to be the major ones where distributed ledger technology could be applied for the sake of security and transparency of corporate actions. In this context, it needs to be underlined that even though blockchain might help to eliminate certain problems,[4] it will at the same time create new ones (related to events such as failure of the code governing the database). Both the former and the latter are subject to analysis in later parts of this chapter.

The chapter is structured as follows: first, it provides a general explanation of problems that could be solved by blockchain technology with respect to share registration and share trading. The next part is aimed at the analysis of the current state of affairs; in particular, it contains a brief comparative examination of several legal orders that recognized blockchain as a tool for the above operations. Third, the chapter describes new dilemmas that are likely to arise on the ground of the law of obligations while distributed ledger technology paves its way towards being used as a technology of keeping corporate records or share trading. The final part presents the main conclusions.

2. Keeping corporate records and share trading: legislators at the crossroads?

As regards corporate law, nowadays we are living in a world of regulatory competition, which is particularly visible within the European Union.[5] Due to a few well-known ECJ rulings,[6] EU nationals are free to select the best (in their opinion) corporate form from the entire palette offered by the domestic legislators and to conduct a business activity within the whole EU under the selected corporate framework. As a result of such a 'race to the top', the legislators are striving to facilitate everyday corporate life, which is achieved, in particular, by way of enhancing corporate digitalization. Application of

3 See eg Gerald Spindler, 'Digitalization and Corporate Law – A View from Germany' (2019) 16 *ECFR* 106, 137–45; Christoph Van der Elst and Anne Lafarre, 'Blockchain and Smart Contracting for the Shareholder Community' (2019) 20 *EBOR* 111.

4 See Sections 2.1 and 2.2 of this chapter.

5 For details see eg Martin Gelter, 'The Structure of Regulatory Competition in European Company Law' (2005) 5 *JCLS* 247; Stefano Lombardo, 'Regulatory Competition in European Company Law. Where Do We Stand Twenty Years after Centros?' (2019) *ECGI Law Working Paper* 452/2019 <https://ssrn.com/abstract=3392502> accessed 14 March 2020.

6 Eg Case C-212/97 *Centros Ltd v Erhvervs- og Selskabsstyrelsen* [1999] *ECR* I-01459, ECLI:EU:C:1999:126; Case C-208/00 *Überseering BV v Nordic Construction Company Baumanagement GmbH (NCC)* [2002] *ECR* I-09919, ECLI:EU:C:2002:632; Case C-167/01 *Kamer van Koophandel en Fabrieken voor Amsterdam v Inspire Art Ltd* [2003] *ECR* I-10155, ECLI:EU:C:2003:512; Case C-106/16 *Proceedings brought by Polbud – Wykonawstwo sp z oo* [2017] ECLI:EU:C:2017:804.

blockchain is, most probably, the next step of that process with respect to share trading and share registration, as it solves several problems that corporate law has been struggling to cope with for a few decades.

2.1 The first problem: traceability and intermediaries

In the era of paper stock, linking specific shares to a specific shareholder was easy, due to the fact that in order to demonstrate (and execute) one's corporate rights a shareholder simply needed to present the document of the share certificate. The same applied to the disposing of shares – generally speaking, at least in most of the major jurisdictions, the sale of shares required the physical transfer of paper stock to the buyer. Share trading based on paper stock generated numerous problems, however. First, due to massive growth in the trading of shares, in 1960s many major stock exchanges (the most significant example being the New York Stock Exchange) were overloaded with documents and therefore were being closed for one additional day during the week (e.g. in New York on Wednesdays) just in order to 'do the paperwork' – that is, to verify, hand on, and simply keep the share certificates in order.[7] Second, in a system based on paper stock, especially in the case of bearer shares, the potential for forging or losing the share certificates involved obvious significant risks. To remedy the first of the two above-described problems, some countries decided to 'immobilize the shares' – that is, they changed the share trading system in a way that share certificates of public companies were no longer physically transferred from one hand to another. Instead, the shares are deposited in the warehouses of special institutions created for that purpose, such as the Depositary Trust and Clearing Corporation (in the USA), Euroclear (Belgium), or Clearstream (Germany and Luxembourg). These institutions often do not, however, conclude any agreements with the actual shareholders of the companies, but rather act via a chain of intermediaries, such as banks, brokerage offices, etc. A result of the aforementioned reform was the fact that at the same time in many jurisdictions (including major ones, like Delaware[8] or Germany[9]) it was not the 'actual' beneficial shareholder but the depositary institution or one of the intermediaries that was indicated in the corporate records as a shareholder. Usually, this does not generate practical problems (as, of course, both the depositary institutions and the intermediaries generally do not execute shareholders' rights on their own, but simply follow the instructions of the beneficial shareholders), but it is not always the case. The most notable examples are those of DNick Holding Plc in Germany[10] and Dell Inc. in

7 George S Geis, 'Traceable Shares and Corporate Law' (2018) 113 *Nw U L Rev* 227, 232.
8 ibid 232–35.
9 Van der Elst and Lafarre (n 3) 112–13.
10 DNick Holding Plc was incorporated in the United Kingdom, but its shares were traded on the German Stock Exchange (*Deutsche Börse*).

Delaware. In both of these companies, minority shareholders intended to execute their appraisal rights, which – according to the relevant laws – were subject to a condition that they could be executed only if earlier the shareholder had voted against the delisting of the company (the case of DNick Holding) or a merger (the case of Dell). In both cases it turned out, however, that the intermediaries were representing large groups of shareholders (which is a standard situation) and when they were voting, they simply took due care only to cast appropriate 'aggregate' numbers of votes, but not to cast specific votes from specific shares (e.g. after receiving instructions to vote 'against' the resolution from the actual beneficial shareholder the intermediaries did not necessarily verify whether they vote 'against' specifically from this shareholder's shares, but rather only whether the aggregate number of votes 'against' is correct). This, in turn, led to dismissal of the cases by the relevant courts, just because of lack of legal standing of the shareholders, as it turned out that the votes cast specifically from their shares were not votes 'against' the general meeting's resolution.[11]

In certain situations, the problem may, however, become even more complicated. In both of the above-described cases, it was at least possible to trace down the way the votes were cast. There are also, however, known certain cases where such 'tracing down' was not possible.[12] The impossibility may be due to legal reasons (such as lack of adequate identification of shares – as, for instance, in certain jurisdictions, especially in private companies, the shares need not be characterized by a number or series)[13] or, more prosaically, simply to lack of necessary information concerning the facts of the case[14] (which may, for instance, be the result of lack of documents indicating all the instructions executed by the intermediary).

2.2 The second problem: transparency

The problem of 'non-traceability' of shares in certain jurisdictions is related primarily to public companies. Nonetheless, the current system of trading shares is also ineffective in certain jurisdictions with respect to private companies. Simple dematerialization of shares (resulting in, naturally, lack of necessity of maintaining any official depository) does not solve the problem. A good example concerning this question may be shown on the basis of the Polish limited liability company (which is, generally, similar to the German GmbH). Its shares are not embodied in any documents – actually, the Polish

11 Van der Elst and Lafarre (n 3) 112–13; Geis (n 7) 245–46.
12 Geis (n 7) 247.
13 Which is the case eg in a Polish limited liability company (*spółka z ograniczoną odpowiedzialnością*).
14 As happened in the *Transkaryotic* case; see Geis (n 7) 247.

Code of Commercial Companies (*Kodeks spółek handlowych*,[15] KSH) forbids issuing documents embodying such shares.[16] On the other hand, there is no central register of shareholders that would determine who is the actual shareholder. The shareholders are, admittedly, entered in the National Court Register conducted by the registry courts,[17] and in the book of shares conducted by the company's management board, but none of these is decisive as regards having the status of the shareholder, due to the fact that, in general, the sole conclusion of share transfer agreement is enough to transfer the title to the shares.[18] This leads to a notable level of legal uncertainty, which can be clearly illustrated by the following example: A, who is the shareholder of the said Polish limited liability company (the 'Company') concludes a share sale agreement with B (which is a party somehow related to him) and – on the basis of this agreement – sells all his shares in the Company to B. The next day neither A nor B reveals that A sold all his shares to B, and A concludes an identical agreement with C. C is afterwards entered into the share book, as well as into the court register, as the Company's shareholder. A year later, C concludes a share transfer agreement with D (the agreement states that C transfers all his shares to D) and therefore – as a result – D is entered into both the share book and the court register. The problem is that despite being entered into both the share book and the court register, in the described situation neither C nor D ever became the Company's shareholder, which is due to the fact that B acquired all the shares on basis of the agreement with A.

2.3 Is blockchain the solution?

One may ask: what does this all have to do with blockchain technology? The answer is that both the problem of lack of transparency and the problem of non-traceability of shares could be solved by way of the introduction of a system where registration and transfers of shares would be conducted within a distributed ledger. This is due to several features of blockchain technology. Because of volume restrictions, the overall technical characteristics of blockchain and distributed ledgers will not be included in this contribution,[19] and only the features that are most significant from the analyzed point of view will be described.

15 Act of 15 September 2000, Code of Commercial Companies (*Ustawa z dnia 15 września 2000 r Kodeks spółek handlowych*) *DzU* 2000, 94, 1037, as later amended.
16 KSH, Art 174 §6.
17 With the exception of the shareholders entitled to shares representing less than 10% of share capital.
18 Unless additional requirements (eg the requirement of the management board's consent) are set out in the articles of association.
19 As regards more detailed description of these issues, see eg Dariusz Szostek, *Blockchain a prawo* (CH Beck 2018) 27-50; Dariusz Szostek, *Blockchain and the Law* (Nomos 2019).

2.3.1 *A few technical remarks*

As the name clearly indicates, blockchain technology consists of connecting separate sets ('blocks') of data into a series ('chain'). What is, however, so specific in it, is that:

(a) First, the data is not stored on one central server (this is why the technology that blockchain is based on is named 'distributed ledger technology').
(b) Second, a new 'block' of data may be added only if it fulfils the criteria that were primarily defined within the source code governing the ledger and – what is also of great importance – whenever a new 'block' of data is added, it is also timestamped, thereby excluding the risk of antedating.
(c) Third, it is incredibly difficult (and, in practice, usually impossible) to remove any data that has already been added to the 'block'.[20]

All these features are of key importance as regards share registration. It is obvious that in the era without paper stock it is necessary to create a reliable and secure model of registration of shares (a system where there is no register generates significant risks already described in Section 2.2). Due to the fact that the shares have no material embodiment, it is the entry in the register that is decisive as to who is the shareholder and how many shares are owned by specific shareholders. The aforementioned features of blockchain make it tailor-made for the aims of registration of shares: (i) lack of centralization of the data generally increases the safety of the data (it is easier to attack one server than the whole network); (ii) the practical impossibility of removing the data from the ledger, as well as time-stamping of the added data, reduce the risk of abuse.

2.3.2 *Blockchain-based registration of shares*

Even though blockchain, as it has been outlined above, may be particularly suitable for the aims of share registration, the paradox is that one of its key advantages – decentralization – cannot be fully utilized with respect to these purposes. This is due to the fact that irrespective of specific legal regulation, there is always one entity 'in control of' the entries in the register, – that is, supervising and making the entries, as well as taking care of uniformity and integrity of the data in the register. In other words, a certain level of centralization is always required. This is due to the fact that share transfer agreements – as any other agreements – may lead to conflicts (in particular related to the validity of agreements), while the company itself should have at least a minimum of certainty as to who should be considered a shareholder (for aims such as conducting general meetings or payment of dividends). Therefore, in practice stock ledgers always need to be centralized to some extent.

20 Geis (n 7) 260; Szostek, *Blockchain a prawo* (n 19) 109.

This constitutes the main difference between the distributed ledger used for the aims of bitcoin and the distributed ledgers used for the aims of keeping corporate records. The former is a permissionless (public) blockchain, which consists in the fact that everybody is entitled to read and add data to the database, without the necessity of being granted individual permission.[21] The latter are permissioned (private) blockchains – that is, only entities having certain authorization (granted by the operator of the database) may access the content of the ledger or add further data. The said authorization may, obviously, take various forms, depending on the scope of rights granted to the participant of the network. The ledger may, for instance, be visible to everybody or only to authorized entities, such as only the company and the shareholders.[22] Generally speaking, however, the difference consists in the fact that while in case of bitcoin blockchain there is no 'operator' governing the blockchain (as everybody is entitled to add the data to the 'chain'), blockchains designed for the aims of maintaining stock ledgers *per se* require a certain level of supervision by an 'operator'. What is, however, of greater importance from the perspective of the law of obligations is that generally the additional rights of the operator are reflected in his additional liability. The legal nature of that liability will be subject to analysis in a later section of this chapter.

2.3.3 Blockchain-based share trading

As regards share trading, the question of the application of blockchain is more complex than with respect to share registration. Blockchain does not, as such, 'break' any of the existing rules concerning share transfers. It may, however, (i) pave the way for smart contracts in the area of share trading, and (ii) facilitate share trading, especially if the system of share trading is linked to the system of share registration. Of course, the idea of automation of share trading is nothing new (one could mention the well-known technique of high-frequency trading), but blockchain provides certain new opportunities in this regard. First, if the system of share trading were to be closely linked to the system of registration of shareholders (e.g. in a way where the conclusion of a share transfer agreement electronically leads to automatic change of the entry in the shareholders' register), the problem of empty voting could be eliminated.[23] Furthermore, blockchain might serve as a technology positively

21 Vincenzo Morabito, *Business Innovation Through Blockchain: The B^3 Perspective* (Springer 2017) 8–9.

22 Such a solution is applied in the Polish simple joint-stock company (*prosta spółka akcyjna*), a new type of company introduced as of 1 March 2021.

23 The problem of empty voting is due to, in particular, the time interval between the record date and the voting date – if a shareholder sells his shares between the record date and the voting date, he is still entitled to vote in spite of not being a shareholder at the moment of voting. For details see Henry TC Hu and Bernard Black, 'The New Vote Buying: Empty Voting and Hidden (Morphable) Ownership' (2006) 79 *S Cal L Rev* 811, 832–35; Geis (n 7) 248–51.

influencing the safety of legal transactions even in the legal systems without blockchain-based share registration, which is due to: (i) the practical impossibility of removing the data from the ledger (in general, it can be only overwritten, without prior removal), and (ii) time-stamping the entered data (and therefore, in particular, the relative simplicity of determining the sequence of concluded agreements). It needs, however, to be underlined that these advantages would be of practical importance only if one could not circumvent the share trading system – that is, if the blockchain-based share trading platform would be the only place where the shares could be transferred (which would be the case if the traditional way of transferring shares – e.g. on the basis of a written agreement – were to be excluded). Such a solution is, however, already possible in many jurisdictions with respect to private companies, as the legal provisions often allow limiting the transferability of shares on the basis of articles of association. Therefore, articles of association could, for instance, state that a share transfer agreement shall be effective *vis-à-vis* the company only if it is concluded within the framework of the said blockchain-based platform.

3. Blockchain-based share registration and share trading versus the existing law of obligations

3.1 General remarks

Before any further analysis is conducted, several general remarks need to be made in order to avoid unnecessary ambiguities. First, it has to be underlined that the role of the code governing the ledger should not be overestimated. Even though the code governing the ledger defines and limits the behaviour of users of the ledger, the code is *not* law,[24] and this assertion remains true also if the legal provisions or company's articles of association require that share registration or share trading be conducted within a distributed ledger. Second, the above conclusion leads to another, perhaps an obvious one, that a 'transaction' registered within the ledger does not necessarily have to be a valid transaction under the governing law. This clearly leads to a conclusion that what is recorded within the distributed ledger does not necessarily have to be consistent with what is the result of the application of the legal provisions. In case of a standard agreement, its nullity usually simply leads to acceptance of fiction that the contract has never been concluded and to return to a situation that occurred before the invalid contract was concluded.

The situation becomes even more complicated in the light of the fact that while in the case of a standard agreement the above-described results arise (which leads to the 'revival' of a situation that occurred before the invalid

24 Dirk A Zetzsche, Ross P Buckley, and Douglas W Arner, 'The Distributed Liability of Distributed Ledgers: Legal Risks of Blockchain' [2018] *U Ill L Rev* 1361, 1386–88.

contract was concluded), in blockchain-based ledgers it is – as already outlined in previous sections of this chapter – practically impossible to restore the previous state of the ledger (as, generally speaking, the data may be added, but not removed, unless a hard fork of the blockchain protocol occurs[25]). Therefore, the traditional remedies applied with respect to invalid or ineffective contracts need to be reassessed, as they may simply be unfit (not applicable) with respect to agreements concluded or registered within distributed ledgers based on blockchain. This is the first, but not the last, reason why the introduction of blockchain-based share registration or share trading should – in most jurisdictions – be accompanied by modification of some of the general rules of the law of obligations. Further reasons will be identified in the following sections of this chapter.

3.2 Blockchain and corporate law – current state of affairs

Even though the development of blockchain within the area of corporate law is in progress, the law, as usual, has not kept pace with technological progress. In many jurisdictions, the question of keeping corporate records in blockchain-based ledgers, as well as the question of share trading via blockchain, is not subject to any specific regulation, so these issues are covered by general provisions of law.[26] This, in turn, leads to a situation where:

(a) If only keeping corporate registers electronically is permitted (which is usually the case), using blockchain technology for these purposes is not prohibited *per se* (on the contrary, in many jurisdictions it seems to be acceptable).
(b) As regards share trading, unless requirements as to the form of share transfer agreement do not preclude it (e.g. requirement of notarial certification of signatures or requirement of concluding the agreement in writing), trading the shares within blockchain-based platforms is also not prohibited.

These two major statements do not, however, lead to a conclusion that there is no need for the introduction of specific provisions regulating blockchain-based share registration and trading. As will be argued in the next sections

25 Hard fork is defined as 'a change in the blockchain protocol that is not backward compatible with the previous protocol – thus creating a separate blockchain that people have to voluntarily switch to'. Wessel Reijers and others, 'Now the Code Runs Itself: On-Chain and Off-Chain Governance of Blockchain Technologies' (2018) 37 *Topoi* 1, 12. See also Fabian Schär, 'Blockchain Forks: A Formal Classification Framework and Persistency Analysis' (2020) *Singapore Econ Rev* 1.

26 As Zetzsche, Buckley, and Arner rightly point out: 'No legal system could afford a carve-out for DLT interactions given the loopholes it would create.' Zetzsche, Buckley, and Arner (n 24) 1388.

of this chapter, conducting these operations within blockchain-based distributed ledgers involves significant risks to the participants of the ledger, in particular the company's shareholders. In order to mitigate these risks, the legislators could depart from standard rules of civil liability with respect to such operations (which will also be described later in this chapter). Until now, however, even if they decided to take any legislative actions, the scope of these actions has been highly limited.

For instance, in Delaware, while keeping corporate records in distributed ledgers is expressly permitted, the law requires only that the records so kept: (i) can be used to prepare the list of stockholders, (ii) record the information required by the law with respect to stock ledgers, (iii) record transfers of stock.[27] There is, however, no detailed, specific regulation concerning liability for malfunctions (e.g. resulting from bugs in the code) of blockchain-based stock ledgers.

In Poland, apart from provisions expressly permitting maintaining shareholders' registers in distributed ledgers,[28] the law does not stipulate any further requirements or rules governing this issue.

In France, the legislator introduced a regulation simply consisting of authorization of the government to enable trading securities by means of distributed ledger technology.[29]

In Vermont, at first sight, the legal regulation seems to be the most far-reaching, as 11 VSA §§ 4171 to 4176 expressly provide for the establishment of blockchain-based limited liability companies (BBLLCs).[30] However, these provisions generally are limited to: (i) stating that BBLLCs are a subtype of standard LLCs (therefore, unless it is expressly provided otherwise, provisions governing LLCs apply to BBLLCs)[31], (ii) declaring what should or could be regulated in the operating agreement of the BBLLC.[32] There are, however, no specific rules concerning, for instance, liability for malfunctions of the code governing the ledger containing corporate records.

What clearly derives from the above examples is that – at least at present – even if the usage of blockchain for the aims of maintenance of stock ledgers is expressly permitted by law, the regulations generally do not provide for

27 See 8 Delaware Code 1953 (Del C) § 224, as last amended with 81 Delaware Laws, c 86, § 7.

28 KSH, Arts 300[31] §4 and 328[1] §3 simply state that: 'The register of shareholders is kept in electronic form, which can be in the form of a distributed and decentralized ledger.'

29 Van der Elst and Lafarre (n 3) 132.

30 Defined in 11 VSA § 4172 as: 'A limited liability company organized [...] for the purpose of operating a business that utilizes blockchain technology for a material portion of its business activities'.

31 11 VSA § 4176.

32 In particular, 11 VSA § 4173 (2) (F) states that the operating agreement might 'specify the rights and obligations of each group of participants within the BBLLC, including which participants shall be entitled to the rights and obligations of members and managers'. No further rules with respect to this issue are, however, provided within that provision.

specific rules concerning civil liability related to the functioning of such ledgers. This, in turn, leads to several major problems in the area of law of obligations.

4. Civil liability for malfunctions of blockchain-based share registers or share trading platforms

4.1 Example

The relevant problems related to the analyzed subject matter may be well illustrated on the basis of the following example (not related to any particular jurisdiction). ABC LLC is a company whose shares are registered in a blockchain-based electronic stock ledger. All the shares of ABC LLC are owned by two shareholders: XYZ plc and XYZ AG. Both are entered in the above-described stock ledger. Despite the lack of any transaction, as a result of a malfunction of the database or a bug in the database's code, a third person managed to change the entries in the stock ledger in a way that the register indicates a third party – DEF Sarl – as the only shareholder of ABC LLC. As a result, the management board of ABC LLC convened the annual general meeting, allowed DEF Sarl's representative as the only one to vote, and, on the basis of a resolution 'adopted' during such general meeting, paid the dividend to DEF Sarl.

Apart from several interesting questions related to 'core' corporate law (e.g. should, in such a situation, the company treat DEF Sarl as a shareholder?), several issues related to the law of obligations arise:

(a) First, who should bear the liability against XYZ plc and XYZ AG? When would such liability be contract liability and when would it be tort liability?
(b) Second, could the third person, who changed the entries in the register, release himself from liability on the basis of an argument that he acted in a way that was allowed by the code (the 'code-as-law' argument)?
(c) Third, should the liability against XYZ plc and XYZ AG be risk-based or fault-based?

4.2 Legal nature of civil liability for fault entries in the stock ledger

A stock ledger may be conducted by various entities, depending on the legislative solution chosen in the specific jurisdiction. In particular, it may be maintained by: (i) registry courts, (ii) authorized entities (e.g. banks, brokerage offices), (iii) the companies themselves. The choice of the entity maintaining a stock ledger is, obviously, of key importance as regards liability for fault entries. If the stock ledger is maintained by the company itself (practically, by the board of directors), there is a corporate relationship between it and its shareholders, and such a relationship can generally be characterized as a contractual or *quasi*-contractual one. In most jurisdictions, corporate relationship, even in the absence of specific rules concerning the maintenance of corporate ledgers, involves general duties such as the duty of care, while improper maintenance of the stock ledger usually could be interpreted as a breach of that duty. If the stock ledger is conducted by the registry court (or any other state entity – in many jurisdictions public administration bodies, not the courts, register companies and keep the registers), there is usually no contractual relationship between the entity maintaining the stock ledger and the shareholder, but the said entity is liable to the shareholder in accordance with the principles typical of state responsibility. The intermediate solution – that is, maintenance of stock ledgers by authorized entities only (as mentioned earlier, banks, brokerage offices, etc.) – is the most complex one, as the variety of legal relationships is possible there.

Generally, however, it is based on an agreement between the company and the entity maintaining the stock ledger. The contractual relationship, therefore, exists, but only between the company and the registry keeper, not between the shareholders and the registry keeper. All in all, this leads to a situation where, most often, improper entries in the stock ledger may lead only to liability based on tort law.

All the above remarks remain valid irrespective of whether the stock ledger is blockchain-based or not. What is, however, specific about blockchain-based stock ledgers, is that apart from the ledger keeper, the company, and the shareholders, several other entities are involved. Even though the ledger is operated by the ledger keeper (who is in charge of granting permissions to the ledger and making the entries), from the technical point of view such an operator may not always be in full control of the ledger. This is due to the decentralized characteristics of blockchain-based ledgers. Such ledgers are recorded in the memories of computers belonging to the users participating in the decentralized network ('nodes'), but the node does not necessarily have to be a shareholder (and *vice versa*). Here, again, what appears is the divergence between the law and the technology – while, in accordance with the law, only the operator of the ledger should be able to add new entries to the ledger, in practice the source code underlying the ledger is conclusive on this issue. The question is what happens if, in accordance with the code, but unlawfully, the nodes change the rules of making further entries in the ledger. It needs to be underlined that, despite the violation of the law, the distributed ledger does not automatically cease to be the company's stock ledger in such a situation. The question that needs to be addressed in such a situation is whether the nodes could be held accountable to the shareholders for their losses incurred – for example, as a result of changes of the code governing the distributed network. What needs to be underlined is that the nodes need not be a party to any agreement with the shareholders. Moreover, they may even never oblige themselves to act otherwise than in accordance with the code. In the absence of specific legislation (which is the case in most jurisdictions), the nodes might therefore even avoid responsibility, unless it could be derived from general provisions, such as the obligation to act in accordance with the principles of social coexistence. The same applies to the potential liability of third persons – for example, those who, due to malfunctions or bugs of the code underlying the ledger, managed to change the entries in the ledger despite not being the nodes or any other users of the decentralized network. What requires analysis in this context is, however, whether they could defend themselves with a 'code-as-law' argument.

4.3 'Code-as-law' (or 'code-as-contract'?) argument

The 'code-as-law' defence has been raised, in particular, by the hacker who seized the assets of The DAO.[33] His argument consisted in claiming that what he did was not prohibited by the code governing The DAO (he, in fact, simply exploited a flaw of the code), and therefore was not unlawful.

From the legal point of view, raising such an argument, of course, cannot be considered legitimate. Nevertheless, modification of the 'code-as-law' argument into a 'code-as-contract' argument significantly changes the optics, as the latter is not manifestly unfounded.[34] Moreover, it can be even strengthened – for example, if access to the stock ledger by the shareholder is preceded by his consent to general terms of the ledger, in particular to its source code.[35] In the case of stock ledgers, the power of such an argument is, however, limited, due to one of the main differences between the bitcoin blockchain and the blockchain used for the aims of maintenance of stock ledgers. Participation in the former is optional in the sense that generally no one is legally obliged to participate in it. On the other hand, participation in the latter is mandatory in the sense that if someone intends to be a shareholder of a company, he, in general, does not decide whether the stock ledger will be blockchain-based or not,[36] while usually both solutions are accepted by law[37] (it is, for instance, possible that a company maintaining a traditional stock ledger will convert it into a blockchain-based one). This issue may be of certain importance when using the 'code-as-contract' argument. Due to the fact that in certain situations the degree of freedom of the user of the ledger as to whether to participate in the ledger or not may be lower than in others (e.g. in the case of blockchain-based stock ledgers it will usually be lower than in the case of bitcoin blockchain), the strength of the 'code-as-contract' defence

33 Zetzsche, Buckley, and Arner (n 24) 1402.
34 Similarly, ibid.
35 Such consent would turn the relationship between the shareholder and the operator of the ledger into a contractual one but based generally on terms and conditions prepared usually unilaterally by the operator.
36 Admittedly, there is, however, a similarity between these two situations, consisting in the fact that both bitcoins and shares are economic rights. Therefore, one could be entitled to these rights only under the condition of participating in certain distributed network.
37 See eg the provisions of 8 Del C § 224, that, of course, do not preclude usage of non-blockchain-based stock ledgers.

should be lower in the latter, as entering the distributed network is, in those cases, usually not a matter of agreement, but rather a matter of a technological decision taken without shareholders' influence (or with limited influence).

4.4 Risk-based or fault-based liability?

In the existing literature, it has been argued with respect to blockchain-based platforms that the traditional European paradigm of liability should be reversed,[38] as instead of the fault-based model of liability (which is currently a standard solution) a risk-based strict liability should be imposed on the operators of blockchain-based platforms. Such a position is justified, *inter alia*, by the fact that it is the operator who creates or at least controls the risks that could result in damage arising from malfunctions of the blockchain-based platforms.[39] This view deserves even more support with respect to blockchain-based stock ledgers, as a consequence of, in particular, the above-mentioned practical requirement of a certain level of centralization. Traditional concepts of fault-based liability are not sufficient to provide due protection to shareholders, which is a result of the following.

First, as it has been already outlined, in many cases the liability of the operator could be based only on tort law, where usually the operator could effectively defend himself on the basis of *culpa in eligendo* provisions – that is, by arguing that he chose a professional entity to prepare the code governing the blockchain-based stock ledger.

Second, if the liability is contractual, the operators usually require acceptance of general terms that usually include indemnity clauses that release the operators from liability for the improper functioning of the code (or at least highly reduce that liability).[40] Whether such clauses are effective or not is dependent on various factors, in particular consumer protection laws. Nevertheless, such protective regulations would rarely apply in cases of corporate relationships.

In this context, leaving the regulation of blockchain-based stock ledgers entirely to freedom of contracts seems to be simply imprudent. The risks involved are very high (and related to fundamental issues, such as the existence and ownership of shares), while the scope of protection is, in practice, significantly limited. That is why legislative intervention is desirable in order to: (i) widen the scope of liability of the operators (with a view to shifting that liability from a fault-based model to a risk-based one), (ii) reduce (or even eliminate) the possibility of limiting operator's liability.

38 Luigi Buonanno, 'Civil Liability in the Era of New Technology: The Influence of Blockchain' (2019) *Bocconi Legal Studies Research Paper* 3454532, 8–9 <https://ssrn.com/abstract=3454532> accessed 14 March 2020.

39 ibid 10–12.

40 Such clauses are mentioned eg by Zetzsche, Buckley, and Arner (n 24) 1394; Buonanno (n 38) 11.

5. Blockchain-based share transfers: smart contracts of sale of shares

As regards share transfers, the development of blockchain may have the greatest impact with respect to: (i) rise of blockchain-based share trading platforms, (ii) facilitation of smart contracts within the area of share trading. As far as the former is concerned, despite the obvious usefulness of blockchain for these aims (e.g. the above-mentioned advantages of time-stamping of the added data), it should not be considered revolutionary. Electronic share trading platforms have already existed for many years and most of the legal 'machinery' developed with respect to them could be applied also to blockchain-based platforms. Most of the remarks made above with regard to share registration (in particular concerning the necessity of the introduction of strict, risk-based liability of operators) remain valid also within this area.

Interestingly, the development of smart contracts also does not constitute any major change with respect to public companies. It may, however, influence share trading in private companies (where automation of share trading has not been so common), as well as other aspects of corporate law, such as procedures for increasing capital, that could be quite easily automatized.[41] Nevertheless, as regards the law of obligations, further analysis must be preceded by several important observations.

First, the term 'smart contracts' is slightly misleading, as actually 'smart contracts' are rarely defined as contracts from the legal point view,[42] but rather as 'computerized transaction protocol that executes the terms of a contract'[43] or 'a sort of computer code which is operated by a computer and is self-executing and self-enforcing'.[44] This could be opposed to traditional definitions of 'traditional' contracts. Irrespective of the view taken, traditional definitions of a contract are generally centred around the moment of conclusion of an agreement,[45] while the definitions of smart contracts centre around the moment of execution of an agreement. This is obviously due to the fact that from the legal perspective smart contracts are simply acts of execution of what has been agreed earlier (in a more or less detailed way) by the humans. With some level of simplification, it could, therefore, be said that the actual (at least from the legal point of view) agreement is generally concluded not in the moment of specifying the performance that will be

41 Spindler (n 3) 143.

42 See detailed analysis of the term by Mateja Durovic and André Janssen, 'Formation of Smart Contracts under Contract Law' in Larry A DiMatteo, Michel Cannarsa, and Cristina Poncibò (eds), *The Cambridge Handbook of Smart Contracts, Blockchain Technology and Digital Platforms* (CUP 2019) 61ff.

43 Nick Szabo, 'Smart Contracts' (1994) <www.fon.hum.uva.nl/rob/Courses/InformationInSpeech/CDROM/Literature/LOTwinterschool2006/szabo.best.vwh.net/smart.contracts.html> accessed 14 March 2020. Cited also by Durovic and Janssen (n 42) 63.

44 Durovic and Janssen (n 42) 63.

45 The well-known concept of 'will theory of contract'.

executed, but earlier – in the moment of specifying all the possible solutions and performances that may take place in the phase of execution (i.e. in the moment of agreeing upon the algorithm).

Having said that, one should again bear in mind that the code is *not* law, and therefore what is registered as a share transfer within the trading platform does not necessarily have to be a valid share transfer in accordance with the law, unless specific legal provisions provide so. Actually, they sometimes do contain a rule that acquisition of shares is effective as of the moment of entry in the securities account or the stock ledger. What would, however, be additionally necessary, if one would intend to ensure permanent compliance of the entries in stock ledgers with the law, is a rule that acquisition of shares from an unauthorized person (i.e. not being the actual shareholder) is valid and effective if that person had been entered into the stock ledger.[46] This, together with automation of entries to the stock ledger, could constitute a significant modernization in the area of share trading.

6. Conclusion

Blockchain technology will strongly influence the reality of share trading and – even more significantly – share registration. It should not, however, be accepted with total optimism. It is true that it will help to eliminate many corporate problems and will facilitate many profitable corporate processes. The current legal framework does not, however, seem to be ready for it. Relying solely on the freedom of contract may lead to results that are difficult to accept. The founder-operator of the distributed ledger enjoys, in practice, a wide range of rights, which is partly due to the fact that he is the one who (at least initially) decides upon the code underlying the ledger. The code obviously is not law, but it may play a *quasi*-contractual role as a part of participants' arrangements (participating in a distributed network is tantamount – in a certain way – to accepting its rules, in particular, the consensus protocols stipulated within the code). It is the founder-operator who is in the position to (i) estimate, (ii) allocate, and (iii) reduce the risks involved. The other users of the distributed ledger are not in a position enabling them to influence the processes of the ledger to a similar extent. The imbalance of power is magnified by the fact that in the case of stock ledgers a certain level of centralization is inevitable, as there is always an entity or board ('ledger keeper') responsible for the content of the ledger.

A major problem occurs in case of divergence between the results of the application of the algorithms included in the code underlying the ledger and

46 A similar rule is present in many legal systems with respect to acquisition of a real estate from an unauthorized person entered into the land and mortgage register. Such rule exists eg in Polish and German legal systems. See § 892(1) of the German Civil Code (*Bürgerliches Gesetzbuch*, in the version promulgated on 2 January 2002, *BGBl* I 42, 2909; 2003 I 738, as later amended) or Art 5 of the Polish Act on Land and Mortgage Registers (*Ustawa z dnia 6 lipca 1982 r o księgach wieczystych i hipotece, DzU* 1982, 19, 147, as later amended).

the results of the application of the law. Even though at first sight the problem may seem trivial (it is obvious that the law prevails over the code), the practical solution of it in the case of blockchain-based ledgers and transactions may be difficult (due to the fact that neither modification of code nor removal of data from the ledger is simple from a technical point of view). All these issues are, at present, either not addressed by the legislators at all or addressed only to a minimal extent. Law is always a step behind technology. It is to be hoped, in case of blockchain-based share registration and share transfers, this step will be as short as possible.

Bibliography

Buonanno L, 'Civil Liability in the Era of New Technology: The Influence of Blockchain' (2019) *Bocconi Legal Studies Research Paper* 3454532 <https://ssrn.com/abstract=3454532> accessed 14 March 2020

Durovic M and Janssen A, 'Formation of Smart Contracts under Contract Law' in DiMatteo LA, Cannarsa M, and Poncibò C (eds), *The Cambridge Handbook of Smart Contracts, Blockchain Technology and Digital Platforms* (CUP 2019) [DOI: https://doi.org/10.1017/9781108592239.004]

Geis GS, 'Traceable Shares and Corporate Law' (2018) 113 *Nw U L Rev* 227

Gelter M, 'The Structure of Regulatory Competition in European Company Law' (2005) 5 *JCLS* 247 [DOI: https://doi.org/10.1080/14735970.2005.11419935]

Hacker P, 'Corporate Governance for Complex Cryptocurrencies? A Framework for Stability and Decision Making in Blockchain-Based Organizations' in Hacker P and others (eds), *Regulating Blockchain: Techno-Social and Legal Challenges* (OUP 2019)

Hu HTC and Black B, 'The New Vote Buying: Empty Voting and Hidden (Morphable) Ownership' (2006) 79 *S Cal L Rev* 811

Kaal WA, 'Blockchain-Based Corporate Governance' (Blockchain and Procedural Law: Law and Justice in the Age of Disintermediation, 2nd Seminar: Automating Legal Instruments, Max Planck Institute Luxembourg, December 2019) <https://ssrn.com/abstract=3441904> accessed 14 March 2020

Lombardo S, 'Regulatory Competition in European Company Law. Where Do We Stand Twenty Years after Centros?' (2019) *ECGI Law Working Paper* 452/2019 <https://ssrn.com/abstract=3392502> accessed 14 March 2020

Morabito V, *Business Innovation Through Blockchain: The* B^3 *Perspective* (Springer 2017)

Reijers W and others, 'Now the Code Runs Itself: On-Chain and Off-Chain Governance of Blockchain Technologies' (2018) 37 *Topoi* 1 [DOI: https://doi.org/10.1007/s11245-018-9626-5]

Schär F, 'Blockchain Forks: A Formal Classification Framework and Persistency Analysis' (2020) *Singapore Econ Rev* 1 [DOI: https://doi.org/10.1142/S0217590820470025]

Spindler G, 'Digitalization and Corporate Law – A View from Germany' (2019) 16 *ECFR* 106 [DOI: https://doi.org/10.1515/ecfr-2019-0009]

Szabo N, 'Smart Contracts' (1994) <www.fon.hum.uva.nl/rob/Courses/InformationInSpeech/CDROM/Literature/LOTwinterschool2006/szabo.best.vwh.net/smart.contracts.html> accessed 14 March 2020

Szostek D, *Blockchain a prawo* (CH Beck 2018)

——— *Blockchain and the Law* (Nomos 2019) [DOI: https://doi.org/10.5771/9783845298290]

Van der Elst C and Lafarre A, 'Blockchain and Smart Contracting for the Shareholder Community' (2019) 20 *EBOR* 111 [DOI: https://doi.org/10.1007/s40804-019-00136-0]
Zetzsche DA, Buckley RP, and Arner DW, 'The Distributed Liability of Distributed Ledgers: Legal Risks of Blockchain' [2018] *U Ill L Rev* 1361

6 Liability for artificial intelligence

Nasir Muftić

1. Introduction

The digital transformation of modern societies relies on the rise of modern technologies such as artificial intelligence (AI). AI will enable humans to complete tasks with unprecedented speed and precision, as well as to spend their time in a different fashion. In 2015, *Foreign Affairs* published an article by Professor Klaus Schwab, the executive chairman of the World Economic Forum, in which he introduced the phrase 'Fourth Industrial Revolution'.[1] The phrase soon became synonymous with the set of technological advancements that are soon going to become reality, including AI. The rise of AI and its popularity among the public have been followed by the increased attention of legislators and lawyers.

This chapter presents the state of affairs in the European Union (EU) with respect to liability for AI. More specifically, it deals with tortious liability (extracontractual liability). In an attempt to outline current issues and trends in this matter as well as to present possible legislative solutions, the chapter is divided into three parts. In Section 2, it addresses the current legal framework relevant to liability in the EU and its Member States. Section 3 addresses the challenges which come from the peculiar nature of AI that lawmakers have to take into consideration. Section 4 suggests a possible legislative response with a focus on the current proposals and suggestions.

In the EU, a wide discussion about the regulation of liability for AI had commenced in recent years. The European Commission published a Data Economy Communication of January 2017[2] and the accompanying Commission Staff Working Document on the free flow of data and emerging issues of the European data economy.[3] The Commission raised the issues that

1 Klaus Schwab, 'The Fourth Industrial Revolution: What It Means and How to Respond' *Foreign Affairs* (Online, 12 December 2015) <www.foreignaffairs.com/articles/2015-12-12/fourth-industrial-revolution> accessed 5 December 2019.

2 European Commission, 'Building a European Data Economy' (Communication) COM (2017) 9 final, 13ff.

3 European Commission, 'Commission Staff Working Document on the free flow of data and emerging issues of the European data economy' SWD (2017) 2 final, 40ff.

DOI: 10.4324/9781003080596-7

new technologies create for the EU data economy and specifically mentioned liability as one of the most challenging issues. The European Parliament afterwards adopted a Resolution on Civil Law Rules on Robotics,[4] inviting the Commission to propose a legislative instrument that would address civil liability for harm caused by AI (along with other technologies). In line with the Data Economy Communication of January 2017[5] and the accompanying Commission Staff Working Document, the Resolution proposed two alternative approaches: the first was labelled as 'the risk management'[6] and second as 'strict liability'.[7] Other ideas the Resolution mentions are the introduction of mandatory liability insurance[8] as well as the possibility of creation of personhood for AI.[9]

The Commission established an Expert Group on Liability and New Technologies[10] with a goal of the revision of the current product liability regime and its applicability to new technologies such as AI, as well as developing principles for possible adaptations if needed. The Expert Group operates in two formations – the Product Liability Directive Formation (PLDF) and the New Technologies Formation (NTF).[11] On 21 November 2019, the NTF published a report on liability for artificial intelligence and other emerging digital technologies[12] (NTF Report) where it presented its findings and recommendations. The NTF Report contains an assessment of extracontractual liability in the EU and general recommendations regarding the adaptations of the existing liability regime for the new technologies, including AI. It is likely that the PLDF is going to propose concrete changes in the existing

4 European Parliament resolution of 16 February 2017 with recommendations to the Commission on Civil Law Rules on Robotics (2015/2103(INL)) [2018] *OJ* C252/239 (Resolution), paras 49ff.

5 COM (2017) 9 final, 13ff.

6 The risk-management approach entails that liability is assigned to the market actor which is best placed to minimize or avoid the realization of the risk or to amortize the costs in relation to those risks: SWD (2017) 2 final, 45.

7 Resolution (n 4) para 53. The Resolution omitted to mention the risk-generating approach as one of the proposals contained in the Commission Staff Working document.

8 ibid, para 57.

9 ibid, para 59.

10 See group details at European Commission, 'Register of Commission expert groups and other similar entities' <https://ec.europa.eu/transparency/regexpert> accessed 24 December 2019.

11 The difference in the roles of the two formations is in that the one is 'looking at the interpretation and possible revision of the PLD and the other one at liability for new technologies from a holistic point of view'. See Sebastian Lohsse, Reiner Schulze, and Dirk Staudenmayer, 'Liability for Artificial Intelligence' in Sebastian Lohsee, Reiner Schulze, and Dirk Staudenmayer (eds), *Liability for Artificial Intelligence and the Internet of Things: Münster Colloquia on EU Law and the Digital Economy IV* (Nomos 2019) 17.

12 Expert Group on Liability and New Technologies – New Technologies Formation, *Liability for Artificial Intelligence and Other Emerging Digital Technologies* (European Commission 2019) (NTF Report).

product liability regime, as well as that both formations will be more specific in their proposals in future.

The interest of the EU in the matter of liability for AI and other new technologies and the struggle to adopt clear rules announces that this issue remains to be solved comprehensively in future.

2. Current legal framework

2.1 Jurisdiction in the EU

Extracontractual liability in the EU is regulated, with a number of exceptions, via the national laws of every Member State. The field of tort law is non-harmonized and differences between national legal regimes are manifold.

The main exception to the aforementioned rule, which is pertinent to AI, exists in the field of product liability, where EU law harmonizes the national laws of Member States with the Product Liability Directive[13] (PLD). Furthermore, certain aspects of liability for violation of data protection law (Art 82 of the General Data Protection Regulation[14]) and competition law (Directive 2014/104/EU[15]) are regulated by the EU law as well. Even though there had been an effort to introduce legislation that would harmonize liability of service providers on the EU level as a parallel set of rules that would coexist with the PLD, the proposed directive failed to become a binding legal instrument,[16] rendering PLD the only EU binding instrument of general application dealing with the matter of extracontractual liability. Related to the regulation of liability, the EU adopted a Directive that regulates insurance against civil liability in respect of the use of motor vehicles.[17]

13 Council Directive 85/374/EEC of 25 July 1985 on the approximation of the laws, regulations and administrative provisions of the Member States concerning liability for defective products [1985] *OJ* L210/29, as amended by Directive 1999/34/EC of the European Parliament and of the Council of 10 May 1999 [1999] *OJ* L141/20.

14 Regulation (EU) 2016/679 of the European Parliament and of the Council of 27 April 2016 on the protection of natural persons with regard to the processing of personal data and on the free movement of such data, and repealing Directive 95/46/EC (General Data Protection Regulation) [2016] *OJ* L119/1.

15 Directive 2014/104/EU of the European Parliament and of the Council of 26 November 2014 on certain rules governing actions for damages under national law for infringements of the competition law provisions of the Member States and of the European Union [2014] *OJ* L349/1.

16 European Commission, 'Proposal for a Council Directive on the liability of suppliers of services' COM (90) 482 final [1991] *OJ* C12/8.

17 Directive 2009/103/EC of the European Parliament and of the Council of 16 September 2009 relating to insurance against civil liability in respect of the use of motor vehicles, and the enforcement of the obligation to insure against such liability [2009] *OJ* L263/11 (Motor Insurance Directive).

Extracontractual liability in the EU is thus characterized by fragmentation and the coexistence of several legal regimes. Even though the EU regulates product liability, the jurisdiction in this matter remains to the greatest extent within the scope of the national legal systems of every Member State.

2.2 Common bases (types) of liability

As regulated individually by Member States to a great extent, the national laws of Member States regulating extracontractual liability differ from each other. Notwithstanding the differences, these liability regimes are based on the same principles,[18] which enable scholars to recognize common building blocks of the European national liability regimes. The European Group on Tort Law, a renowned group of academics, established common principles of tort law in the publication *Principles of European Tort Law* (PETL).[19] The publication recognized that liability consists of the following elements: damage to the protected interest,[20] causation for the damage,[21] and the base for the liability.[22]

Typical bases for liability are fault-based liability and strict liability (an abnormally dangerous activity and other activities recognized by national law); vicarious liability (liability for an auxiliary acting on behalf of the person deemed liable, or, more generally, being in charge of another[23]), and product liability. Thereby, it is possible, to a certain extent, to compare classic bases of liability that exist throughout the national laws of Member States.[24]

2.2.1 Fault-based liability and strict liability

Fault-based liability is applicable in cases when certain activity is not covered by strict liability. Fault-based liability operates as a default liability regime in

18 Gerhard Wagner, 'Robot Liability' in Sebastian Lohsee, Reiner Schulze, and Dirk Staudenmayer (eds), *Liability for Artificial Intelligence and the Internet of Things: Münster Colloquia on EU Law and the Digital Economy IV* (Nomos 2019) 33.

19 European Group on Tort Law (ed), *Principles of European Tort Law: Text and Commentary* (Springer 2005). The similarities between the tort law regimes in Europe are recognized in the Book VI of the Draft Common Frame of Reference (DCFR).

20 PETL, Art 2:101.

21 PETL, Art 3:101.

22 PETL, Title III.

23 PETL, Title III. See also: Ioannis Revolidis and Alan Dahi, 'The Peculiar Case of the Mushroom Picking Robot: Extra-contractual Liability in Robotics' in Marcelo Corrales, Mark Fenwick, and Nikolaus Forgó (eds), *Robotics, AI and the Future of Law* (Springer 2018).

24 This chapter does not discuss the contractual liability that might coexist with extracontractual liability. For more information, see Miquel Martín-Casals (ed), *The Borderlines of Tort Law: Interactions with Contract Law* (Intersentia 2019).

that respect.[25] A Member State is entitled to declare that a certain activity shall be subject to either fault-based liability or strict liability. Usually, the applicable base of liability depends on the severity of risks that a certain activity bears. If the risks are higher, it is more likely that such an activity will be covered by strict liability. Furthermore, the problems related to fault-based liability, such as proof of defect or slow adoption of technical standards in certain industries,[26] are also dealt with by the introduction of strict liability as it provides higher incentives to the responsible persons to be concerned about the performance of AI. Strict liability places a victim in an advantageous position compared to fault-based liability since she does not have to prove intention or negligence on side of the tortfeasor.

Usually, fault-based liability and strict liability coexist and might be applicable to the same harmful event in cases where multiple tortfeasors exist.[27] The rules on whether fault-based liability or strict liability shall be applied to particular cases are not harmonized in Europe. It is thus hard to claim that each of these bases of liability would be applicable in all national regimes in similar cases. The NTF Report suggests that strict liability should cover emerging technologies (including AI) as they may typically cause significant harm in the current state of affairs.[28] Moreover, the NTF Report advocates for the continuation of the coexistence of strict liability and fault-based liability as that provides the victim with 'more than one basis to seek compensation against more than one person'.[29]

2.2.2 Vicarious liability

Vicarious liability is a liability for an auxiliary acting on behalf of the person deemed liable, or, more generally, being in charge of another.[30] This basis of liability lies on the principle *respondeat superior, ubi commoda et eius incommode*, whereby the person in charge who extends control or influence over its agent ought to be liable for the actions of the agent. If AI bears characteristics that separate it from other traditional technical means employed by humans, vicarious liability enables the extension of the liability of humans in charge by treating AI as auxiliary. The employment of vicarious liability relies on the

25 Ernst Karner, 'Liability for Robotics: Current Rules, Challenges, and the Need for Innovative Concepts' in Sebastian Lohsee, Reiner Schulze, and Dirk Staudenmayer (eds), *Liability for Artificial Intelligence and the Internet of Things: Münster Colloquia on EU Law and the Digital Economy IV* (Nomos 2019) 117.

26 Gerald Spindler, 'User Liability and Strict Liability in the Internet of Things and for Robots' in Sebastian Lohsee, Reiner Schulze, and Dirk Staudenmayer (eds), *Liability for Artificial Intelligence and the Internet of Things: Münster Colloquia on EU Law and the Digital Economy IV* (Nomos 2019) 143.

27 NTF Report (n 12) 37.

28 ibid 43.

29 ibid 6.

30 See PETL, Title III, Ch 6. See also Revolidis and Dahi (n 23).

presumption that AI is functionally comparable to human labour insofar as it is empowered to conduct an autonomous decision-making process. The purpose of the application of this basis of liability would be to disallow the avoidance of liability from the principal in spite of the autonomous behaviour of the agent.

2.2.3 Product liability

The only general basis of liability harmonized on the European Union level is product liability, regulated by the PLD. It provides for the liability of producers of defective products that cause damage to persons or their property.[31] As a pillar of consumer protection in the EU, the PLD is technology-neutral and regulates the liability of manufacturers by providing victims with an easy way to recover. The producer's fault is irrelevant[32] and the victim has to prove the defect in the product, the damage, and the causal link between the defect and the damage.[33] The PLD provides for the joint and several liability in a case where two or more persons are liable for the same damage,[34] thereby providing the victim with a favourable position.[35]

The definition of product is limited to movables with the exception of primary agricultural products and game, even though incorporated into another movable or an immovable, and it includes electricity.[36] The PLD provides that the damage recoverable via product liability is limited to death or personal injuries, or damage to any item of property other than the defective product itself that is intended for private use and that is was used mainly in such fashion.[37] The limitation of recovery is set to the amount of 500 euros.[38]

A product is defective when it does not provide the safety which a person is entitled to expect, measured at the time when the product was put into circulation. The exact meaning of such a defined safety standard is not considered well settled in scholarship.[39]

31 Producer is defined in Art 3(1) PLD as 'the manufacturer of a finished product, the producer of any raw material or the manufacturer of a component part and any person who, by putting his name, trade mark or other distinguishing feature on the product presents himself as its producer'.

32 PLD, recital 2.

33 PLD, Art 4.

34 PLD, Art 5.

35 Jacob Turner, *Robot Rules: Regulating Artificial Intelligence* (Palgrave Macmillan 2019) 94.

36 PLD, Art 2.

37 PLD, Art 9.

38 Wagner mentions a different interpretation of the recovery threshold by Member States: 'Some Member States have transposed this threshold as a deductible applicable to all claims for compensation of property damage, while others allow the victim to sue for full compensation, provided only that the threshold has been overcome.' Wagner (n 18) 36.

39 Simon Whittaker, *Liability for Products: English Law, French Law, and European Harmonisation* (OUP 2005) 481–94.

Although all EU Member States have transposed the PLD into their national legal systems, product liability is not entirely harmonized throughout the EU. There are differences in the transposition of the PLD as well as the differences in compensation avenues that coexist along with the product liability.[40]

3. Challenges to the current liability regime

This part of the chapter will outline (a) the relevant peculiar characteristics of AI and (b) the challenges it poses for the aforementioned current liability regimes.

3.1 Characteristics of AI

Until the development of AI, human creations have never possessed such a degree of autonomy, nor have they been capacitated to learn and improve based on their prior experiences to this extent. The technology itself is not new. It emerged in the 1950s as an attempt to simulate human reasoning. AI has developed over time and nowadays it is immensely sophisticated.[41] However, AI is today a great enigma since it is unclear exactly how it operates and what its autonomy means. This field is in its 'infancy and a greater understanding of their societal implications is needed'.[42] Even with several definitions of AI, not one is generally accepted as it is hard to capture the essence of AI as it is prone to great and unpredictable improvements.[43]

As the goal of this section is not to define AI, it will turn to address AI's functional characteristics pertinent for the regulation of liability.

The role of the law is to be adaptable to new circumstances and applicable to new phenomena. Not all human inventions require the special attention of lawmakers as the current law is capable of addressing new issues successfully. Although some of the characteristics of AI do not require rethinking the existing liability concepts and rules, certain characteristics of AI bear the potential to challenge fundamental liability concepts and rules. Many authors have already recognized specific characteristics of AI with such potential.[44]

40 NTF Report (n 12) 27.

41 See Herbert Zech, 'Liability for Autonomous Systems: Tackling Specific Risks of Modern IT' in Sebastian Lohsee, Reiner Schulze, and Dirk Staudenmayer (eds), *Liability for Artificial Intelligence and the Internet of Things: Münster Colloquia on EU Law and the Digital Economy IV* (Nomos 2019) 187.

42 Council of Europe – The Committee of Experts on Internet Intermediaries (MSI-NET), 'Algorithms and Human Rights: Study on the human rights dimensions of automated data processing techniques and possible regulatory implications: Council of Europe study DGI(2017)12' (Council of Europe 2018) 4.

43 Turner (n 35) 7.

44 For instance, Ryan Calo argues that a technology, such as AI, is exceptional when it poses a challenge to fundamental doctrinal concepts. See Ryan Calo, 'Robotics and the Lessons

The NTF Report endeavoured to addresses the most important characteristics of the emerging digital technologies (AI included) that are potentially disruptive.

It seems that the NTF Report managed to enumerate these features credibly and comprehensively. It recognized the following characteristics: complexity, opacity, openness, autonomy, predictability, data-drivenness, and vulnerability.[45]

Complexity means the multi-layered interaction of many technological parts with a high degree of technical sophistication. Opacity addresses the often unclear modus operandi of AI since it operates as a black box, a combination of the code written by its creators and self-learned cognition. Openness means that AI (as well as many new digital technologies) ought to be open by design and allow for external inputs as it is essential for its proper operation. AI is enabled to operate autonomously – with less, or entirely without, human control or supervision. Due to the complexity and self-learning capacity, the operation of AI might be unpredictable. AI is data-intensive technology as it depends on the analysis of data sets in order to utilize its total potential. Due to the need for constant interaction with outside information, there is a proclivity to cybersecurity breaches.

3.2 Challenges

As mentioned above, the specific characteristics of AI give rise to challenges to the current liability regime. This part addresses some of these.

3.2.1 Who should be responsible?

Two sets of persons might be responsible for a tortious event which occurred as a consequence of the use of a certain product. First are those actors who participate in the creation of AI (also referred to as 'manufacturers'), such as producers, manufacturers, designers, programmers, and others. The second set of actors includes persons who in any way use the product, such as owners, keepers, and operators (also referred to as 'users').[46] Traditionally, liability regimes hold the second set of actors responsible in cases where the use of a certain product gave rise to extracontractual liability as they are in control of the product and reap the benefits of its utilization.

However, due to specific characteristics of AI, it seems that the well-established rule is undermined. Unlike traditional products, AI possesses a

of Cyberlaw' (2015) 103 *CLR* 513; Herbert Zech recognized self-learning (autonomy) and multi-layered neural networks (deep learning) and associated new AI-specific risks to them. See Zech (n 41). Jacob Turner argues that AI is exceptional due to the two characteristics: it makes moral choices and it can develop independently. See Turner (n 35) 64.

45 NTF Report (n 12) 32.

46 Lohsse, Schulze, and Staudenmayer (n 11) 32.

degree of autonomy and a significant cognitive apparatus. It is enabled to conduct independent and sophisticated decision-making process, potentially unknown to humans. The problem is that the degree of control of the second set of actors over AI is lower than over traditional products with potential that they sometimes cannot affect the operation of AI at all. Furthermore, a risk of injury caused by AI might not be foreseeable to any set of potential defendants.[47] The second set of actors might not be able to predict the behaviour of AI due to lack of understanding of the technology. Also, despite being creators of the original code, the influence of the first set of actors is diminished due to AI's self-learning capacity. In such circumstances, it is hard to select the most appropriate party to bear responsibility. Notwithstanding the unprecedented autonomy of AI, it is necessary to hold some of the involved actors liable for injuries.

Naturally, if AI is abused or misused by users, it seems appropriate that they ought to bear the loss. The hard case is when there is no misuse or abuse by any party involved. Since the second set of persons extend no control or a very low level of control over AI, it seems that the first set of actors is in the best position to influence AI's tortious behaviour (ideally to prevent it). Moreover, the manufacturers are the best cost avoiders.[48]

Some scholars predict that, for the aforementioned reason, the liability of manufacturers ought to increase in size and relevance, and the responsibility of users will diminish proportionally.[49] Even if the liability falls on the manufacturers as a policy choice, there might be a problem with crafting of proper measures that would ensure that manufacturers are going to retain it. They might tend to pass the costs on the second set of actors through the pricing mechanism since manufacturers can, for instance, increase the price of products in order to offset liability costs.

On the other hand, the second set of users are those who utilize the benefits of the new technology. They are in a position to determine the specific purpose and the place of the activities of AI. For instance, users of autonomous vehicles are enjoying the benefits of a ride and they are in a position to define the destination and potentially other characteristics of a specific ride, such as the preferred route. From that perspective, it seems that they should not be excused from bearing at least a portion of the risk.

3.2.2 Which basis of liability should be employed?

If one attempts to apply fault-based liability, it will be hard to demonstrate that the intent to harm or knowledge that harm will occur was present in

47 Jack M Balkin, 'The Path of Robotics Law' (2015) 6 *Cal L Rev Circ* 45, 52.

48 NTF Report (n 12) 40.

49 Mark A Geistfeld, 'A Roadmap for Autonomous Vehicles: State Tort Liability, Automobile Insurance, and Federal Safety Regulation' (2017) 105 *CLR* 1611, 1691.

both sets of actors in most cases.[50] In the case of AI, the concept of negligence is strained due to the lack of comprehensive understanding of the proper functioning of AI and its self-learning ability. Also, there might be an issue with an understanding of what would constitute fault as the rules regarding safety standards that one might expect from AI have not yet been established.[51]

The application of a basis of liability that does not involve fault or negligence seems a logical solution. Historically, the liability of producers of new technologies that carry potential to cause significant damage has changed over time. Traditional liability regimes for producers were based on the fault of producers. With the emergence of new technologies that bear the potential of causing harm, states around Europe introduced strict liability for their manufacturers. An example from the nineteenth century is an introduction of potentially dangerous technologies such as a 'steam train chugging along the tracks and endangering fields and forests with its sparks',[52] and an example from the twentieth century is the introduction of the large scale of production systems due to which products became available to a great number of users and therefore created an increased potential of causing damage of great magnitude.[53]

3.2.3 Regulatory level

As mentioned before, extracontractual liability in the EU is in general regulated on the level of Member States with the exception of product liability. In general, the EU has an *ad hoc* approach when it comes to the regulation of private law. It sees 'private law from a functional rather than a formal, and from a fragmented rather than a systematic, point of view, and only regulated areas which it deemed to be necessary in order to create the internal market'.[54] Despite the strong initiative of the academic community and EU lawmakers to adopt a set of rules covering many areas of private law, several of the previous unification and harmonization efforts were marked by pertinent setbacks.[55]

AI might bring a new perspective. As a data-intensive technology, its unique characteristics entail the availability of large sets of data for processing

50 Wagner (n 18) 45.
51 NTF Report (n 12) 23.
52 Lohsse, Schulze, and Staudenmayer (n 11) 14.
53 Cristina Amato, 'Product Liability and Product Security: Present and Future' in Sebastian Lohsee, Reiner Schulze, and Dirk Staudenmayer (eds), *Liability for Artificial Intelligence and the Internet of Things: Münster Colloquia on EU Law and the Digital Economy IV* (Nomos 2019) 83.
54 Cees van Dam, *European Tort Law* (2nd edn, OUP 2013) 156.
55 See eg Peter AJ van den Berg, *The Politics of European Codification: A History of the Unification of Law in France, Prussia, the Austrian Monarchy and the Netherlands* (Europa Law Publishing 2007).

in order to achieve fast and steady advancements of the technology. AI relies on borderless data flows and lack of hurdles in obtaining and processing data that dictate the pace of improvement.[56] Therefore, there is a practical reason for having rules on AI on a level above the national legal systems. Also, since the EU currently lags behind the US and China in AI development,[57] it ought to avoid fragmentation of the legal system. It ought to pursue a policy that provides the fast and steady growth which entails a harmonized set of rules. However, the harmonization of tort law is a complex task as it cannot be treated in isolation but must take 'into account other compensation systems, such as private insurance and social security systems',[58] as well as harmonization of administrative and criminal law.[59]

3.2.4 Proper time and scope of regulation

Timely regulation of new technology is very sensitive in its nature. A lawmaker faces a question of whether to regulate a phenomenon that it does not understand due to its novelty and sophistication. Moreover, the situation is even more complex when the process of the development of technology is not completed in the time of regulation as well as when the direction in which the development will go cannot be anticipated. Development of AI fits the latter category of technological advancements. In such situations, the time lawmakers have to regulate depends on the current and imminent impact of new technology on society.

Timely regulation is important for the development of technology. 'At the early stages of a technology, it is particularly important to provide incentives to take care as manufacturers still have a lot to learn.'[60] Adoption of new liability rules can be understood as an expression of understanding of new phenomena that cannot be encompassed by the existing liability rules.[61] It can be claimed that, due to the ambiguous nature of AI in the present day, lawmakers are not ready to assess whether the current liability rules are fit for the proper regulation of AI.

A related question is whether new liability rules ought to be rules of general application or rules applicable to particular sectors where AI is present, and which are at higher stages of development compared to other sectors. The adoption of sector-specific rules might seem favourable as it is easier to select

56 Lohsse, Schulze, and Staudenmayer (n 11) 15.

57 See Max Craglia (ed), *Artificial Intelligence: A European Perspective* (Publications Office of the European Union 2018) 12.

58 Amato (n 53) 161.

59 ibid.

60 Wagner (n 18) 52.

61 Jean-Sébastien Borghetti, 'How can Artificial Intelligence be Defective?' in Sebastian Lohsee, Reiner Schulze, and Dirk Staudenmayer (eds), *Liability for Artificial Intelligence and the Internet of Things: Münster Colloquia on EU Law and the Digital Economy IV* (Nomos 2019) 72.

particular sectors where AI is increasingly employed and where the patterns and specific risks related to liability might be recognized. It is easier to assess specific risks of sectors where AI is already in use and to adopt specific rules pertaining to them than to endeavour to discern rules of general application related to AI used in general.

Coupled with the vague nature of AI, the urge of the adoption rules of general application ought to be resisted as the time to face this issue will be more favourable in future. In other words, the search for the general rules of liability for AI can be deemed as a multi-step process:

> As a first step at the European level, therefore, there is a need to produce sectoral, risk-based liability rules for specific autonomous systems of particular practical importance (e.g. motor vehicles and medical robots). A second step would see these sectoral rules expanded into a general liability rule based on risk, which would, as far as possible, exclude gaps in protection and value contradictions.[62]

Liability rules alone would not be sufficient as they need to be coupled with product security and technical standards which, in turn, are easier to be identified on the level of particular sectors than in general.

3.2.5 Product Liability Directive

The adequacy of the PLD for facing the challenges of the digital age has been questioned recently. As mentioned above, the Commission has assigned to a formation of the Expert Group a task to assess the PLD and identify the specific shortcomings it might have. At the time of writing this chapter, the formation has not issued a report on this issue. Therefore, the current standing of the Expert Group on this issue is limited to the general recommendations contained in the NTF Report.

Apart from criticism of the PLD over issues that are not technology-related, such as the 500 euros threshold,[63] or the exclusion of property losses related to the property that in general is not 'ordinarily intended for private use or consumption and was used by the injured person mainly for his own private use or consumption',[64] the scholarship has identified several shortcomings the PLD has when it comes to its application to AI.

62 Revolidis and Dahi (n 23) 123.

63 Bernhard A Koch, 'Product Liability 2.0 – Mere Update or New Version?' in Sebastian Lohsee, Reiner Schulze, and Dirk Staudenmayer (eds), *Liability for Artificial Intelligence and the Internet of Things: Münster Colloquia on EU Law and the Digital Economy IV* (Nomos 2019) 103.

64 Gerhard Wagner in Mathias Habersack (ed), *Münchener Kommentar zum Bürgerlichen Gesetzbuch: Band 6: Schuldrecht: Besonderer Teil IV* (7th edn, CH Beck 2017) § 1 ProdHaftG, para 14.

The PLD defines a product as a movable with the exception of primary agricultural products and game, even though incorporated into another movable or an immovable and includes electricity. It does not define whether the intangible objects are covered by this definition. AI might appear as embodied and unembodied object. If it does appear as a part of a corporeal object, there is no doubt that such product fits the definition. On the other hand, if AI appears as software that is distributed separately from the hardware, it is doubtful whether one might rely on the PLD. A ray of hope in the current definition of a product lies in the explicit reference the PLD makes to electricity. It provides a certain leeway for the expansion of the definition to intangible objects that might include AI.[65] However, the grounds for such an interpretation do not seem to be apt to resist criticism and the current ambiguity will be resolved by virtue of the adoption of a clear definition.

The definition of a defect in the PLD is determined through reference to the standard of safety which a person is entitled to expect, measured at the time when the product was put into circulation. A distinction ought to be made between defects in AI, on one hand, and defects in the objects that are governed or animated by AI, on the other hand. Defects in the objects will be covered by the existing definition of a defect in the PLD and they are therefore not troublesome. If defects exist due to human error or failure, such as errors in manufacturing or design, or failure to provide proper information or warnings to the users, manufacturers should be attributed with liability for damage. But what if there is no human error or failure, and the damage has been created due to AI's autonomous decision-making?

Another question is how to define the safety standard with which AI ought to comply. The PLD does not provide instructions in that respect. Traditional methods of establishing defect employed by the courts are not well suited to be applied to AI.[66] The most common method is to compare the performance of a product with comparable products. It is uncertain, however, whether the performance of AI should be compared to the performance of humans or the performance of other AI in similar situations.[67] Notwithstanding the selected method of determining the safety standard, it is clear that the notion of a defect in the PLD needs to be adjusted to respond to the challenges of AI.

3.2.6 Burden of proof and causation

A general rule is that a person who seeks compensation bears a burden of proof for her claim. PLD is not an exception to this rule, as the injured party

65 Wagner (n 18) 42.

66 Borghetti (n 61) 67, notes that courts establish the defect in one of the following ways and elaborates why none of them are appropriate: proof that the product malfunctioned, proof of the violation of safety standards, balancing the product's risks and benefits, and comparing the product with other products.

67 ibid 71.

demanding compensation has to prove the defect, damage, and the causal relationship between defect and damage.[68] The problem brought by AI, along with other new digital technologies, is the increased complexity of the duties of the claimant. As mentioned above, proving defect under the PLD appears to be challenging due to the complexity and opacity of AI as well as the fact that the applicable tests are ambiguous and require a high degree of technical expertise. A similar problems might also appear under Member States' procedural rules governing bases of liability completely under their sovereignty where the claimant usually bears the burden of proof.

Another anticipated problem might be proving the causal relationship between the defect and the damage. The success of the claimant depends, *inter alia*, on the applicable standard of proof. As the NTF Report provides:

> The standard of proof determines the degree to which a court must be persuaded of some assertion in order to hold it as true. This standard is quite different throughout Europe. Legal systems require that the judge ought to be convinced to something equivalent to a certainty, or at least a high degree of probability, to decide in favour of the party with the burden of proof. By contrast, common law countries require that there be a probability greater than 50% (or a preponderance of the evidence) to satisfy the burden of proof.[69]

The PLD also does not define a standard of proof for product liability, thereby leaving the gap to be filled by the national law of Member States.[70]

The complexity of interactions involving modern technologies constitutes an obstacle in itself. Very often they act in concert when executing an operation or a task, thereby creating an environment of complex mutual relations affecting the user and third parties. In such a setting, it might be hard to assess whether an action or omission of a manufacturer or a user contributed to the damage. If harm occurs as a result of such a complex set of factors, the duty to prove the causal link might be hard to meet.[71]

The number of possible complex situations that might pose a challenge to the issue of causality is myriad – for instance, how one ought to prove causation in a situation when AI makes a decision based on the flawed data it processed, or when harm was caused by a device whose hardware and software are purchased from different manufacturers separately due to the

68 PLD, Art 4.
69 NTF Report (n 12) 20.
70 Miquel Martín-Casals, 'Causation and Scope of Liability in the Internet of Things (IoT)' in Sebastian Lohsee, Reiner Schulze, and Dirk Staudenmayer (eds), *Liability for Artificial Intelligence and the Internet of Things: Münster Colloquia on EU Law and the Digital Economy IV* (Nomos 2019) 206.
71 See Donald G Gifford, 'Technological Triggers to Tort Revolutions: Steam Locomotives, Autonomous Vehicles, and Accident Compensation' (2017) 11 *J Tort L* 71.

openness of digital environments, or when the user added software to the programs already installed by the original equipment manufacturer or tampered with the operation of the pre-installed software.[72] Moreover, private parties are usually not required to record and protocol all activities of their devices, which is why the evidence required for proving causality might be hard to collect.[73]

For several reasons that render the task of proving causation very burdensome for the party who has to prove it, it is widely suggested that the implementation of measures which ought to enhance her position and alleviate the burden of proof is needed for the achievement of effective access to justice.[74] Even if lawmakers agree with the aforementioned assertion, exact measures which might be adopted might be different since the jurisdiction in matters of the procedure is regulated mainly by the national laws of Member States who might decide to apply different measures to reach the same goal and thereby create further fragmentation of the applicable procedural laws.

4. Possible solutions

4.1 Proper allocation and basis of liability

4.1.1 Electronic personality

Due to the current limitations of the PLD and the possibility of insufficient solution that it might provide in specific cases, recourse to national legal systems might be necessary. Even then, the proper allocation of liability between manufacturers and users puts lawmakers between a rock and a hard place. After all, the lawmaker needs to make a decision weighing between persuasive *pro et contra* arguments. The idea of the introduction of separate legal personhood of AI appears to be ground-breaking since it might terminate debate over which of the involved parties ought to be responsible for harm by avoiding placing the burden on any of the currently existing persons.

According to this idea, AI would be regarded as a separate (electronic) person and it ought to be held responsible for the harm it causes since it acts with less or no human control and conducts a separate decision-making process. AI would have a separate pool of assets from its manufacturers and users and this would be used when the duty to remunerate harm it created arises. Since lawmakers have already recognized certain human creations as persons, such as corporations, the idea of the coexistence of other types of persons along with humans does not seem to be completely new. Moreover, due to AI's ability to interact with third parties autonomously or otherwise

72 Wagner (n 18) 47.
73 Martín-Casals, *The Borderlines of Tort Law* (n 24) 132.
74 NTF Report (n 12) 34.

independently, the case for its separate personhood might be even stronger than of legal persons who always have humans who conduct decision-making in background.

This idea received attention from the Parliament, as the Resolution on Civil Law Rules on Robotics calls on the Commission to assess the introduction of legal personhood for electronic persons as a solution for issues of liability.[75] It, however, did not receive the strong support of the experts. First, philosophical and ethical considerations of recognizing electronic entities as persons fired the debate about the status and understanding of humans and their peculiarities in modern societies. It is suggested that the introduction of electronic persons might create disturbance as the current concepts of personhood are anthropocentric and not suited for electronic entities such as AI.[76] Apart from philosophical and ethical considerations, even if understood as a pure liability question without any potentially negative implications beyond, this idea possesses several shortcomings. If an electronic person is deemed responsible, it needs a pool of assets in order to provide compensation to injured parties for harms it creates.[77] The composition and maintenance of an electronic person's assets emerge as a problem. Manufacturers or users or a third party inevitably ought to provide at least initial assets which will be used for the compensation and a certain method of maintenance of assets needs to be used, such as some sort of initial capital or mandatory insurance. If manufacturers or users will bear the cost of establishing and maintaining the assets of an electronic person, then why is there a need for a separate legal person at all? For instance, insurance can be purchased even without the existence of an electronic person. Also, the question of whether manufacturers or users ought to bear the cost of establishing and maintaining the assets of an electronic person since it is possible that they might re-allocate any lawmaker's rule through the freedom of contract.

Furthermore, the electronic personality of AI provides a shield to the manufacturers who will no longer be responsible, which is why they will have no incentive to endeavour to reduce the risk of harm.[78] Separate assets of the electronic person could be seen as a liability cap for the parties who have to provide them. In the case of manufacturers, electronic personhood would create leeway for irresponsible manufacturers not willing to invest time to render products safe due to the limited responsibility (or even absence thereof). The responsibility of the electronic person would not provide an incentive for the improvement of its performance, as its learning capacity

75 Resolution (n 4) 59.

76 For further discussion see Horst Eidenmüller, 'Machine Performance and Human Failure: How Shall We Regulate Autonomous Machines?' (2019) 15 *J Bus & Tech L* 109.

77 Jan-Erik Schirmer, 'Artificial Intelligence and Legal Personality: Introducing "Teilrechtsfähigkeit": A Partial Legal Status Made in Germany' in Thomas Wischmeyer and Timo Rademacher (eds), *Regulating Artificial Intelligence* (Springer 2019) 131.

78 Wagner (n 18) 57.

for improvement is based on programming. Thereby, the effect of liability deterrence of the tortfeasor would not be accomplished.[79] Finally, the introduction of electronic persons would require adoption of 'standards of "conduct" [...] in order to hold them liable individually, which could hardly be brought in line with negligence standards for humans'.[80]

Certain halfway forms of electronic personhood, which ought to mitigate the aforementioned shortcomings, have also been introduced. An extension of a German concept of *Teilrechtsfähigkeit* has been proposed as a suitable solution.[81] It would provide AI with 'a status of partial legal subjectivity based on certain legal capabilities'[82] which would be limited to specific rights and obligations needed for the performance of its tasks. There is also a proposal whereby AI that would resemble the status of slaves in the Roman Empire, who

> were not considered human beings for a long time, nor did they have human rights. They had the possibility of *peculium* though, to have and hold a certain amount of property as their own private property that their masters allowed them to spend or use as their own. Still, they were considered to be property; legal objects that could be bought or sold.[83]

The master/owner of a slave could be sued for harm caused by the slave, but his liability was limited to the amount of property covered by *peculium*.

The introduction of legal personhood has also been rejected in the NTF Report due to the aforementioned reasons. The idea seems to be too complex to implement as it requires several steps to be taken in order to adjust the legal system, whereas it possesses many shortcomings. Moreover, since there is currently no pressing need to make a radical change in the existing liability regime due to the lack of the presence of harm caused by AI, separate legal personality for AI does not seem to be an appropriate measure.

4.1.2 Manufacturers and users

Provided that AI is excluded as a responsible party, the focus shall be on manufacturers and users. We might expect to see the rise of liability of manufacturers in future.[84] As mentioned above, there are several reasons that would affect such a decision. They can make an impact on the per-

79 ibid.

80 Koch, 'Product Liability 2.0' (n 63) 115.

81 See Schirmer (n 77).

82 ibid 140.

83 Robert van den Hoven van Genderen, 'Do We Need New Legal Personhood in the Age of Robots and AI?' in Marcelo Corrales, Mark Fenwick, and Nikolaus Forgó (eds), *Robotics, AI and the Future of Law* (Springer 2018) 21.

84 Wagner (n 18) 41.

formance of AI and take precautionary measures. They can determine the goal of performance and, eventually, they enjoy the benefits of the utilization of the technology. Determining whether manufacturers or users ought to be responsible is a hard question that does not allow for a simple answer. The manufacturers are the best cost avoiders and the only ones capable of foreseeing potential issues in the performance of AI and preventing harm. In the case of fully automated devices, the user is completely out of control of AI and her responsibility ought to be limited to proper maintenance and use. If the manufacturer was in control of updates or upgrades to the technology, it is the one who ought to be responsible. The more control the user extends over the device, the more responsible they ought to be, and *vice versa*.

When AI is connected with increased dangerousness, the NTF Report advises the expansion of strict liability as an appropriate response.[85] Strict liability ought to lie with the person who is in control of the operation. In the case of a defect in a product, liability of a manufacturer can continue to apply along with strict liability since they are based on 'different theories'.[86] The NTF Report also suggests that fault liability of users ought to continue to coexist with other bases of liability, thereby providing for a range of duties of care as triggers.[87] Furthermore, since the principles on which auxiliary liability is based can be found in the relationship between users and AI, this liability can continue to apply. Product liability, auxiliary liability, strict liability, and fault liability can continue to coexist, although each retains its specific purpose and value in a liability regime.

Thus far, the exact set of measures a lawmaker needs to undertake is hard to define since AI devices still have not become an integral part of everyday life of humans and it is uncertain what the risks exactly are going to be. Existing publications usually focus on the anticipation of risks arising out of generalized knowledge about AI and provide for general recommendations. Specific risks are identified and specific measures are proposed in a small number of cases and they are usually related to a specific sector in which AI operates. The sector of autonomous vehicles is one of the frontrunners when it comes to the application of AI and there are several discussions and measures already undertaken. For example, the United Kingdom has already passed the Automated and Electric Vehicles Act of 2018, dealing with issues in that sector.[88]

85 NTF Report (n 12) 3.
86 Koch, 'Product Liability 2.0' (n 63) 116.
87 The NTF Report mentions the following: 'Operators of emerging digital technologies should have to comply with an adapted range of duties of care, including with regard to (a) choosing the right system for the right task and skills; (b) monitoring the system; and (c) maintaining the system.' NTF Report (n 12) 6–7.
88 See Francesco Paolo Patti, 'The European Road to Autonomous Vehicles' (2019) 43 *Fordham Intl LJ* 125.

4.2 Position of injured persons

Notwithstanding the difficulty involved in providing a proper response to the allocation of responsibility for harm, injured persons ought to be in a position that enables full compensation within a reasonable time that would not be overly burdensome or costly to achieve.

The identification of the responsible party ought not to be a hard task for the injured party. The injured party needs to be able to promptly seek compensation from any of the parties who might be responsible, without the need to be involved in the process of identification of the actual responsible party in a particular case. Potentially responsible parties ought to be jointly and severally liable as a general rule as a one-stop-shop solution.[89] Naturally, responsible parties need to have a right of recourse, and parties in the interest of efficiency ought to be 'incentivized to make contractual arrangements for tort claims in advance'.[90] The NTF Report advises joint and several liability of manufacturers who produce different components of a 'commercial and technological unit' who 'cooperate on a contractual or similar basis'. It seems that the user of AI is not involved in the group of jointly and severally liable parties mentioned in the NTF Report, which is a measure that would enhance the position of the injured party even more. Furthermore, since there is a requirement of cooperation of manufacturers 'on a contractual or similar basis', it is possible that manufacturers who are not aware of other manufacturers are not covered by this requirement and cannot be jointly and severally liable. In the case of open digital environments, parts of which can be assembled by the user, it is unlikely that manufacturers of different parts will be aware of such cooperation in every particular case. Inclusion of the user of AI in a group of jointly and severally liable parties as well as the elimination of the criterion of cooperation 'on a contractual or similar basis' would enhance the position of injured parties.

The liability system ought to take into account the heavy burden of proof a victim bears and provide for measures that would alleviate it. Several measures suitable for reaching this goal have been proposed. First, the increased use of strict liability in the case of AI and other complex emerging new technologies would provide an injured party with a favourable position insofar as she does not have to prove negligence or fault of the tortfeasors. Second, as collection of evidence is a hard task in digital environments in present times, an obligation of manufacturers to design devices to record information related to the operation of the device and an obligation to make the recorded information available should be imposed (logging by design). The NTF Report proposes the same measure and takes it a step further: it provides that 'failure to comply with a logging and disclosure duty should lead to a rebuttable presumption that the information would, if logged and disclosed,

89 NTF Report (n 12) 58.
90 ibid.

have revealed that the relevant element of liability is fulfilled'.[91] Sometimes, in spite of the availability of the information about the operation of a device, the burden of proof remains heavy. A number of measures are available, such as the application of *res ipsa loquitur* theory, whereby the occurrence of harm is enough for the inference of negligence.[92] Other known measures involve lowering the standard of proof,[93] the application of *prima facie* evidence,[94] judicial presumptions,[95] or adverse inferences of the failure of manufacturers or users to produce evidence in their control about the harmful event.[96] The NTF Report even suggests a reversal of the burden of proof of causation and fault[97] (where that is the applicable basis of liability) if the position of the claimant is characterized by the 'disproportionate difficulties or costs'[98] and the fact that the defendant is in a much more favourable position to provide proof.

A victim ought to be in a position to obtain compensation without hardship and in a reasonable time. The application of joint and several liability fosters this goal as the injured party might select the most solvent defendant. The European Parliament suggested in the Resolution that there might be a need for the introduction of mandatory liability insurance. This is a well-known mechanism that already exists in Europe and provides certain indemnification to the victims of traffic accidents.[99] Since the EU has already harmonized the rules on the mandatory insurance scheme for vehicles by virtue of the Motor Insurance Directive, there is already significant experience on the part of Member States that would facilitate the adoption of such mechanism for AI. Mandatory insurance could prevent the risk of the insolvency of the tortfeasor as well as increase the process of compensation.[100] For damages not covered by mandatory insurance, a fund that would cover the residual losses might be introduced. This idea has been also supported in the Resolution.[101] Apart from fostering total compensation of the victim, this measure could limit the liability of potentially responsible parties.

91 ibid 48.
92 Borghetti (n 61) 67.
93 For instance, liability law in the medical sector employs some of these measures. See Bernhard A Koch, 'Medical Liability in Europe: Comparative Analysis' in Bernhard A Koch (ed), *Medical Liability in Europe: A Comparison of Selected Jurisdictions* (De Gruyter 2011) 611.
94 Martín-Casals, 'Causation and Scope of Liability in the IoT' (n 70) 206.
95 ibid.
96 NTF Report (n 12) 51.
97 ibid 49–55.
98 ibid 6.
99 Wagner (n 18) 51.
100 Georg Borges, 'New Liability Concepts: the Potential of Insurance and Compensation Funds' in Sebastian Lohsee, Reiner Schulze, and Dirk Staudenmayer (eds), *Liability for Artificial Intelligence and the Internet of Things: Münster Colloquia on EU Law and the Digital Economy IV* (Nomos 2019) 156.
101 Resolution (n 4) para 59.

Just like mandatory insurance, the concept of a fund that would supplement mandatory insurance is not new as it already exists in Member States' national legal systems, which reduces the risk of having to face an unknown mechanism.[102] Furthermore, since society reaps the benefits of technological progress, compensation funds 'could perhaps be used to cushion the transformation risks in the development of our transforming society'.[103] The issue of who ought to bear the cost of mandatory insurance and who ought to contribute to the fund does not have a clear answer at the present time. However, since one of the main goals of the technological advancement is to create flawless machines that perform tasks better than humans, or at least with a smaller number of errors, the price of insurance and the contribution to the fund ought not to be high as the occurrence of tortious events is expected to be diminished.

5. Conclusion

As a transformative technology, AI poses many challenges to modern societies. The adoption of proper measures that provide a fair and timely allocation of losses ought not to disincentivize further technological developments, but also must not lead to the moral hazard of any involved actors. The introduction of changes to the existing liability regime is a sensitive task that entails a thorough and comprehensive assessment of the phenomena that require intervention.

Modest adaptation of the current rules could be done by focusing on the rules that today can be anticipated as problematic or obsolete, such as the adaptation of the PLD or the enhancement of the position of the victim. New rules could be adopted in sectors with the significant presence of AI or where it could soon be impactful. It is currently uncertain whether it is even possible to find one-size-fits-all rules for AI at all. If that is achievable, a long-term goal should naturally be the adoption of general rules of liability, but the processes must not be rushed. Improper general rules might turn out to be Law of the Horse – a set of incoherent rules without clear logic apart from the subject matter they regulate. The creation of new rules could take into account already existing mechanisms in the legal system such as mandatory insurance or compensation funds. These are favourable over new mechanisms since they are well tested and as such they will, to some degree, eliminate uncertainty.

Current knowledge about AI is insufficient to render bold and radical changes in the hitherto well-functioning extracontractual liability system. It remains to be seen what changes the Fourth Industrial Revolution will bring

102 The idea of the introduction of a compensation fund that would not supplement but replace a liability system has also been assessed in the scholarship. It, however, did not receive strong support. See Borges (n 100) 158.

103 ibid 163.

forth – AI has not become an integral part of our lives yet. It seems that the new pertinent regulatory action can be prolonged as there is neither immediate appetite nor sufficient knowledge to regulate now.

Bibliography

Amato C, 'Product Liability and Product Security: Present and Future' in Lohsee S, Schulze R, and Staudenmayer D (eds), *Liability for Artificial Intelligence and the Internet of Things: Münster Colloquia on EU Law and the Digital Economy IV* (Nomos 2019) [DOI: https://doi.org/10.5771/9783845294797-77]

Balkin JM, 'The Path of Robotics Law' (2015) 6 *Cal L Rev Circ* 45

Borges G, 'New Liability Concepts: the Potential of Insurance and Compensation Funds' in Lohsee S, Schulze R, and Staudenmayer D (eds), *Liability for Artificial Intelligence and the Internet of Things: Münster Colloquia on EU Law and the Digital Economy IV* (Nomos 2019) [DOI: https://doi.org/10.5771/9783845294797-145]

Borghetti JS, 'How can Artificial Intelligence be Defective?' in Lohsee S, Schulze R, and Staudenmayer D (eds), *Liability for Artificial Intelligence and the Internet of Things: Münster Colloquia on EU Law and the Digital Economy IV* (Nomos 2019) [DOI: https://doi.org/10.5771/9783845294797-63]

Calo R, 'Robotics and the Lessons of Cyberlaw' (2015) 103 *CLR* 513

Council of Europe – The Committee of Experts on Internet Intermediaries (MSI-NET), 'Algorithms and Human Rights: Study on the human rights dimensions of automated data processing techniques and possible regulatory implications: Council of Europe study DGI(2017)12' (Council of Europe 2018)

Craglia M (ed), *Artificial Intelligence: A European Perspective* (Publications Office of the European Union 2018) [DOI: https://doi.org/10.2760/936974]

Eidenmüller H, 'Machine Performance and Human Failure: How Shall We Regulate Autonomous Machines?' (2019) 15 *J Bus & Tech L* 109

European Commission, 'Proposal for a Council Directive on the liability of suppliers of services' COM (90) 482 final [1991] *OJ* C12/8

——— 'Building a European Data Economy' (Communication) COM (2017) 9 final

——— 'Commission Staff Working document on the free flow of data and emerging issues of the European data economy' SWD (2017) 2 final

European Group on Tort Law (ed), *Principles of European Tort Law: Text and Commentary* (Springer 2005) [DOI: https://doi.org/10.1007/3-211-27751-X]

Expert Group on Liability and New Technologies – New Technologies Formation, *Liability for Artificial Intelligence and Other Emerging Digital Technologies* (European Commission 2019) [DOI: https://doi.org/10.2838/25362]

Geistfeld MA, 'A Roadmap for Autonomous Vehicles: State Tort Liability, Automobile Insurance, and Federal Safety Regulation' (2017) 105 *CLR* 1611 [DOI: https://dx.doi.org/10.15779/Z38416SZ9R]

Gifford DG, 'Technological Triggers to Tort Revolutions: Steam Locomotives, Autonomous Vehicles, and Accident Compensation' (2017) 11 *J Tort L* 71 [DOI: https://doi.org/10.1515/jtl-2017-0029]

Habersack M (ed), *Münchener Kommentar zum Bürgerlichen Gesetzbuch: Band 6: Schuldrecht: Besonderer Teil IV* (7th edn, CH Beck 2017)

Karner E, 'Liability for Robotics: Current Rules, Challenges, and the Need for Innovative Concepts' in Lohsee S, Schulze R, and Staudenmayer D (eds), *Liability for Artificial Intelligence and the Internet of Things: Münster Colloquia on EU Law and the Digital Economy IV* (Nomos 2019) [DOI: https://doi.org/10.5771/9783845294797-117]

Koch BA, 'Medical Liability in Europe: Comparative Analysis' in Koch BA (ed), *Medical Liability in Europe: A Comparison of Selected Jurisdictions* (De Gruyter 2011) [DOI: https://doi.org/10.1515/9783110260168.611]

——— 'Product Liability 2.0 – Mere Update or New Version?' in Lohsee S, Schulze R, and Staudenmayer D (eds), *Liability for Artificial Intelligence and the Internet of Things: Münster Colloquia on EU Law and the Digital Economy IV* (Nomos 2019) [DOI: https://doi.org/10.5771/9783845294797-97]

Lohsse S, Schulze R, and Staudenmayer D, 'Liability for Artificial Intelligence' in Lohsee S, Schulze R, and Staudenmayer D (eds), *Liability for Artificial Intelligence and the Internet of Things: Münster Colloquia on EU Law and the Digital Economy IV* (Nomos 2019) [DOI: https://doi.org/10.5771/9783845294797-9]

Martín-Casals M (ed), *The Borderlines of Tort Law: Interactions with Contract Law* (Intersentia 2019) [DOI: https://doi.org/10.1017/9781780689135]

——— 'Causation and Scope of Liability in the Internet of Things (IoT)' in Lohsee S, Schulze R, and Staudenmayer D (eds), *Liability for Artificial Intelligence and the Internet of Things: Münster Colloquia on EU Law and the Digital Economy IV* (Nomos 2019) [DOI: https://doi.org/10.5040/9781509925841.0018]

Patti FP, 'The European Road to Autonomous Vehicles' (2019) 43 *Fordham Intl LJ* 125

Revolidis I and Dahi A, 'The Peculiar Case of the Mushroom Picking Robot: Extra-contractual Liability in Robotics' in Corrales M, Fenwick M, and Forgó N (eds), *Robotics, AI and the Future of Law* (Springer 2018) [DOI: https://doi.org/10.1007/978-981-13-2874-9_3]

Schirmer JE, 'Artificial Intelligence and Legal Personality: Introducing "Teilrechtsfähigkeit": A Partial Legal Status Made in Germany' in Wischmeyer T and Rademacher T (eds), *Regulating Artificial Intelligence* (Springer 2019) [DOI: https://doi.org/10.1007/978-3-030-32361-5_6]

Schwab K, 'The Fourth Industrial Revolution: What It Means and How to Respond' *Foreign Affairs* (Online, 12 December 2015) <www.foreignaffairs.com/articles/2015-12-12/fourth-industrial-revolution> accessed 5 December 2019

Spindler G, 'User Liability and Strict Liability in the Internet of Things and for Robots' in Lohsee S, Schulze R, and Staudenmayer D (eds), *Liability for Artificial Intelligence and the Internet of Things: Münster Colloquia on EU Law and the Digital Economy IV* (Nomos 2019) [DOI: https://doi.org/10.5771/9783845294797-125]

Turner J, *Robot Rules: Regulating Artificial Intelligence* (Palgrave Macmillan 2019) [DOI: https://doi.org/10.1007/978-3-319-96235-1]

Van Dam C, *European Tort Law* (2nd edn, OUP 2013)

Van den Berg PAJ, *The Politics of European Codification: A History of the Unification of Law in France, Prussia, the Austrian Monarchy and the Netherlands* (Europa Law Publishing 2007)

Van den Hoven van Genderen R, 'Do We Need New Legal Personhood in the Age of Robots and AI?' in Corrales M, Fenwick M, and Forgó N (eds), *Robotics, AI and the Future of Law* (Springer 2018) [DOI: https://doi.org/10.1007/978-981-13-2874-9_2]

Wagner G, 'Robot Liability' in Lohsee S, Schulze R, and Staudenmayer D (eds), *Liability for Artificial Intelligence and the Internet of Things: Münster Colloquia on EU Law and the Digital Economy IV* (Nomos 2019) [DOI: https://doi.org/10.5771/9783845294797-25]

Whittaker S, *Liability for Products: English Law, French Law, and European Harmonisation* (OUP 2005)

Zech H, 'Liability for Autonomous Systems: Tackling Specific Risks of Modern IT' in Lohsee S, Schulze R, and Staudenmayer D (eds), *Liability for Artificial Intelligence and the Internet of Things: Münster Colloquia on EU Law and the Digital Economy IV* (Nomos 2019) [DOI: https://doi.org/10.5771/9783845294797-185]

Part II

Contract law challenges posed by smart contracts

7 What are smart contracts?

An attempt at demystification

Mateja Durovic

1. Introduction

This chapter represents an extended and revised version of the paper on smart contracts presented at the first Zagreb International Conference on the Law of Obligations in December 2019.[1] The chapter examines smart contracts in an attempt to understand better this rather unclear and innovative concept that is disrupting the existent legal system. The rise of smart contracts is just one of the signs of a rising tendency of automation of contracts and contract law as part of the Fourth Industrial Revolution.[2] Accordingly, in the era of the Fourth Industrial Revolution, the regulatory framework needs, on the one hand, to ensure that law continues to protect fundamental values (e.g. protection of a weaker party or the legality of commercial transactions); on the other side, however, the regulatory framework must not unreasonably inhibit innovation and further digitalization of the market by the imposition of unreasonable burdens. In practice, the balance between these values is very difficult to secure and, today, that seems to be one of the main challenges for legal systems worldwide.

Contract law rules, accordingly, must not inhibit the development of new technologies and smart contracts, but they still need to secure protection of some of the fundamental principles, such as justice, fairness, and protection of vulnerable parties. In that context, the question of proper regulation and contract law understanding of smart contracts is very important as smart contracts are becoming widely adopted in diverse commercial contexts and the digitalization of contract law has already widely spread.[3]

1 The author would like to thank to the conference participants for their useful comments on the paper. The usual disclaimer applies.

2 Florian Möslein, 'Legal Boundaries of Blockchain Technologies: Smart Contracts as Self-Help?' in Alberto De Franceschi and Reiner Schulze (eds), *Digital Revolution – New Challenges for Law* (CH Beck and Nomos 2019) 313.

3 See Stefan Grundmann (ed), *European Contract Law in the Digital Age* (Intersentia 2018).

DOI: 10.4324/9781003080596-9

2. The notion of smart contracts

To start with, in order to understand smart contracts properly, the name 'smart contracts' itself is confusing and inadequate as the notion of the smart contract itself is a misnomer.[4] As an initial observation, it is important to emphasize that smart contracts are neither smart nor contracts in the legal sense, so the terminology used to explain this form of new technology is wrong and has led to confusion. Smart contracts are not smart because the current stage of technological development does not allow the use of smart contracts in more complex commercial transactions.

As it stands now, smart contracts can be used in straightforward transactions where simple and clear 'if' and 'then' parameters are used. In other words, smart contracts cannot include any term that is ambiguous in any way; they can only be used for a simple transaction where the situation is straightforward. For example, a smart contract can be used in the situation: if trader A delivers 100 tonnes of wool, trader B will pay 100,000 euros, without the possibility of any kind of alternation.

However, smart contracts cannot be applied to situations where the situation is more complicated, such as commercial transactions containing a condition as a requirement for fulfilment – for example, if we add to the previous hypothetical transaction some kind of requirement related to the quality of the purchased goods or requirements related to transportation or delivery. However, what is important to note here is that smart contracts cannot cover these kinds of situations *at this moment*; this does not mean that they will not be able to include them in the future as technological developments are constantly evolving and smart contract technology is continually improving.

3. Are smart contracts in fact contracts at all?

Smart contracts are neither contracts in the strict legal sense, but rather computer codes stored and replicated on the system and supervised by the network of computers that run the blockchain.[5] In the common law legal world, contracts are understood as legally enforceable agreements between two or more parties. In the civil law jurisdictions, contracts are a consensus of expressed consents whose aim is to produce certain legal effects: to establish, modify, or abolish diverse rights and obligations. However, smart contracts are not legal contracts at all in any of these two meanings; they are just a

4 Jeffrey M Lipshaw, 'Persistence of "Dumb" Contracts' (2019) 2 (1) *Stanford J Blockchain L & Pol'y* 1, 12.

5 Nikolas Guggenberger, 'The Potential of Blockchain for the Conclusion of Contracts' in Reiner Schulze, Dirk Staudenmayer, and Sebastian Lohsse (eds), *Contracts for the Supply of Digital Content: Regulatory Challenges and Gaps* (Nomos 2017) 83ff.

form of new technology that is used to execute promises established through a legal contract.[6]

Typically, smart contracts are agreements which are stored on an immutable blockchain that is time-stamped and distributed across potentially millions of nodes.[7] This feature of smart contracts makes it almost impossible to modify in any manner the contents of the contract as smart contracts cannot be altered retroactively. This is what makes them very desirable to the businesses: the issue of certainty – parties can be reassured that the established promises will eventually be executed and that nothing can stop that.

4. The history of smart contracts

The concept of smart contracts is itself not radically new as it is almost three decades old. It was developed in the last decade of the twentieth century by computer scientist and cryptographer Nick Szabo. Szabo defined a smart contract as a computerized transaction protocol that executes the terms of a contract.[8] The first example of a smart contract used by Szabo was the vending machine as an automated machine that provides diverse items, such as chocolates, drinks, or snacks in exchange for money as an automated transaction that does not require the involvement of a third party and happens automatically.

However, smart contracts have become popular only in the last few years as technological developments, particularly blockchains, have enabled their application in practice. Since then, we can follow the incredible growth of smart contract technology throughout the world. The existence of blockchain technology is of existential importance to smart contracts as smart contracts exist across a distributed, decentralized blockchain network and it is the code that controls the execution. Smart contracts can be encoded on any blockchain, but, in reality, they are typically written on Ethereum blockchain.[9] This is because Ethereum gives them unlimited processing capacity. As a platform, Ethereum runs smart contract code when a user sends it a message that some condition has been fulfilled (e.g. purchased goods have been delivered).

6 Alexander Savelyev, 'Contract Law 2.0: "Smart" Contracts as the Beginning of the End of Classic Contract Law' (2016) *Higher School of Economics Research Paper* WP BRP 71/LAW/2016, 10 <https://ssrn.com/abstract=2885241> accessed 13 May 2020.

7 Georgios Dimitropoulos, 'The Law of Blockchain' 95 (2020) *Wash L Rev* 1117, 1135 <https://digitalcommons.law.uw.edu/wlr/vol95/iss3/3> accessed 27 May 2021.

8 Nick Szabo, 'Smart Contracts' (1994) <www.fon.hum.uva.nl/rob/Courses/InformationInSpeech/CDROM/Literature/LOTwinterschool2006/szabo.best.vwh.net/smart.contracts.html> accessed 13 May 2020.

9 See 'Ethereum' <https://ethereum.org/> accessed 13 May 2020.

5. The relevance of smart contracts

Currently, the most important question posed in the context of smart contracts is the issue of their validity in the eyes of the law.[10] The enforceability of contractual transactions using smart contracts is relevant not only from the perspective of the contractual parties using them but also in respect of investments in line with the growing interest in smart contracts.[11]

Smart contracts represent one of the forms of new technology that is currently being developed and investors want to be sure that their investments are justified and their investment will pay off – that is, that parties will use smart contracts in practice and pay for them. And parties will use smart contracts only if they are fully in line with the applicable law and they know that such transactions are safe and enforceable. Accordingly, legal systems have to confirm that the transactions using smart contracts are actually enforceable in the eyes of the law.[12] All this will result in increased legal certainty followed by confidence of market participants and investors in smart contracts.

The reason why smart contracts are becoming popular for businesses and why parties would use them is the fact that they guarantee the security, permanence, efficiency, and immutability of a commercial transaction.[13] In that manner, a party to a contract is ensured that the particular promise established on a contract will be executed. It is important to note that, as it stands now, there is no technological or theoretical way for a transaction coded in the form of a smart contract to be stopped.

Smart contracts enable the performance of promises established through a contract without the involvement of a third party (e.g. a bank or a judge). Smart contracts are saving money and time: smart contracts are established on blockchains as decentralized systems that exist between all permitted parties; there is no need to involve an intermediary or the contractual parties themselves to execute the promises. In that sense, smart contracts help contractual parties exchange money, property, shares, or anything they want in a conflict-free way without the involvement of a third party. This is a huge advantage of smart contracts as they significantly reduce the chances of non-performance of the contract. However, this may also be a disadvantage, in the event of a justified reason for failure to perform (e.g. *force majeure*,

10 Chamber of Digital Commerce, 'Smart Contracts: Is the Law Ready?' (2018) 35 <https://digitalchamber.org/smart-contracts-whitepaper> accessed 13 May 2020.

11 See UK Jurisdiction Task Force, 'Legal statement on cryptoassets and smart contracts' (*Tech Nation*, November 2019) <https://technation.io/about-us/lawtech-panel> accessed 13 May 2020.

12 Mateja Durovic and Franciszek Lech, 'The Enforceability of Smart Contracts' (2019) 5 *Ita LJ* 493.

13 Mateja Durovic and André Janssen, 'Formation of Smart Contracts under Contract Law' in Larry A DiMatteo, Michel Cannarsa, and Cristina Poncibò (eds), *The Cambridge Handbook of Smart Contracts, Blockchain Technology and Digital Platforms* (CUP 2019) 61ff.

something very relevant in the period of coronavirus pandemic) as the execution of smart contracts cannot be modified.

Smart contracts are being applied in diverse sectors. For example, they turned out to be very successful and practical in the case of tenancy agreements.[14] In the case of a tenancy agreement, it can be agreed that the front door of the leased apartment can only be opened with an automated key that can only be used if the monthly rent is paid. If not, the smart contract automatically blocks the key to the door and the tenant cannot enter the flat due to the unpaid rent. A similar situation is with a leased car that can be used only if the monthly lease has been correctly paid.

6. Smart contracts v legal contracts

In short, the main difference between smart contracts and legal contracts is that legal contracts define the relationship between the contractual parties, whereas smart contracts define the execution of promises between parties. However, there are more substantial differences between smart contracts and legal contracts, and they will be explained below.

The first difference is the manner in which smart contracts and legal contracts are expressed and the deployed language:[15] smart contracts are written in a programming language, such as Solidity, and presented in a code that a machine can read, whereas legal contracts are presented in natural languages such as English, Italian, or French.

The second difference is who is expected to perform: in case of smart contracts, it is always the software that performs without the need to involve anyone else, whereas in the case of legal contracts performance is carried out by humans.

Third, the difference is in the content in which the contract is contained: a machine will carry out a contract that is contained in the software, whereas in the case of legal contracts legal language and terms are being used.

Fourth, the difference is related to execution and flexibility: smart contracts carry out the action literally and there is no possibility for a change or correction of errors, whereas in the case of legal contracts there is more flexibility and possibility for correction of contract errors, if any.

Fifth, there is a different outcome in the event of ambiguity of a contract: in the case of ambiguous code, it may happen that the machine does not execute at all the action encoded in a smart contract or executes the action improperly, whereas in the case of ambiguous terms of legal contracts, there is much more flexibility to fix the the lack clarity and it is more likely that the promises will be executed in the form they were initially planned.

14 See Midasium, 'Smart Tenancy Contracts' <https://midasium.herokuapp.com/smart-tenancy> accessed 13 May 2020.

15 Jason G Allen, 'Wrapped and Stacked: "Smart Contracts" and the Interaction of Natural and Formal Language' (2018) 14 *ERCL* 307.

7. The issues with smart contracts

The problem is that smart contracts cannot deal with more complex transactions. They cannot solve the problem in situations when, for instance, a seller does not deliver or a buyer does not pay the price for the goods. Likewise, the question is what happens in case of a defect of delivered goods, which is not answered by a smart contract. Similarly, smart contracts cannot be used, as already pointed out above, for more complex contracts – for example, those containing provisions on after-sales service.

Moreover, smart contracts open up other legal questions.[16] For example, as smart contracts are typically programmed by IT experts and not lawyers, but under lawyers' instructions, the issue is who is liable in the event of a programming mistake? Likewise, a number of problems may arise in relation to the coding of the smart contract. In addition, the challenge is how to ensure that smart contracts are not used to unlawfully circumvent rules and protection provided by the legal system – for example, to be deployed for transactions involving illegal weapons or drugs. The self-enforceability and inability of courts to stop the performance of a smart contract could in principle also result in illegal contracts being performed, exacerbating the already anxious reservations about cryptocurrency and blockchain being used for illicit means. The computer code does not consider a possible nullity of a legal contract (unless programmed to do so) and discrepancies can occur between the legal and the informatics systems, which then may result in unfair or even unlawful smart contracts being enforced.

Another issue is related to cybersecurity. As it stands now, from the cybersecurity perspective, smart contracts are safe, but the question is what will happen in the future with the development of new technologies that will enable, possibly, hacking of smart contracts and result in increasing of risk for smart contracts, emphasizing the question of liability. This is an area where, almost certainly, we can expect developments in the future.

A further open question in relation to smart contracts is the issue of applicable law as well as a forum for disputes arising from smart contracts.[17] The question of applicable law is something that makes the regulation of smart contracts very challenging due to their likely transnational nature. This is because smart contracts can be operated by different computers located in different jurisdictions and thus have a very strong cross-border dimension. Accordingly, in practice, this may make it more difficult to identify the law applicable to the smart contract.[18]

16 Roberto Pardolesi and Antonio Davola, 'What is Wrong in the Debate About Smart Contracts' (2019) *Luiss Guido Carli University Working Paper* <https://ssrn.com/abstract=3339421> accessed 13 May 2020.

17 Giesela Ruhl, 'Smart (Legal) Contracts, or: Which (Contract) Law for Smart Contracts?' in Benedetta Cappiello and Gherardo Carullo (eds), *Blockchain, Law and Governance* (Springer 2020).

18 Mateja Durovic, 'How to Resolve Smart Contract Disputes – Smart Arbitration as a Solution' (*Oxford Business Law Blog*, 1 June 2018) <www.law.ox.ac.uk/business-law-blog/

Another open question is the issue of interpretation of a smart contract's contents.[19] In addition, what is also relevant is to determine the application of diverse contract law standards to smart contracts. An excellent example is the requirement of good faith – the challenge is how to secure that the requirement of good faith is fulfilled, as it is required by many legal systems worldwide.[20] Another standard, especially relevant in the context of the coronavirus pandemic, is the *force majeure*: parties are excused from a failure to perform their contractual promises if the failure is a result of *force majeure*. The challenge is how to ensure that smart contracts take into consideration the occurrence of *force majeure* as the execution of the encoded promise into a smart contract can be neither stopped nor postponed.

8. Regulation of smart contracts

As smart contracts are still in their nascent stage, many more questions in relation to them are posed than there are answers provided. A lot of clarity in relation to smart contracts will need to be provided in the future, primarily because smart contracts are still to be tested by judges and lawyers.

The approach towards smart contracts also includes three policy options from the perspective of contract law:

(a) *Keeping contract law as it is* – traditional contract law is sufficient and adequate to address smart contracts, so no changes are needed.
(b) *Revising contract law* – the existing contract law needs to be modified and adapted to address challenges brought by smart contracts.
(c) *Contract law will become redundant* – this is in line with the principle 'code as law', in the sense that code (software) is replacing the law.

It seems that the most likely option, as it stands now, is the combination of options (a) and (b) as traditional contract law will be maintained with some modification to adapt it to the challenges and particularities brought by smart contracts and to secure the validity of commercial transactions that deploy smart contracts.

Smart contracts are to be understood in the context of freedom of contract as the most fundamental principle of contract law that allows the contractual parties to regulate their contractual relationship in line with their desires and possibilities. In that sense, it seems unproblematic to allow the use of smart contracts in order to secure partial or full execution of promises established on the ground of a legal contract.

---

blog/2018/06/law-and-autonomous-systems-series-how-resolve-smart-contract-disputes> accessed 13 May 2020.

19 Michel Cannarsa, 'Interpretation of Contracts and Smart Contracts: Smart Interpretation or Interpretation of Smart Contracts?' (2018) 26 *ERPL* 773.

20 See Reinhard Zimmermann and Simon Whittaker (eds), *Good Faith in European Contract Law* (CUP 2000).

From the perspective of freedom of contract, the soil of common law jurisdictions is more favourable for smart contracts than in civil law jurisdictions. This is because common law contains fewer regulatory requirements than the civil law (e.g. absence of a general principle of good faith in contract law) which makes their application easier in practice. More complications are to be faced in cases of business-to-consumer transactions where regulatory requirements are much more demanding (e.g. due to the requirements related to the fairness and transparency of contract terms).[21] Smart contracts are certainly disrupting consumer markets and the existing framework of consumer protection.[22]

An essential question is how smart contracts fit into the existing framework of contract law. The applicable law is a very important issue as the enforceability of smart contracts will depend on the applicable law. Some jurisdictions, such as Italy, have already introduced special laws securing the enforceability of smart contracts.[23] This has also been done in some of the US states, such as Arizona and Tennessee.

In Arizona, the law states that 'Smart Contracts may exist in commerce. A contract relating to a transaction may not be denied legal effect, validity or enforceability solely because that contract contains a smart contract term.'[24]

In another US state, Tennessee, the newly adopted law states:

> 'Smart contract' means an event-driven computer program, that executes on an electronic, distributed, decentralized, shared, and replicated ledger that is used to automate transactions, including, but not limited to, transactions that:
>
> (A) Take custody over and instruct transfer of assets on that ledger;
> (B) Create and distribute electronic assets;
> (C) Synchronize information; or
> (D) Manage identity and user access to software applications.[25]
>
> (a) A cryptographic signature that is generated and stored through distributed ledger technology is considered to be in an electronic form and to be an electronic signature.
> (b) A record or contract that is secured through distributed ledger technology is considered to be in an electronic form and to be an electronic record.

21 See Council Directive 93/13/EEC of 5 April 1993 on unfair terms in consumer contracts [1993] *OJ* L95/29.

22 Joshua AT Fairfield, 'Smart Contracts, Bitcoin Bots, and Consumer Protection' (2014) 71 *Wash & Lee L Rev Online* 35 <https://scholarlycommons.law.wlu.edu/wlulr-online/vol71/iss2/3> accessed 13 May 2020.

23 Law Decree 135, 'Urgent provisions on support and simplification for businesses and the public administration' (*Decreto-legge* 135, '*Disposizioni urgenti in materia di sostegno e semplificazione per le imprese e per la pubblica amministrazione*') *GU* 290 of 14 December 2018.

24 Arizona Revised Statutes (ARS) § 44-7061 C.

25 Tennessee Code (TN Code) § 47-10-201(2).

(c) Smart contracts may exist in commerce. No contract relating to a transaction shall be denied legal effect, validity, or enforceability solely because that contract is executed through a smart contract.[26]

All these jurisdictions have adopted such pieces of legislation in order to demonstrate that they are commercial and investment-friendly and that they are open to supporting the deployment of new technologies, including smart contracts, in the commercial transactions.

However, it is possible to imagine jurisdictions where the legal system might not recognize smart contracts, or might restrictively allow them, prohibiting them, for example, in case of business-to-consumer transactions. This is why statutory intervention is certainly important.

In the past, the development of new forms of contractual transactions also attracted regional and international legal responses. For example, parallel with the development of online trade and e-commerce, it is possible to observe the development of the common European rules in this area: Directive 2000/31/EC on electronic commerce[27] or Directive 97/7/EC on distance selling[28] (subsequently replaced by Directive 2011/83/EU on consumer rights[29]). Similarly, on a global level, UNCITRAL developed the UNCITRAL Model Law on Electronic Commerce in 1996.

The European E-Commerce Directive, adopted some twenty years ago, at the dawn of e-commerce development, points out that:

> Member States shall ensure that their legal system allows contracts to be concluded by electronic means. Member States shall in particular ensure that the legal requirements applicable to the contractual process neither create obstacles for the use of electronic contracts nor result in such contracts being deprived of legal effectiveness and validity on account of their having been made by electronic means.[30]

It is possible to imagine that the EU in the near future will develop a similar piece of legislation, like the one on e-commerce, requiring its Member States to recognize the enforceability of commercial transactions using smart contracts. Moreover, UNIDROIT and UNCITRAL have been working together on smart contracts and what the international legal

26 TN Code § 47-10-202, (a) to (c).

27 Directive 2000/31/EC of the European Parliament and of the Council of 8 June 2000 on certain legal aspects of information society services, in particular electronic commerce, in the Internal Market [2002] OJ L178/1 (E-Commerce Directive).

28 Directive 97/7/EC of the European Parliament and of the Council of 20 May 1997 on the protection of consumers in respect of distance contracts [1997] OJ L144/19.

29 Directive 2011/83/EU of the European Parliament and of the Council of 25 October 2011 on consumer rights, amending Council Directive 93/13/EEC and Directive 1999/44/EC of the European Parliament and of the Council and repealing Council Directive 85/577/EEC and Directive 97/7/EC of the European Parliament and of the Council [2011] OJ L304/64.

30 E-Commerce Directive, Art 9(1).

response should be.[31] The conclusion reached was to continue work in this area in the future and to come up, possibly, with a joint international legal instrument.[32]

9. Concluding remarks

This chapter examined smart contracts from a contract law perspective. It was possible to observe in this chapter that smart contracts are neither smart nor contracts in the legal sense. Smarts contracts are rather a form of new technology, a code, used to secure the execution of promises established through a legal contract.

As it stands now, the discussion of smart contracts means much more opening and posing different questions in relation to smart contracts than providing the answers. This is still a new form of technology that is increasingly being used by businesses, and it is yet to be seen how it fits in traditional contract law and legal systems. What is certain is that this new form of contracting has certainly opened some new important legal questions. Smart contracts are not yet sufficiently tested and assessed, especially before the courts, and it is interesting to see what kind of answers case law will provide in the future. When it comes to the enforceability of smart contracts, that does not yet seem to be problematic as they are to be understood in line with the principle of freedom of contract.[33] As correctly concluded in the United Kingdom:

> A smart contract is capable of satisfying those requirements just as well as a more traditional or natural language contract, and a smart contract is therefore capable of having contractual force. Whether the requirements are in fact met in any given case will depend on the parties' words and conduct, just as it does with any other contract.[34]

Future developments will depend a lot on how judges, lawyers, and policymakers decide to interpret and apply smart contracts in the context of traditional contract law. Their approach is uncertain, but what is certain is that exciting smart contract times are ahead of all of us.

31 UNIDROIT, 'UNCITRAL/UNIDROIT Workshop on Smart Contracts, Artificial Intelligence and Distributed Ledger Technology – Summary of conclusions published' (*UNIDROIT: News and events*, 2019) <www.unidroit.org/89-news-and-events/2663-uncitral-unidroit-workshop-on-smart-contracts-artificial-intelligence-and-distributed-ledger-technology-summary-of-conclusions-published%20(last> accessed 13 May 2020.

32 UNCITRAL and UNIDROIT, 'Joint UNCITRAL/UNIDROIT Workshop: Rome, Seat UNIDROIT, 6 and 7 May 2019: Summary of the Discussion and Conclusion', 7 (*UNIDROIT: News and events*, 2019) <www.unidroit.org/english/news/2019/190506-unidroit-uncitral-workshop/conclusions-e.pdf> accessed 13 May 2020.

33 Durovic and Lech (n 12) 510–11.

34 UK Jurisdiction Task Force (n 11) 8.

Bibliography

Allen JG, 'Wrapped and Stacked: "Smart Contracts" and the Interaction of Natural and Formal Language' (2018) 14 *ERCL* 307 [DOI: https://doi.org/10.1515/ercl-2018-1023]

Cannarsa M, 'Interpretation of Contracts and Smart Contracts: Smart Interpretation or Interpretation of Smart Contracts?' (2018) 26 *ERPL* 773

Chamber of Digital Commerce, 'Smart Contracts: Is the Law Ready?' (2018) 35 <https://digitalchamber.org/smart-contracts-whitepaper> accessed 13 May 2020

Dimitropoulos G, 'The Law of Blockchain' 95 (2020) *Wash L Rev* 1117 <https://digitalcommons.law.uw.edu/wlr/vol95/iss3/3> accessed 27 May 2021

Durovic M, 'How to Resolve Smart Contract Disputes – Smart Arbitration as a Solution' (*Oxford Business Law Blog*, 1 June 2018) <www.law.ox.ac.uk/business-law-blog/blog/2018/06/law-and-autonomous-systems-series-how-resolve-smart-contract-disputes> accessed 13 May 2020

———. and Janssen A, 'Formation of Smart Contracts under Contract Law' in DiMatteo LA, Cannarsa M, and Poncibò C (eds), *The Cambridge Handbook of Smart Contracts, Blockchain Technology and Digital Platforms* (CUP 2019) [DOI: https://doi.org/10.1017/9781108592239.004]

———. and Lech F, 'The Enforceability of Smart Contracts' (2019) 5 *Ita LJ* 493 [DOI: https://doi.org/10.23815/2421-2156.ITALJ]

Fairfield JAT, 'Smart Contracts, Bitcoin Bots, and Consumer Protection' (2014) 71 *Wash & Lee L Rev Online* 35 <https://scholarlycommons.law.wlu.edu/wlulr-online/vol71/iss2/3> accessed 13 May 2020

Grundmann S (ed), *European Contract Law in the Digital Age* (Intersentia 2018) [DOI: https://doi.org/10.1017/9781780686431]

Guggenberger N, 'The Potential of Blockchain for the Conclusion of Contracts' in Schulze R, Staudenmayer D, and Lohsse S (eds), *Contracts for the Supply of Digital Content: Regulatory Challenges and Gaps* (Nomos 2017) [DOI: https://doi.org/10.5771/9783845281391-83]

Lipshaw JM, 'Persistence of "Dumb" Contracts' (2019) 2 (1) *Stanford J Blockchain L & Pol'y* 1

Midasium, 'Smart Tenancy Contracts' <https://midasium.herokuapp.com/smart-tenancy> accessed 13 May 2020

Möslein F, 'Legal Boundaries of Blockchain Technologies: Smart Contracts as Self-Help?' in De Franceschi A and Schulze R (eds), *Digital Revolution – New Challenges for Law* (CH Beck and Nomos 2019) [DOI: https://doi.org/10.17104/9783406759048-313]

Pardolesi R and Davola A, 'What is Wrong in the Debate About Smart Contracts' (2019) *Luiss Guido Carli University Working Paper* <https://ssrn.com/abstract=3339421> accessed 13 May 2020

Ruhl G, 'Smart (Legal) Contracts, or: Which (Contract) Law for Smart Contracts?' in Cappiello B and Carullo G (eds), *Blockchain, Law and Governance* (Springer 2020) [DOI: https://doi.org/10.1007/978-3-030-52722-8_11]

Savelyev A, 'Contract Law 2.0: "Smart" Contracts as the Beginning of the End of Classic Contract Law' (2016) *Higher School of Economics Research Paper* WP BRP 71/LAW/2016 <https://ssrn.com/abstract=2885241> accessed 13 May 2020

Szabo N, 'Smart Contracts' (1994) <www.fon.hum.uva.nl/rob/Courses/InformationInSpeech/CDROM/Literature/LOTwinterschool2006/szabo.best.vwh.net/smart.contracts.html> accessed 13 May 2020

UK Jurisdiction Task Force, 'Legal statement on cryptoassets and smart contracts' (*Tech Nation*, November 2019) <https://technation.io/about-us/lawtech-panel> accessed 13 May 2020

UNCITRAL and UNIDROIT, 'Joint UNCITRAL/UNIDROIT Workshop: Rome, Seat UNIDROIT, 6 and 7 May 2019: Summary of the Discussion and Conclusion' (*UNIDROIT: News and events*, 2019) <www.unidroit.org/english/news/2019/190506-unidroit-uncitral-workshop/conclusions-e.pdf> accessed 13 May 2020

UNIDROIT, 'UNCITRAL/UNIDROIT Workshop on Smart Contracts, Artificial Intelligence and Distributed Ledger Technology – Summary of conclusions published' (*UNIDROIT: News and events*, 2019) <www.unidroit.org/89-news-and-events/2663-uncitral-unidroit-workshop-on-smart-contracts-artificial-intelligence-and-distributed-ledger-technology-summary-of-conclusions-published%20(last> accessed 13 May 2020

Zimmermann R and Whittaker S (eds), *Good Faith in European Contract Law* (CUP 2000)

8 The 'contracting problem' revisited

Explaining the formation of algorithmic contracts under the common law

Nicholas Liu

1. Introduction[1]

The foundations of English contract law were laid on the assumption that transactions were necessarily concluded between humans. We now inhabit a different world, one in which transactions can be effected by computer algorithms operating autonomously on one or sometimes both sides. This raises questions as to how such contracts can fulfil the requirements of contract formation. Collectively, the challenge posed by these questions is referred to as the 'contracting problem'.[2]

Responses to the contracting problem have been diverse, but commentators and the courts broadly agree that the problem should have a solution; the conclusion cannot be that such contracts are simply invalid. This is consistent with the modern recognition that courts and laws 'are there to help businessmen, not to hinder them; [...] to give effect to their transactions, not to frustrate them'.[3] Commercial parties and consumers regularly engage in trading through algorithms, expecting that their transactions will be upheld. The law would be inadequate if it had to disappoint that expectation. Further, treaties and statutes applicable in many jurisdictions appear to mandate that such contracts be upheld. Against this backdrop, it may even be thought that the contracting problem is a paper tiger.

1 This chapter was prepared with the benefit of discussions with Goh Yihan, Vincent Ooi, Yao Qinzhe (who provided comments on an early draft), and Gan Jhia Huei. The usual disclaimers apply.

2 The term appears to have been coined by Samir Chopra and Laurence White, 'Artificial Agents and the Contracting Problem: A Solution via an Agency Analysis' [2009] *U Ill JL Tech & Pol'y* 363.

3 Lord Goff, 'Commercial Contracts and the Commercial Court' [1984] *LMCLQ* 382, 391. See also Lord Steyn, 'Contract Law: Fulfilling the Reasonable Expectations of Honest Men' (1997) 113 *LQR* 433 ('A thread runs through our contract law that effect must be given to the reasonable expectations of honest men.'); Lord Bingham, 'The Law as the Handmaid of Commerce' in *Lives of the Law: Selected Essays and Speeches: 2000–2010* (OUP 2011) 295 ('the law acts as the handmaid of commerce and not as an adversary, a fetter or an irritant').

DOI: 10.4324/9781003080596-10

I argue that the contracting problem is real, in that there is at least an *apparent* doctrinal gap in contract formation that must be bridged by either a new rationalization of the existing authorities or an extension of the law proper. However, the gap is narrower than is sometimes thought. It encompasses only one of the four requirements for contract formation: that is, agreement. Further, I argue that the gap can be bridged without extending the existing law;[4] it suffices to apply the decided cases, albeit with some reinterpretation of their underlying rationale.

2. Algorithmic contracts defined

This chapter focuses on contracts incorporating terms generated by autonomous software and where the offer, acceptance, or both have been transmitted by that software, without any direct input from or review by a human. Such contracts have been referred to by various names, including 'contracts formed by software'[5] and 'contracts reached through artificial agents'.[6] For convenience, I will call them 'algorithmic contracts', borrowing the term coined by Scholz to refer to 'contracts that contain terms that were determined by algorithm rather than a person'.[7] In adopting this term, I am conscious of the risk that, as Eliza Mik has argued, technology-specific labels may create a misleading impression that the things so labelled are necessarily so different that the orthodox rules cannot apply.[8] As will be apparent from the analysis in the fourth part of the chapter, no such implication is intended here.

Algorithmic contracts can be further sub-divided into three types: offeror-side (where the offeror contracts through software), offeree-side (where the offeree contracts through software), and pure algorithmic contracts (where both parties contract through software). This division is helpful because the

4 This conclusion parallels that reached by Giusella Finocchiaro concerning (from a civil law perspective) the conventional and statutory positions in her article: Giusella Finocchiaro, 'The conclusion of the electronic contract through "software agents": A false legal problem? Brief considerations' (2003) 19 *Computer L & Secur Rep* 20.

5 Vincent Ooi, 'Contracts formed by software: An approach from the law of mistake' (2019) *SMU Centre for AI & Data Governance Research Paper* 2019/02 <https://ssrn.com/abstract=3322308> accessed 7 May 2020. 'Software' and 'algorithms' are used interchangeably in this context.

6 Chopra and White (n 2) 365.

7 Lauren Henry Scholz, 'Algorithmic Contracts' (2017) 20 *Stan Tech L Rev* 128, 134. I use the term in a slightly different sense from Scholz, as she treats smart contracts as necessarily falling under this umbrella (see ibid 147–48). Yet not all smart contracts meet Scholz's stated definition of algorithmic contracts – it is entirely possible to have a smart contract that merely embodies or implements terms that were wholly human-determined.

8 Eliza Mik, 'The *Un*importance of being "electronic" or – popular misconceptions about "Internet contracting"' (2011) 19 *IJLIT* 324, 325 (warning against 'the propensity to depart from the principles of contract law and to devise technology-specific rules (and new nomenclature) once a technological factor is present').

role played by software in a transaction affects the software-specific formation issues that arise at each stage of the analysis.

Further, two types of algorithmic contracts are excluded from consideration in this chapter.

First, there are what Ooi refers to as '"passive" contract forming mechanisms', which merely 'relay [...] the representations of the user without altering [them] in any way' – for instance, email or instant messaging software.[9] 'Passive' contract forming mechanisms pose no difficulties for contract formation and require no further discussion. The contracting problem arises only with respect to what Ooi terms '"active" contract forming mechanisms', which execute transactions without human intervention.[10]

Second, this chapter also excludes software that is not 'deterministic', to use the terminology chosen by the Court of Appeal of Singapore in *Quoine Pte Ltd v B2C2 Ltd*.[11] An algorithm is deterministic if, once programmed, it 'will always produce precisely the same output given the same input'.[12] Non-deterministic algorithms include those incorporating unsupervised machine learning, especially (but not only) if they take the form of 'black box' algorithms the behaviour of which cannot be predicted in advance and may not be humanly explicable even in retrospect.[13] At the extreme end, one encounters (as yet hypothetical) 'strong' artificial intelligences that might be considered to possess personhood of their own.[14]

Without definitively concluding that the analysis in this chapter cannot apply to non-deterministic algorithms, it must be acknowledged that the greater degree of uncertainty and autonomy inherent in such algorithms requires consideration of a correspondingly broader set of considerations. The case for a fundamental reimagining of the law (drawing on agency analogies,[15]

9 Ooi (n 5) 3, citing Jane Winn and Benjamin Wright, *The Law of Electronic Commerce* (4th edn, Aspen Law & Business 2000).

10 Ooi (n 5) 4. Ooi's terminology should not be confused with the terminology of 'active agents' and 'passive agents' used by Kees Stuurman and Hugo Wijnands, 'Software Law – Intelligent agents: a curse or a blessing? A survey of the legal aspects of the application of intelligent software systems' (2001) 17 *Computer L & Secur Rep* 92.

11 [2020] SGCA(I) 02 [15], endorsing a distinction drawn below by the Simon Thorley QC, sitting as an International Judge of the Singapore International Commercial Court, in *B2C2 Ltd v Quoine Pte Ltd* [2019] SGHC(I) 3; [2019] 4 SLR 17 [82].

12 *Quoine* (n 11) [15]. The sense in which 'deterministic' is used in *Quoine*, and which this chapter adopts for convenience, differs from that borne by the same term of art used in computer science. The consternation this may cause to some is regretted.

13 Scholz (n 7) 150, 152.

14 Lawrence B Solum, 'Legal Personhood for Artificial Intelligences' (1992) 70 *NC L Rev* 1231, discussed in Tom Allen and Robin Widdison, 'Can Computers Make Contracts?' (1996) 9 *Harv JL & Tech* 25, 35–36; Robert van den Hoven van Genderen, 'Do We Need New Legal Personhood in the Age of Robots and AI?' in Marcelo Corrales, Mark Fenwick, and Nikolaus Forgó (eds), *Robotics, AI and the Future of Law* (Springer 2018).

15 Ian R Kerr, 'Ensuring the Success of Contract Formation in Agent-Mediated Electronic Commerce' (2001) 1 *Electron Commer Res* 183; Chopra and White (n 2); Faye Fangfei

Roman law master–slave analogies,[16] or perhaps even endowing sufficiently sophisticated software with legal personality[17]) appears more compelling in that context, and is beyond the scope of this chapter.

3. What makes the contracting problem a problem?

The contracting problem poses this question: what is the doctrinal mechanism by which the interaction of a human and a computer system, or of two computer systems without any human intervention, produces a binding contract? In other words, how can an algorithmic contract satisfy the requirements for contract formation? I will first show that the existing conventional and statutory framework does not make these questions redundant, before defining the scope of the problem as a matter of common law.

3.1 The insufficiency of statutory provisions in non-American common law jurisdictions

Internationally, electronic transactions are covered by the United Nations Convention on the Use of Electronic Communications in International Contracts[18] (CUECIC) and the UNCITRAL Model Law on Electronic Commerce[19] (MLEC). Many jurisdictions have enacted domestic legislation giving effect to these conventions. Consequently, one sometimes hears suggestions from sceptical regulators and practitioners that the game of solving the contracting problem is not worth the candle: if we know that an algorithmic contract can be valid because a statute tells us so, debates over how we explain its validity in terms of common law doctrine are (arguably) mere hair-splitting.

Wang, *Law of Electronic Commercial Transactions: Contemporary Issues in the EU, US and China* (2nd edn, Routledge 2014) 14 (briefly discussed). The interested reader may also wish to consult Chopra and White's expanded argument for an agency analysis: Samir Chopra and Laurence F White, *A Legal Theory for Autonomous Artificial Agents* (University of Michigan Press 2011).

16 Andrew Katz, 'Intelligent Agents and Internet Commerce in Ancient Rome' (*SCL*, 15 October 2008) <www.scl.org/articles/1095-intelligent-agents-and-internet-commerce-in-ancient-rome> accessed 5 May 2020. This could also be combined with an agency analogy: Chopra and White (n 6) 377–78.

17 Sam N Lehman-Wilzig, 'Frankenstein unbound: Towards a legal definition of Artificial Intelligence' (1981) 13 *Futures* 442; Solum (n 14); Allen and Widdison (n 14) 35–36; Emily M Weitzenboeck, 'Electronic Agents and the Formation of Contracts' (2001) 9 *IJLIT* 204, 213–14; van den Hoven van Genderen (n 14).

18 United Nations Convention on the Use of Electronic Communications in International Contracts (adopted 23 November 2005, entered into force 1 March 2013) 2898 *UNTS* 3 (CUECIC).

19 UNCITRAL, 'UNCITRAL Model Law on Electronic Commerce with Guide to Enactment 1996: with additional article 5 bis as adopted in 1998' (United Nations 1999) <https://uncitral.un.org/sites/uncitral.un.org/files/media-documents/uncitral/en/19-04970_ebook.pdf> accessed 7 May 2020 (MLEC).

Unhappily for commerce, the sceptics are mistaken. The MLEC, the CUECIC, and their domestic implementations generally lack a comprehensive framework for the formation of algorithmic contracts and are uncertain in their scope, leaving a lacuna that the common law must fill. The exceptions are the United States and Canada, which have each arguably rendered the contracting problem moot through the Uniform Electronic Transactions Act 1999 and the Uniform Electronic Commerce Act 1999, respectively. These acts provide more detailed provisions than the MLEC and have been enacted in state or provincial law throughout most of the United States and Canada. In addition, the United States also has the Uniform Computer Information Transaction Act,[20] which goes further still (though it has only been enacted in two states and is no longer being promoted, due to resistance to its licensor-friendly positions with regard to software licensing[21]). For these reasons, this chapter does not further discuss the current position in the United States and Canada.[22]

Turning then to the MLEC, Art 13 provides a rule of attribution by which 'a data message is deemed to be that of the originator if it was sent [...] (b) by an information system programmed by, or on behalf of, the originator to operate automatically'.[23] This rule helps to narrow the inquiry as it bypasses debate as to whether messages sent by software, without human intervention, can be attributed to the user of the software. However, as with mundane, non-electronic disputes over contract formation, attribution of a message is only the beginning, and cannot resolve the contracting problem on its own.[24] As regards the CUECIC, the relevant provision is Article 12, which states that:

> A contract formed by the interaction of an automated message system and a natural person, or by the interaction of automated message systems, shall not be denied validity or enforceability on the sole ground that no natural person reviewed or intervened in each of the individual actions carried out by the automated message systems or the resulting contract.[25]

Similar language is found in domestic implementing statutes of the CUECIC, such as Singapore's Electronic Transactions Act 2010 and Australia's Electronic Transactions Act 1999. The effect is simply to clarify that the lack of human review/intervention is not in itself a bar to contract formation.

20 Uniform Computer Information Transaction Act (National Conference of Commissioners on Uniform State Laws 2002) <www.uniformlaws.org> accessed 5 May 2020 (UCITA).

21 Michael L Rustad and Elif Kavusturan, 'A Commercial Law for Software Contracting' (2019) 76 *Wash & Lee L Rev* 775, 781–82.

22 See eg Kerr (n 15) 193–97; Weitzenboeck (n 17) 224–31.

23 MLEC, Art 13.

24 See Section 4.1.

25 CUECIC, Art 12.

Article 12 is of limited help in solving the contracting problem. Eliza Mik argues that the article is 'redundant' because it purports to remove a bar that did not exist at common law to begin with.[26] Further, Article 12 tells us what cannot prevent contract formation, but not how to discern when a contract *has* been validly formed: as Ooi points out, Article 12 and other provisions of the CUECIC and MLEC 'do not explain the theoretical legal basis or rule of attribution through which these contracts are given validity or enforceability'.[27] The *travaux préparatoires* to the CUECIC confirm this, endorsing the statement that 'the use of fully automated systems for commercial transactions should not alter traditional rules on contract formation and legal capacity'.[28]

Having established that the current statutory and conventional frameworks in the non-American common law world do not solve the contracting problem, we are now in a position to examine the nature and scope of the contracting problem as a matter of common law doctrine.

3.2 The doctrinal nature of the contracting problem

The requirements for contract formation can be summarized as follows:

> To constitute a valid contract (1) there must be two or more separate and definite parties to the contract; (2) those parties must be in agreement, that is there must be a consensus ad idem; (3) those parties must intend to create legal relations in the sense that the promises of each side are to be enforceable simply because they are contractual promises; (4) the promises of each party must be supported by consideration. ...[29]

Various commentators have taken the view that algorithmic contracts may have difficulty satisfying some combination of these requirements. I will first show that there is no real difficulty (solvable or otherwise) with the first, third, and fourth requirements, in order to focus the bulk of this chapter on the more problematic second requirement.

Regarding the first requirement, commentators have pointed out that software currently cannot be a party to a contract due to lack of legal

26 Eliza Mik, 'Evaluating the Impact of the UN Convention on the use of Electronic Communications in International Contracts on Domestic Contract Law: The Singapore Example' (2010) 28 *Chinese (Taiwan) YB Intl L & Aff* 43, 60–61.

27 Ooi (n 5) 14.

28 UNCITRAL, 'Report of the Working Group on Electronic Commerce on its thirty-eighth session' (24 April 2001) UN Doc A/CN 9/484, para 106, endorsed in UNCITRAL, 'Report of the Working Group on Electronic Commerce on its thirty-ninth session' (21 March 2002) UN Doc A/CN 9/509, para 102. The statement was made in the context of possible treatment of software as an agent but carries broader implications.

29 *Halsbury's Laws of England* (4th edn, Butterworths 1974) vol 9, para 203 (footnotes omitted), quoted in Allen and Widdison (n 14) 30.

personality.[30] This is undeniable as a matter of *lex lata* and only means that we need to identify a contract between the persons behind the software. It sets the stage for the difficulties surrounding the second requirement but is not a problem in itself.

Regarding the third requirement, the problem identified by Allen and Widdison, and Chopra and White, is that a party arguably cannot be said to intend to create legal relations when she was, at the time of the purported conclusion of the contract, ignorant of the offer's existence and terms.[31] However, this problem does not warrant separate consideration because it is resolved (one way or the other) in the course of analyzing the second requirement of agreement through offer and acceptance.

For a statement to amount to an offer at all, it has to be 'made with the intention that it is to become binding as soon as it is accepted by the person to whom it is addressed'.[32] This requirement, an aspect of the second requirement, substantially overlaps with the third requirement and often makes the latter otiose.[33] The only situation where separately analyzing the intention to create legal relations adds to the analysis is where, on the facts, agreement is assumed without much inquiry (for example, where 'the fact of agreement [...] is not disputed since the parties have in fact signed a written document').[34] In such cases, separately analyzing the intention to create legal relations verifies that there is substance to what might otherwise remain a 'mere *form* of agreement'.[35] That consideration is unlikely to apply to algorithmic contracts, as the task of identifying an agreement in that context invariably engages the question of whether the communications from both parties evidenced an intention to be bound (as the analysis in the fourth part of the chapter will show).

In any event, even if it is thought that the inquiry as to agreement leaves some lingering doubt as to the parties' intention to create legal relations, applying the 'usual presumption' that such intention is present in a commercial context would ordinarily resolve the matter.[36] Hence, the third requirement is academic or easily met, and need not vex us either way.

30 Allen and Widdison (n 14) 30; Chopra and White (n 2) 365; Kerr (n 15) 188; Weitzenboeck (n 17) 210–11; Wang (n 15) 41.

31 Allen and Widdison (n 14) 34; Chopra and White (n 2) 366.

32 Hugh G Beale (ed), *Chitty on Contracts*, vol 1 (32nd edn, Sweet & Maxwell 2015) para 2-003.

33 See eg Robert Bradgate, 'Formation of Contracts' in Michael Furmston (ed), *The Law of Contract* (Butterworths Common Law Series, 3rd edn, LexisNexis Butterworths 2007) at para 2.169; Pey Woan Lee, 'Intention to Create Legal Relations' in Andrew Boon Leong Phang (ed), *The Law of Contract in Singapore* (Academy Publishing 2012) paras 05.002–05.003.

34 Lee (n 33) para 05.004.

35 ibid.

36 Allen and Widdison (n 14) 34. See also the observations of the UK Jurisdiction Task Force's Legal Statement on Cryptoassets and Smart Contracts, noting that a party 'will struggle to displace the presumption that she did indeed intend to be bound' by a transaction produced by interacting with code deployed on a publicly accessible platform, and

In respect of the fourth requirement, consideration, Scholz argues that it may not be satisfied because any purported consideration in an algorithmic contract would not be the result of 'a bargaining process between the parties'.[37] If the requirement that consideration be the result of a bargaining process were unique to the contract law of the United States, it would not trouble us.[38] In fact, the requirement is mirrored to some extent in the English tradition by the requirement that consideration must be requested by the promisor,[39] so Scholz's point must be addressed.

The answer to it is that a 'request' or 'bargain' in the relevant sense will necessarily be found wherever the consideration takes the form of a counter-performance required by the terms of the offer itself. The only cases in which the requirement has been seriously disputed, whether ultimately satisfied or not, are cases where the purported consideration was not mentioned or implied in the offer.

In *Combe v Combe*, a wife sought to enforce her husband's promise to pay her a certain sum in maintenance, the purported consideration for his promise being her forbearance to apply to court for maintenance.[40] It is clear from Lord Denning's judgment, and indeed from the wife's counsel's arguments (as reported), that her forbearance was never discussed: '[t]here was [...] clearly no promise by the wife, express or implied, to forbear from applying to court',[41] and she had refrained from applying to court 'in consequence of her husband's promise',[42] not because forbearance had been agreed.[43] Similarly, in *Alliance Bank v Broom*, the defendant debtor had provided security to the plaintiff bank, despite there being no promise from the plaintiff bank to forbear from suing for the debt owed to them.[44] Rather inconsistently with *Combe*, Kindersley VC found that there was good consideration in the

that this might apply even to interactions with a Decentralized Autonomous Organization on a blockchain: UK Jurisdiction Task Force, 'Legal statement on cryptoassets and smart contracts' (*Tech Nation*, November 2019) <https://technation.io/lawtech-uk-resources/#cryptoassets> accessed 10 December 2019, paras 147–48.

37 Scholz (n 7) 155–56.

38 See Section 3.1 above.

39 Pey Woan Lee, 'Consideration' in Andrew Boon Leong Phang (ed), *The Law of Contract in Singapore* (Academy Publishing 2012) para 04.008, citing *Gay Choon Ing v Loh Sze Ti Terence Peter and Another Appeal* [2009] 2 SLR(R) 332; [2009] SGCA 3 [82]. See also Peter Benson, 'The Idea of Consideration' (2011) 61 *UTLJ* 241, 249, 253–54; Mindy Chen-Wishart, *Contract Law* (6th edn, OUP 2018) 113.

40 [1951] 2 KB 215 (CA), 221.

41 ibid 221.

42 ibid 218 (submissions of Peter Robinson, counsel for the respondent).

43 Lord Denning also observed that had the wife promised, there would still have been no consideration as the promise would have been unenforceable, as her right to apply to court could not be waived: ibid 221. That would, however, have been on the ground of a lack of benefit or detriment, and not on the ground that the consideration had not been requested.

44 (1864) 2 *Drewry & Smale* 289 (CH), discussed in *Chitty on Contracts* (n 32) 4-061.

form of the bank's actual forbearance from suing. The different result was subsequently rationalized as resting on the basis of an implied request for forbearance.[45] In any event, these two cases illustrate the point that whether consideration had been requested/bargained for is a question that arises only when the offer is silent on what the promisee is supposed to do in return for the promise. Put differently, the true requirement is that 'the consideration is referable to the promise',[46] with a request being but one way to identify that referability. In an algorithmic contract, what each party is to contribute to the transaction is necessarily spelt out in the offer (and, in that sense, 'requested'), and the question does not even arise.

This leaves us with the second requirement, agreement. This is the real crux of the contracting problem. Since agreement traditionally requires an offer from one party and a corresponding acceptance from another party,[47] a preliminary question is whether the (purported) offer and (purported) acceptance can be attributed to the parties. An answer is provided by what Ooi describes as the '"Mere Tools" Theory', which is simply the proposition that 'the representations made by the software are deemed to be the representations made by the user'.[48] This proposition is doubtless correct under the MLEC[49] and unobjectionable under a common-sense application of the common law as well, including the presumption (no longer a rule of law, but at least an evidential guide) that persons intend the natural and probable consequences of their acts. If a person issues instructions to software, knowing that these instructions will cause the software to send messages to other parties, it seems obvious that those messages are attributable to the user (though their *significance* is a separate question); we do not need a special rule to tell us that.

One may then wonder whether attribution disposes of the matter entirely. Ooi, for one, suggests that the 'Mere Tools' Theory is indeed a complete answer to the contracting problem.[50] To him, this is actually a demerit, for it leads him to conclude that the 'Mere Tools' Theory should be *rejected* as 'a blunt instrument which is at odds with commercial reality and which unfairly allocates a considerable amount of risk to the user'.[51] Similarly, Emad Abdel Rahim Dahiyat argues that if one treats software as 'merely pure tools of communication', this 'implies that the requisite intention to be bound in this case is actually generated by human users but transmitted automatically

45 In *Fullerton v Provincial Bank of Ireland* [1903] AC 309 (HL), 313, discussed in *Chitty on Contracts* (n 32) 4-061.

46 Jack Beatson, Andrew Burrows, and John Cartwright, *Anson's Law of Contract* (30th edn, OUP 2016) 95.

47 *Chitty on Contracts* (n 32) para 2-001.

48 Ooi (n 5) 3, citing Weitzenboeck (n 17) 226 (see also 214). See also Chopra and White (n 2) 370.

49 MLEC, Art 13.

50 Ooi (n 5) 3, 5.

51 ibid 6.

by a computer'.[52] For that reason, he finds it appropriate to attribute messages to deterministic software, but not non-deterministic software.[53]

This is, with respect, a misunderstanding of the consequences of attributing a message, which is all the 'Mere Tools' Theory in its MLEC and common law form does.[54] Ooi's and Dahiyat's criticisms are based on a misapprehension that once we have decided that an algorithm's messages *are* the user's messages, the user is bound without further inquiry. In fact, determining that a message originates from a party is but the starting point in identifying a valid agreement, even when the message is directly spoken or written by a human. Imagine that Richard III's line, 'A horse! a horse! my kingdom for a horse!',[55] had been followed by one of his subjects giving him a horse. The king's statement would no doubt be attributable to him, and the act of handing over the horse attributable to the subject, but it would still be necessary to ask whether the king's words constituted an offer and whether the subject's handing over of the horse constituted acceptance.[56] The same exercise must be done with messages sent by software, even after one has decided that those messages are attributable to their respective users.

Offer and acceptance, then, constitute the main difficulty in the contracting problem, and each requires separate analysis. For convenience, I will summarize the potential difficulties that apply at each stage, dealing with the detailed doctrinal basis together with my proposed solutions in the fourth part of the chapter.

In an offeror-side algorithmic contract, the offer stage may be thought to pose difficulties because of the counter-intuitiveness of the idea that one can intend to be bound upon acceptance of an offer one does not realize one is making. The user might only know that she has set in motion software that may subsequently send an offer out into the world at some undefined point, and that the terms of that offer will be determined according to whatever programming has gone into the software. Even by an objective standard, can that be enough?

In an offeree-side algorithmic contract, acceptance poses a different set of difficulties. Although an offeror's intention to be bound upon acceptance is a purely objective inquiry, an offeree's acceptance of an offer appears to have a subjective requirement of actual knowledge of the existence of the offer at the time of acceptance, at least in the case of a unilateral contract. How can this be surmounted when the offeree's knowledge of the offer lags behind the purported acceptance?

52 Emad Abdel Rahim Dahiyat, 'Intelligent agents and intentionality: Should we begin to think outside the box?' (2006) 22 *Computer L & Secur Rep* 472, 473.

53 ibid 473.

54 We are not concerned here with the stronger variant found in UCITA, which Chopra and White strenuously criticize: Chopra and White (n 2) 370–72.

55 William Shakespeare, *The Tragedy of King Richard III*, Act V, Scene IV (Project Gutenberg, uploaded 1 October 1998) <www.gutenberg.org/ebooks/1503> accessed 19 May 2020.

56 Perhaps a reasonable subject would have perceived that the king was speaking hyperbolically and did not intend to be bound, or the subject did not hear the king's declaration and the delivery of the horse was coincidental.

4. The vending machine, refurbished – a solution in two parts

The customary academic approach to the contracting problem has been to take an inventory of the possible solutions or models that other commentators have put forth, examine the pros and cons of each, and finally explain why one's preferred solution is the best one. This is sensible if one sees the contracting problem as a multi-faceted one requiring a holistic solution. Given that the contracting problem is (as earlier argued) much narrower than commonly thought, I will instead proceed directly to what I see as the minimally invasive doctrinal solution to the offeror's and then the offeree's sides of the contracting problem. As it happens, that is a combination of the unilateral contract analysis with a version of what Ooi calls the 'Extended Objective Theory of Contract',[57] although I suggest that 'Extended' is a misnomer. Properly understood, the doctrines are adequate as is.

4.1 The offer

In seeking an explanation for an offeror-side algorithmic contract, one need not start from scratch. Because the offeror does not have a specific offeree in mind, but instead deploys the software so as to potentially contract with any person who can access the offers generated by the software, the obvious analogy is to *Thornton v Shoe Lane Parking Ltd*.[58] There, Lord Denning held that a sale of a parking ticket through an automatic ticket-vending machine:

> can be translated into offer and acceptance in this way: the offer is made when the proprietor of the machine holds it out as being ready to receive the money. The acceptance takes place when the customer puts his money into the slot. The terms of the offer are contained in the notice placed on or near the machine stating what is offered for the money. The customer is bound by those terms as long as they are sufficiently brought to his notice before-hand, but not otherwise.[59]

Commentators have argued that this reasoning could also apply to algorithmic contracts.[60] The analogy seems apt: though the company that owned the machine in *Thornton* knew the price per hour, it could not have known the duration of a particular contract (and thus the total contract price),[61] the

57 Ooi (n 5) 2. Ooi credits the theory to Allen and Widdison (n 14) 43–44, who do not use the phrase, but do advocate 'modify[ing] contract doctrine by relaxing the requirements on intentionality in contract-making' (ibid 43).
58 [1971] 2 QB 163 (CA).
59 ibid 169.
60 Chopra and White (n 2) 373 (albeit expressing doubt, at 374, whether this would work where the software 'plays a role in determining the content of the offer for a particular contract'); Dahiyat (n 52) 472; Ooi (n 5) 13.
61 Chopra and White (n 2) 373.

identity of the counterparty, and when a contract would be entered into. Those features are shared with algorithmic contracts, and, indeed, the vending machine could be considered to be a simple algorithm embodied in a primitive form.

Similar analysis has been judicially accepted by the High Court of England and Wales in *R (on the application of Software Solutions Partners Ltd) v Her Majesty's Commissioners for Customs and Excise*[62] and by the Court of Appeal of Singapore in *Quoine*,[63] both of which applied *Thornton* to explain the formation of algorithmic contracts.

In *Software Solutions*, insurers allowed insurance brokers to use a designated information system to generate the terms under which the insurers were willing to insure their ultimate customers.[64] Once a broker had input a customer's relevant information into the system, the system would analyze that information and automatically generate the terms of an offer of insurance from the insurers, which the customer could then choose to accept.[65] There were thus two contracts, one a contract between the insurers and the broker authorizing the broker to bind the insurers to an insurance contract with the customer, and the other the contract of insurance between the insurers and the customer (if the customer accepted the offer). The court held that as far as the contract between the insurers and the broker was concerned, the offer was made when the insurers 'h[e]ld out the [system] as the automatic medium for contract formation', and acceptance was done by the act of entering a customer's information into the system.[66] The fact that the terms and existence of any given contract between the insurers and the broker could not have been known by the insurers in advance did not trouble the court.

Quoine concerned traders on a cryptocurrency exchange who ended up entering into contracts with each other for the sale and purchase of Ether in exchange for Bitcoin. The sellers had programmed their proprietary trading software to place sell orders for Ether at the pre-defined price of ten Bitcoins per Ether in the event that the book of sell orders were to be depleted[67] (which could happen for reasons including a sudden drop in liquidity or some sort of error in the exchange platform software[68]). The buyers had contracted with the operator of the cryptocurrency exchange to make use of the latter's margin trading facilities, borrowing Ether from the operator for that purpose.[69] This also entailed allowing the exchange operator's software to place

62 [2007] EWHC 971 (Admin), [66]–[68].
63 *Quoine* (n 11) [95], citing *Software Solutions* (n 62).
64 *Software Solutions* (n 62) [2], [15].
65 ibid [16].
66 ibid [67].
67 *Quoine* (n 11) [18].
68 ibid [157]–[158].
69 ibid [12], [14].

buy orders for Ether, at the best available market price, on behalf of the buyers in the event of a margin call.[70]

This system hit a snag when human error on the part of the exchange operator led to a series of unfortunate events, including a massive drop in liquidity (triggering the seller's software to place the sell orders for Ether at the pre-defined high price) and, in turn, an erroneous margin call (triggering the operator's software to place buy orders for Ether at market price on behalf of the buyers).[71] This led to the buyers automatically buying Ether at the extraordinarily high price set by the sellers (about 250 times the external market rate at the time), as the sellers' sell orders had become the only ones on the market.[72]

The facts of *Quoine* gave rise to some fascinating issues, especially concerning possible vitiation on the ground of mistake (which ultimately failed).[73] For present purposes, the relevant point is that the Court of Appeal of Singapore held that the analysis in *Software Solutions* and *Thornton* should apply, with the consequence that the transactions between the buyers and the sellers were valid contracts.[74] The court did not see fit to analyze the formation process in detail, so it is unclear whether the sell orders were the offers and the buy orders the acceptances, or *vice versa*, or some other, novel possibility. What is clear is that the parties' lack of knowledge of existence of and terms of the offers 'did not here prevent the formation of a contract at the point of time when an offer made by one algorithm was accepted by the other'.[75]

The argument is sufficiently supported by authority, but does the analysis make sense? I believe it does, and this can be more easily seen when the distinctive features of an offeror-side algorithmic contract such as that in *Quoine* and *Software Solutions* are separated into its three distinctive facets:

(a) Delay in transmission – the software may not send an offer immediately when set in motion, but at some later time when certain conditions are triggered.
(b) Uncertainty of transmission – if the conditions are not triggered, the software may never send an offer at all.
(c) Unknowability of some of the precise terms at the time the software is set in motion – for instance, the price or quantity of a good to be bought or sold.

70 ibid [12].
71 ibid [27]–[29].
72 ibid [159].
73 For an illuminating case comment focusing on the mistake issue in *Quoine*, see Kelvin FK Low and Eliza Mik, 'Lost in Transmission: Unilateral Mistakes in Automated Contracts' (2020) 136 *LQR* 563 <https://ssrn.com/abstract=3591657> accessed 20 May 2020.
74 *Quoine* (n 11) [94]–[96].
75 ibid [96].

Since this is a question of principle and not a weighing of factors, it suffices to ask whether these facts would prevent contract formation individually; if not, they should not prevent it in combination, either.

The first fact is trivial. An intention to be bound by an offer upon acceptance is not less firm just because an offeror has built in a transmission delay.

The second fact also should not be problematic. Say my email software or internet connection is very unreliable. I know that for any given email, there is an even chance that my clicking the 'send' button will not cause it to be sent; it may instead get permanently stuck in my outbox until I delete or re-attempt to send it. If I type an offer in an email and click the 'send' button, it is unreal to suggest that my uncertainty as to whether the offer will be transmitted undermines my firm intention that *if* the offer is transmitted, and the recipient accepts, I will be bound by that acceptance.

The third fact – unknowability of the precise terms in advance – raises a more involved point. Chopra and White argue that the vending machine analogy breaks down when it comes to algorithmic contracts 'where the artificial agent plays a role in determining the content of the offer for a particular contract'.[76] In their view, for the unilateral contract analysis to work, 'the machine operator [must have] assented to a rule for determining the terms of particular contracts, which is notified in advance to users'.[77] They argue that the lack of 'a simple, unchanging offer communicated directly by the principal'[78] in an algorithmic contract means that the unilateral contract analysis cannot explain such contracts.[79]

It is difficult to discern the doctrinal basis of Chopra and White's argument. They cite no authority for their propositions; in addition (though this is no fault of the authors), they did not have the benefit of considering *Software Solutions* and *Quoine*, which support the contrary conclusion. Authority aside, the logic and principle of the argument are also not apparent. If the concern is one of attribution,[80] this would be solved by attribution of the statement under the 'Mere Tools' Theory.[81] If the concern is certainty of terms, the scenario has a familiar analogue in conventional gap-filling mechanisms. As Scholz points out, it is common for an offer to leave out the exact price of a good, but state that the price will be (for instance) the market price on a given future date.[82] The offeror does not know what that price will be, but she does know the nature of the transaction and how the price will be determined. It is trite law that this type of offer is capable of giving rise to a valid contract.[83]

76 Chopra and White (n 2) 373.
77 ibid.
78 ibid 374.
79 ibid.
80 ibid.
81 See Section 3.2.
82 Scholz (n 7) 136.
83 *Chitty on Contracts* (n 32) para 2-137, citing (among others) *Hillas & Co Ltd v Arcos Ltd* [1932] UKHL 2; (1932) 147 LT 503.

Scholz rightly suggests that at least some software used for contracting falls squarely into this category, such as dynamic pricing software and even 'clear box' algorithms that go beyond strictly gap-filling, at least 'if their behavior is foreseeable and limited in scope'.[84] She argues that 'black box' algorithms, however, involve such uncertainty that the existing contract law cannot easily accommodate them, and a new model based on agency law is required.[85]

Scholz's analogy to conventional gap-filling mechanisms appears sound, but contrary to her reservations, 'black box' algorithms can also be dealt with by the same reasoning. It is already established that an offeror can be bound even where she signs a document in blank and leaves key terms of the offer to be filled in by the ultimate unpredictable actor: another human being, who is not the offeree and not an agent of the offeror.[86] If that other person chooses to fill in the blanks and pass the document to the offeree, and the offeree accepts the offer, the offeror will still be bound, unless she can show that the transaction is 'essentially different in substance or in kind from the transaction intended';[87] the third party effectively acts as a pre-contractual gap-filling mechanism chosen by the offeror. The justification for this position is that there is no 'great difference between signing blind a completed document the contents of which one has not read and signing a printed document [...] with the blanks for the particular transaction not filled in but agreeing to, or authorising, another to fill in those blanks and the figures later'.[88] The same should apply where one puts one's fate (in respect of a given type of transaction) in the hands of an unpredictable 'black box' algorithm rather than an unpredictable human. Although 'black box' algorithms fall outside the scope of this chapter, the point is still a significant one as it would apply *a fortiori* to the more limited and predictable kinds of software we are concerned with.

Thus, there is no obstacle to an offer being effective even though its existence and precise terms were unknown to the offeror at the time of the offer. This conclusion is reached through proper application of the existing machinery of contract law to the facts of offeror-side algorithmic contracts; no extension is needed.

4.2 The acceptance

On the offeree's side, a different problem looms: the supposed rule that in a unilateral contract, unlike a bilateral contract, an offer can only be accepted by a person with knowledge of the offer.

84 Scholz (n 7) 136.

85 ibid 164–69.

86 *United Dominions Trust Ltd v Western* [1976] QB 513 (CA), 519–22 (per Megaw LJ), 523 (per Scarman LJ), 524 (per Bridge LJ).

87 *Chitty on Contracts* (n 32) para 3-053, citing (among others) *United Dominions Trust Ltd* (n 85). In that exceptional case, the offeror may be able to avail herself of the *non est factum* doctrine.

88 *United Dominions Trust Ltd* (n 86) 523 (per Scarman LJ).

A unilateral contract is defined as follows:

> An offer of a unilateral contract is made when one party promises to pay the other a sum of money (or to do some other act, or to forbear from doing something) if the other will do (or forbear from doing) something without making any promise to that effect: for example where A promises to pay B £100 if B will walk from London to York or find and return A's lost dog or give up smoking for a year. The contract in these cases is called "unilateral" because it arises without B's having made any counter-promise to perform the stipulated act or forbearance; it is contrasted with a bilateral contract under which each party undertakes an obligation.[89]

Offers leading to the conclusion of unilateral contracts are sometimes referred to as unilateral offers.[90]

As earlier argued, algorithmic contracts are similar to vending machine contracts like that in *Thornton*. Although neither *Thornton* itself nor the recent cases applying *Thornton* to algorithmic contracts[91] describe the contract in *Thornton* as a unilateral contract, commentators have generally considered it and similar transactions to be instances of unilateral contracts.[92] Some have also expressly argued that algorithmic contracts are or can be assimilated to unilateral contracts. Allen and Widdison suggest that the offer made by an electronic merchant is like the promise, 'If you go to York, I will give you £100', which can be accepted by going to York.[93] The electronic merchant's offer can be understood as, 'If you order goods from my computer, I promise to supply those goods', which can be accepted by placing the order.[94] Ooi takes substantially the same view.[95] Although Chopra and White, and Dahiyat, view this analysis as viable for simpler algorithmic contracts but not others,[96] their reservations are based on substantially the same reasons I discussed and dismissed in Section 4.1 of this chapter.

There is, however, some difficulty with characterizing algorithmic contracts as purely unilateral contracts. As the definition given earlier reflects, a unilateral contract is one where *only the offeror makes a promise*, such as to pay a reward – that is what is 'unilateral' about a unilateral contract. Consequently, an offeree in a unilateral contract never incurs any detriment beyond having done the act that constituted acceptance. Yet some algorithmic contracts involve both parties taking on obligations upon entry into the contract. In

89 *Chitty on Contracts* (n 32) para 2-082 (citations omitted).
90 See eg ibid paras 2-078, 2-085.
91 *Quoine* (n 11) and *Software Solutions* (n 62).
92 Chopra and White (n 2) 373; Kerr (n 15) 188; Dahiyat (n 52) 472–73; Ooi (n 5) 13.
93 Allen and Widdison (n 14) 33.
94 ibid.
95 Ooi (n 5) 13.
96 Chopra and White (n 2) 372–74; Dahiyat (n 52) 472–73.

Allen and Widdison's example, the buyer must pay for the order once he has placed it, and in *Quoine*, parties were obliged to settle the trades after the conclusion of the contracts (albeit this was done automatically).[97] It is not possible, therefore, to explain *all* algorithmic contracts as purely unilateral contracts.

The better view, and one that leads to the same outcome, is that algorithmic contracts can be either unilateral contracts or contracts that begin as unilateral contracts but then become bilateral contracts. The law recognizes the latter as a possibility. For instance, in *The Eurymedon*,[98] the House of Lords held that a contract between shippers and stevedores began as a unilateral one (the stevedores had no obligation to discharge the goods, though they could accept the offer by discharging the goods) and shifted from unilateral to bilateral once the stevedores had discharged the goods.[99] The ticket sale in *Thornton* is best understood in these terms as well, given that purchasing a ticket (unlike purchasing a newspaper or a can of soda) often will not purely confer benefits on the driver, but will also impose obligations or detriments (such as, but for the ineffective incorporation on the facts of *Thornton*, exclusion of tortious liability that would otherwise exist[100]).

Even with the above qualification, an algorithmic contract is unilateral at the point at which acceptance is to be assessed, and so must satisfy the requirements for acceptance of unilateral contracts. Critically, this would seem to include a requirement of knowledge of the offer, established in the High Court of Australia's decision in *R v Clarke*.[101] Clarke had been arrested for murder and provided information on the true murderers in order to save himself. He later tried to claim a reward that had been offered by the Crown for such information.[102] Justice Higgins, in one of three judgments employing broadly similar reasoning, held that:

> Clarke had seen the offer, indeed; but it was not present to his mind – he had forgotten it, and gave no consideration to it, in his intense excitement as to his own danger. There cannot be assent without knowledge of the offer; and ignorance of the offer is the same thing whether it is due to never hearing of it or to forgetting it after hearing.[103]

The claim failed for lack of a valid acceptance.

A significant point in *Clarke* is that the requirement of knowledge of the offer is a consequence of the requirement of assent: one must know of an offer because one could not otherwise assent to it. This is stated even more clearly

97 *Quoine* (n 11) [2].
98 *New Zealand Shipping Co Ltd v A N Satterthwaite Ltd (The Eurymedon)* [1975] AC 154 (PC).
99 ibid 167–68.
100 *Thornton* (n 58) 168.
101 (1927) 40 CLR 227 (HCA).
102 ibid 231.
103 ibid 241.

in the American case of *Fitch v Snedaker* (which was cited with approval in *Clarke*):

> To the existence of a contract there must be mutual assent, or in another form offer and consent to the offer. The motive inducing consent may be immaterial, but the consent is vital. Without that there is no contract. How then can there be consent or assent to that of which the party has never heard?[104]

The better view is thus that knowledge of the offer is not an independent requirement, but a precondition for fulfilment of the true requirement, which is assent to the offer.

If there is any doubt as to the correctness of *Clarke* as a statement of the existing law, that doubt stems from *Gibbons v Proctor*,[105] another reward case. The offer there was to pay for information concerning a fugitive. A policeman, Gibbons, had information and, in ignorance of the offer, shared it with an intermediary who then relayed it to the offeror. Gibbons's performance was found to constitute acceptance, so the case has sometimes been thought to be authority that a unilateral offer may be accepted in ignorance of the offer.[106] The contemporary consensus is that this is a mistaken interpretation because, according to one reported version of the case, Gibbons had learned of the offer by the time the information had reached the offeror, which was the point of acceptance.[107]

David Pugsley's meticulous comparison of the three available reports of the case shows that this explanation is unsustainable.[108] He observes that the sole report containing this purported fact is much less reliable than the other two, as it was prepared at a later date, apparently by rephrasing one of the earlier two reports, and contains notable inaccuracies (including as to the name of the plaintiff).[109] The specific sentence containing the purported fact of Gibbons's knowledge appears to be one such inaccuracy, introduced in the course of a paraphrase.[110] Hence, the other two reports – which are silent as to Gibbons's knowledge of the offer – should

104 *Fitch v Snedaker* (1868) 38 NY 248, cited in *Clarke* (n 101) 241.

105 (1891) 64 LT 594.

106 Including in *Clarke*, in which Higgins J understood Gibbons to stand for that proposition but chose not to follow it: *Clarke* (n 101) 240.

107 See eg Michael J Fisher and Desmond G Greenwood, *Contract Law in Hong Kong* (HKU Press 2007) 60; *Chitty on Contracts* (n 32) para 2-040; Edwin Peel, *Treitel on the Law of Contract* (13th edn, Sweet & Maxwell 2011) para 2-048; Ewan McKendrick, *Contract Law* (12th edn, Palgrave 2017) 37.

108 David Pugsley, 'Gibbons v Proctor' (1977) 10 *Bracton LJ* 69.

109 ibid 69–70. See also Elizabeth Macdonald, 'When is a contract formed by the browse-wrap process?' (2011) 19 *IJLIT* 285, 290 (describing *Gibbons*, and the authorities relied on therein, as 'unsatisfactorily reported, elderly, English case law', and preferring *Clarke*).

110 Pugsley (n 108) 69–70.

be taken as accurately reflecting what the case decided.[111] The real reason *Gibbons* does not stand for the proposition that acceptance in ignorance of a unilateral offer is effective is that, as Pugsley points out, we simply do not know whether Gibbons knew of the offer or not. That was not even in issue – the case turned instead on whether the offer had been made at the time the information reached the offeror.[112] *Gibbons* has nothing to say about the knowledge requirement, and that is sufficient reason to reject it as a statement of the existing law on this point and to follow *Clarke* instead.

It thus appears that knowledge of the offer is generally required for acceptance of unilateral offers. We must either find an exception to that requirement or find a way to impute the software's 'knowledge' to the offeree. Although the second option is also viable (and could be achieved by solutions such as an agency-inspired analysis), the first option is preferable as it better accords with the rationale for the requirement and is justifiable as a matter of existing authority.

As earlier argued, knowledge of an offer is not an independent requirement, but a stepping stone to finding assent. Immediately, one detects dissonance between the notion that the offeree's knowledge is required, and the fundamental principle in English contract law that agreement is determined objectively, not subjectively: 'The parties are to be judged, not by what is in their minds, but by what they have said or written or done.'[113] Outward assent is enough.

How, then, can we reconcile *Clarke* with this fundamental principle? The question deserves deeper consideration than this chapter can give it, but I will attempt a brief answer. The key lies in the context of *Clarke*. When Clarke gave up the information regarding the murderers, he did not mention the reward and, given that he had been charged with the same murders for which the culprits were sought, an obvious and sufficient explanation, to a reasonable person in the offeror's position, would have been that Clarke intended to clear his name.[114] In those circumstances, even though the act performed coincided with the act stipulated, it could have been just that – coincidence. The act of sharing the information being objectively ambiguous, it could not constitute outward assent. The same was true in the other reward cases and might also be said of other classic examples such as using a medicinal 'smoke ball'[115] or travelling to York.

Viewed in that context, the inquiry into the offeree's knowledge and subjective intention is understandable. When nothing objective links the act and the offer, the law must either deny relief outright (which may be more

111 ibid 70.

112 ibid.

113 Michael P Furmston, *Cheshire, Fifoot and Furmston's Law of Contract* (15th edn, OUP 2007) 38, quoted in *Chitty on Contracts* (n 32) para 1-017. See also Allen and Widdison (n 14) 32; Dahiyat (n 52) 477–80.

114 Which Clarke himself admitted was the reality: *Clarke* (n 101) 238–39.

115 *Carlill v Carbolic Smoke Ball Co* [1892] EWCA Civ 1; [1893] 1 QB 256.

principled, but hard on deserving claimants), or seek some extra element to rule out serendipity and transform the ambiguous act into unambiguous acceptance. Thus it is that subjective assent to the offer, when shown, is allowed to fill in for the lack of assent on the usual objective standard.

If the foregoing explanation is correct, *Clarke* should not be understood as imposing a further requirement in unilateral contract cases, but as extending a lifeline to claims that would otherwise certainly fail for want of objective assent. The fact that claimants under offeree-side and pure algorithmic contracts may not be able to avail themselves of that lifeline only matters if they need that lifeline in the first place. But an algorithmic contract, by its nature, is vanishingly unlikely to ever need that lifeline. For software to autonomously accept an offer, that offer must have been encoded by or for the offeror and pushed on to a platform that the offeree's software could access. The only way for the offeree's software to signal acceptance would be to interact with the very code embodying the offer, creating an objective correspondence between the offer and the acceptance. The act is as self-explanatory as signing on a dotted line or inserting coins into a vending machine. Since outward assent is present, the inquiry can stop there, without any need to ask whether the offeree had subjective knowledge of the offer and a subjective intention to assent.

This removes the last potential obstacle to formation of a valid algorithmic contract. As we have seen, though the analysis of agreement in an offeree-side or pure algorithmic contract is not straightforward, a solution is possible on the state of the existing authorities, properly considered.

5. Conclusion

Much of the analysis above draws on work that has already been done, particularly by commentators focusing on the unilateral contract analysis and/or the objective theory of contract formation. What this chapter set out to establish was that:

(a) The contracting problem is narrower than it is often thought to be. It is confined to the requirement of agreement.
(b) Within those confines, there are nonetheless a handful of difficulties, including some that have not previously been noticed (such as the *Clarke* requirement).
(c) Despite the difficulties, the contracting problem is solvable with the existing tools of contract law. The solution involves some reinterpretation of the authorities, but no true extension of the law.

If I have succeeded in the above, the search for an explanation of the validity of algorithmic contracts as a matter of the existing common law of contracts is at an end. Considering the issue *de lege ferenda*, however, there are virtues other than simplicity to be weighed, and a conservative, incremental approach may not always produce the most satisfying answers to other contractual questions. In particular, vitiating factors and interpretation of terms bring questions of knowledge and intention to the fore again, and it is there that that other proposed models (such as those derived from the law of agency) appear to offer advantages. Further exploration is needed, and it is hoped that the journey will go more smoothly with the undergrowth of the contracting problem cleared away.

Bibliography

——— *Halsbury's Laws of England* (4th edn, Butterworths 1974) vol 9

Allen T and Widdison R, 'Can Computers Make Contracts?' (1996) 9 *Harv JL & Tech* 25

Beale HG (ed), *Chitty on Contracts*, vol 1 (32nd edn, Sweet & Maxwell 2015)

Beatson J, Burrows A, and Cartwright J, *Anson's Law of Contract* (30th edn, OUP 2016)

Benson P, 'The Idea of Consideration' (2011) 61 *UTLJ* 241 [DOI: https://doi.org/10.3138/utlj.61.2.241]

Bingham TH, 'The Law as the Handmaid of Commerce' in *Lives of the Law: Selected Essays and Speeches: 2000–2010* (OUP 2011)

Bradgate R, 'Formation of Contracts' in Furmston M (ed), *The Law of Contract* (Butterworths Common Law Series, 3rd edn, LexisNexis Butterworths 2007)

Chen-Wishart M, *Contract Law* (6th edn, OUP 2018)

Chopra S and White L, 'Artificial Agents and the Contracting Problem: A Solution via an Agency Analysis' [2009] *U Ill JL Tech & Pol'y* 363

——— and White LF, *A Legal Theory for Autonomous Artificial Agents* (University of Michigan Press 2011) [DOI: https://doi.org/10.3998/mpub.356801]

Dahiyat EAR, 'Intelligent agents and intentionality: Should we begin to think outside the box?' (2006) 22 *Computer L & Secur Rep* 472 [DOI: https://doi.org/10.1016/j.clsr.2006.09.001]

Finocchiaro G, 'The conclusion of the electronic contract through "software agents": A false legal problem? Brief considerations' (2003) 19 *Computer L & Secur Rep* 20 [DOI: https://doi.org/10.1016/s0267-3649(03)00105-5]

Fisher MJ and Greenwood DG, *Contract Law in Hong Kong* (HKU Press 2007)

Furmston MP, *Cheshire, Fifoot and Furmston's Law of Contract* (15th edn, OUP 2007)

Goff R, 'Commercial Contracts and the Commercial Court' [1984] *LMCLQ* 382

Katz A, 'Intelligent Agents and Internet Commerce in Ancient Rome' (*SCL*, 15 October 2008) <www.scl.org/articles/1095-intelligent-agents-and-internet-commerce-in-ancient-rome> accessed 5 May 2020

Kerr IR, 'Ensuring the Success of Contract Formation in Agent-Mediated Electronic Commerce' (2001) 1 *Electron Commer Res* 183 [DOI: https://doi.org/10.1023/A:1011587932113]

Lee PW, 'Consideration' in Phang ABL (ed), *The Law of Contract in Singapore* (Academy Publishing 2012)

——— 'Intention to Create Legal Relations' in Phang ABL (ed), *The Law of Contract in Singapore* (Academy Publishing 2012)

Lehman-Wilzig SN, 'Frankenstein unbound: Towards a legal definition of artificial intelligence' (1981) 13 *Futures* 442 [DOI: https://doi.org/10.1016/0016-3287(81)90100-2]

Low KFK and Mik E, 'Lost in Transmission: Unilateral Mistakes in Automated Contracts' (2020) 136 *LQR* 563 <https://ssrn.com/abstract=3591657> accessed 20 May 2020

Macdonald E, 'When is a contract formed by the browse-wrap process?' (2011) 19 *IJLIT* 285 [DOI: https://doi.org/10.1093/ijlit/ear009]

McKendrick E, *Contract Law* (12th edn, Palgrave 2017)

Mik E, 'Evaluating the Impact of the UN Convention on the use of Electronic Communications in International Contracts on Domestic Contract Law: The Singapore Example' (2010) 28 *Chinese (Taiwan) YB Intl L & Aff* 43 [DOI: https://doi.org/10.1163/9789004425019_004]

——— 'The *Un*importance of being "electronic" or – popular misconceptions about "Internet contracting"' (2011) 19 *IJLIT* 324 [DOI: https://doi.org/10.1093/ijlit/ear011]

Ooi V, 'Contracts formed by software: An approach from the law of mistake' (2019) *SMU Centre for AI & Data Governance Research Paper* 2019/02 <https://ssrn.com/abstract=3322308> accessed 7 May 2020

Peel E, *Treitel on the Law of Contract* (13th edn, Sweet & Maxwell 2011)

Pugsley D, '*Gibbons v Proctor*' (1977) 10 *Bracton LJ* 69

Rustad ML and Kavusturan E, 'A Commercial Law for Software Contracting' (2019) 76 *Wash & Lee L Rev* 775

Scholz LH, 'Algorithmic Contracts' (2017) 20 *Stan Tech L Rev* 128

Shakespeare W, *The Tragedy of King Richard III*, Act V, Scene IV (Project Gutenberg, uploaded 1 October 1998) <www.gutenberg.org/ebooks/1503> accessed 19 May 2020

Solum LB, 'Legal Personhood for Artificial Intelligences' (1992) 70 *NC L Rev* 1231

Steyn J, 'Contract Law: Fulfilling the Reasonable Expectations of Honest Men' (1997) 113 *LQR* 433

Stuurman K and Wijnands H, 'Software law – Intelligent agents: a curse or a blessing? A survey of the legal aspects of the application of intelligent software systems' (2001) 17 *Computer L & Secur Rep* 92 [DOI: https://doi.org/10.1016/S0267-3649(01)00203-5]

UK Jurisdiction Task Force, 'Legal statement on cryptoassets and smart contracts' (*Tech Nation*, November 2019) <https://technation.io/lawtech-uk-resources/#cryptoassets> accessed 10 December 2019

UNCITRAL, 'UNCITRAL Model Law on Electronic Commerce with Guide to Enactment 1996: with additional article 5 bis as adopted in 1998' (United Nations 1999) <https://uncitral.un.org/sites/uncitral.un.org/files/media-documents/uncitral/en/19-04970_ebook.pdf> accessed 7 May 2020

——— 'Report of the Working Group on Electronic Commerce on its thirty-eighth session' (24 April 2001) UN Doc A/CN 9/484

——— 'Report of the Working Group on Electronic Commerce on its thirty-ninth session' (21 March 2002) UN Doc A/CN 9/509

Van den Hoven van Genderen R, 'Do We Need New Legal Personhood in the Age of Robots and AI?' in Corrales M, Fenwick M, and Forgó N (eds), *Robotics, AI and the Future of Law* (Springer 2018) [DOI: https://doi.org/10.1007/978-981-13-2874-9_2]

Wang FF, *Law of Electronic Commercial Transactions: Contemporary Issues in the EU, US and China* (2nd edn, Routledge 2014) [DOI: https://doi.org/10.4324/9780203628812]

Weitzenboeck EM, 'Electronic Agents and the Formation of Contracts' (2001) 9 *IJLIT* 204 [DOI: https://doi.org/10.1093/ijlit/9.3.204]

Winn J and Wright B, *The Law of Electronic Commerce* (4th edn, Aspen Law & Business 2000)

9 Addressing contemporary challenges in contract law through millenary concepts

Andrea Faraci and Luigi Lonardo

1. Introduction

The opposition between rigidity and flexibility of law, as a mirror of the contrast between what is unjust and what is just, is as old as the law itself – as Sophocles' *Antigone* witnesses.[1] Painting with very broad strokes, the struggle between rigidity and flexibility is enhanced by the constant need of the law to adapt itself to social and economic changes – and it is also evident in contract law. Some kind of flexibility of law will be required. To be clear: we believe that these issues are old enough that they warrant treatment through millenary categories. It is in fact on a short journey through these millenary concepts – rather than on presenting actual solutions – that this paper focuses. What we set out to do is precisely settle a reflection on certain ancient – and not so ancient – conceptions of equity and justice as tools for law's changes.

Smart contracts are a 'computerized transaction protocol that executes the terms of a contract'.[2] They are based on software languages, or 'codes': the set of instructions forming the software which is executed by a machine (now, mostly a computer)[3] in an abstract manner to produce real-world output. Smart contracts, as Jelena Madir says, are better thought of as 'conditional transactions' because they refer to the logic written in code that has 'IF this, THEN that' conditions.[4] Distributed ledger technologies (DLT) have facilitated the efficacy and reliability of smart contracts. Blockchain, for example, is being increasingly looked at with interest by states as well as private individuals, for its application to cryptocurrencies as well as other forms of

1 In similar terms: Aristotle, *Rhetoric* in *Ars Rhetorica* (William David Ross ed, Clarendon Press 1959) (Perseus Digital Library <www.perseus.tufts.edu> accessed 23 March 2020) 1.15 [5–6].

2 Nick Szabo, 'Smart Contracts' (1994) <www.fon.hum.uva.nl/rob/Courses/InformationInSpeech/CDROM/Literature/LOTwinterschool2006/szabo.best.vwh.net/smart.contracts.html> accessed 23 March 2020.

3 That with a vending machine is also a smart contract.

4 Jelena Madir, 'Smart Contracts: (How) Do They Fit Under Existing Legal Frameworks?' (2018) 1 <https://ssrn.com/abstract=3301463> accessed 23 March 2020.

DOI: 10.4324/9781003080596-11

contracts.[5] In one sentence, for the purposes of the present contribution, a blockchain is a ledger which allows for an anonymous, decentralized, and highly sophisticated maths-backed system (an illustrious example of which is the cryptocurrency Bitcoin).[6] The appeal of smart contracts is undeniable, their diffusion unstoppable. They promise efficiency, lower legal and transactional costs, as well as, for those using blockchain technology, transparency, and anonymity.[7]

More concretely, smart contracts – especially those using cutting edge technology, such as blockchain or other highly sophisticated forms of encryption for distributed ledger – give rise to an important set of issues, concerning the applicability of general rules to govern their definition, creation, and execution, touched upon in the fourth part of the chapter. For example, are smart contracts to be defined as a different object to traditional contracts? But also: what exactly is smart about them? How can we handle legal gaps in the legal regulation of smart contracts? Moreover, how can we guarantee legal protection that can be considered conforming to the values of social justice – and why should we care about the issue at all?

Traces of interactions between a strict set of laws and the concept of equity can be found in Mesopotamian legal tradition between the end of the third millennium BC and the second half of the second millennium BC. For example, Iranian legal experience presents the concept of justice, which belonged to the king, as an instrument to correct or integrate awards made by the *databares* (the travelling judges charged with applying the laws strictly).[8] In Babylonian law (in Ur-Nammu or Hammurabi's codes) equity is always one of the main characteristics of the rulers.[9]

Essentially, it seems that human beings have always been quite aware of the fact that law (i.e. a legal system) is a living creature as well as the fact that it is shaped by personal and social issues, economic needs, and moral and religious opinions that the law itself is called upon to regulate. Consequently, a most important question has been, in ancient times as well and probably since the very idea of law was born, how to 'handle' changes and regulatory gaps (which are often caused by social, economic, or technological change). All these matters lead to another essential question – namely,

5 Alexander Savelyev, 'Contract Law 2.0: "Smart" Contracts as the Beginning of the End of Classic Contract Law' (2017) 26 *I & CTL* 116, 117; Reena SenGupta, 'The Great Integration of Data, Technology and Services' (*Financial Times*, 23 October 2019) <www.ft.com/content/99f6f334-eab7-11e9-85f4-d00e5018f061> accessed 18 November 2019.

6 Savelyev defines blockchain as 'a decentralized distributed database of all verified transactions that take place across a P2P-network system operating on cryptographic algorithms'. Savelyev (n 5) 119.

7 As summed up by Mark Giancaspro, 'Is a "Smart Contract" Really a Smart Idea? Insights from a Legal Perspective' (2017) 33 *CLS Rev* 825, 829.

8 See Onorato Bucci, *Il principio di equità nella storia del diritto* (Edizioni Scientifiche Italiane 2000) 15–24.

9 ibid.

how to face the conflict between general rules and concrete facts, something especially relevant when it comes to contemporary challenges to the law of obligations, such as smart contracts. This conflict is often created by the usual, and actually quite natural, generality and abstractness of laws' dispositions.

2. *Epieikeia* and *Aequitas*

Reference to the concept of equity abounds. It may be spotted in virtually any age and in most ancient societies. However, the most systematic speculation on equity is probably the one offered by Aristotle. The concept of *epieikeia* (sometimes translated as fairness) is present also in previous Greek sources, but as mentioned Aristotle is the most sophisticated.

Aristotle told us that equity is not contrary to law, nor to justice itself, but that it is an ulterior tool necessary in order to tackle – and this is a crucial point – the incompleteness as well as the rigidity of the law. This specific perspective is firstly shown in the *Nicomachean Ethics*:

> The source of the difficulty is that equity, though just, is not legal justice, but a rectification of legal justice. The reason for this is that law is always a general statement, yet there are cases which it is not possible to cover in a general statement.[10]

In addition, always with reference to the relationship between law and equity, Aristotle adds:

> When therefore the law lays down a general rule, and thereafter a case arises which is an exception to the rule, it is then right, where the lawgiver's pronouncement because of its absoluteness is defective and erroneous, to rectify the defect by deciding as the lawgiver would himself decide if he were present on the occasion, and would have enacted if he had been cognizant of the case in question.[11]

This was not merely Aristotle's 'personal' philosophy of law. He was expressing, instead, a shared understanding. Several scholars (see Biscardi and Bearzot[12]) correctly emphasized that, instead, Aristotle's understanding of *epieikeia* was deeply connected to legal practice.

10 Aristotle, *Nicomachean Ethics* in *Aristotle in 23 Volumes*, vol 19 (Harris Rackham tr, HUP and William Heinemann 1934) (Perseus Digital Library <www.perseus.tufts.edu> accessed 23 March 2020) 1137b [4]–[5].

11 ibid 1137b [6].

12 Arnaldo Biscardi, 'On *Aequitas* and *Epieikeia*' in Alfredo Mordechai Rabello (ed), *Aequitas and Equity: Equity in Civil Law and Mixed Jurisdictions* (Hebrew University of Jerusalem 1993) 1–11; Cinzia Bearzot, *La giustizia nella Grecia antica* (Carocci 2008) 56ff.

For example, one may take into consideration what Aristotle discusses again about *epieikeia* in his *Rhetoric*:

> For that which is equitable seems to be just, and equity is justice that goes beyond the written law. These omissions are sometimes involuntary, sometimes voluntary, on the part of the legislators; involuntary when it may have escaped their notice, voluntary when, being unable to define for all cases, they are obliged to make a universal statement, which is not applicable to all, but only to most, cases; and whenever it is difficult to give a definition owing to the infinite number of cases, as, for instance, the size and kind of an iron instrument used in wounding; for life would not be long enough to reckon all the possibilities.[13]

Therefore, in this part of the *Rhetoric* Aristotle expresses another specific thought that looks like a reference to his own legal reality:

> [I]f the written law is counter to our case, we must have recourse to the general law and equity, as more in accordance with justice; and we must argue that, *when the dicast takes an oath to decide to the best of his judgement*, he means that he will not abide rigorously by the written laws; that equity is ever constant and never changes, even as the general law, which is based on nature, whereas the written laws often vary [...][14]

As mentioned above, it is believed that Aristotle was referring to an essential part of the oath of the Athenian Supreme Tribunal, the Heliaia, requiring judges to decide 'with due respect of the law and decrees of the city (*kata tous nomous*), or according to the fairest opinion (*gnome dikaiotate*)'.[15]

The precise extension of this concept's application in the Greek court is still very much an object of debate.[16] In fact, as scholars observed, according to some version of the oath's text, some discretion was allowed for judges only if there were not applicable laws deciding the concrete case.

13 Aristotle, *Rhetoric* in *Aristotle in 23 Volumes*, vol 22 (John Henry Freese tr, HUP and William Heinemann 1926) (Perseus Digital Library <www.perseus.tufts.edu> accessed 23 March 2020) 1.13 [13].

14 ibid 1.15 [4]–[6] (emphasis added).

15 Bearzot (n 12) 56. About the history of this concept and its relationship with the *epieikeia*, see also Biscardi, 'On Aequitas and Epieikeia' (n 12) 1–11; James L O'Neil, 'Was the Athenian Gnome *Dikaiotate* a Principle of Equity? (2001) 35 *Antichthon* 20; Edward Harris, 'How Strictly Did the Athenian Courts Apply the Law? The Role of Epieikeia' (2013) 56 *Bull Inst Class Stud* 27.

16 This particular expression was actually present in several other Greek legal systems. See again O'Neil (n 15); Edward M Harris, 'The Rule of Law in Athenian Democracy: Reflections on the Judicial Oath' (2006) 9 *Dike* 157; Cinzia Bearzot, 'La *gnome* del giudice nell'oratoria attica' in Emmanuele Vimercati and Cinzia Bearzot (eds), *La giustizia dei greci tra riflessione filosofica e prassi giudiziaria* (Vita e Pensiero 2013) 85–98.

Moreover, the Aristotelian interpretation of the oath – where *gnome* is interpreted as an extension of *epieikeia* – seems to have no confirmation in Attic oratory.[17]

However, other scholars identified a well-spread use of the term *gnome* associated with argumentations which implied a most flexible relationship with the law.[18] In addition, it has been also argued that even if there is not a perfect correspondence between *epieikeia* and *gnome dikaiotate*, it can be considered quite sure that the two concepts are quite similar, as a response to a specific need for law's flexibility.[19]

In conclusion, scholars noticed also that *Rhetoric* was probably, or even certainly, addressed to those who dealt with practical justice regularly, such us logographers, judges, or politicians. It is quite unlikely Aristotle was talking about something that was actually only in his mind.[20]

The concept of equity was fundamental also in the other most important legal traditions, namely the Roman one. *Aequitas* (equity, fairness) was so important as to be considered the essence of law itself. In fact, as the famous definition offered by Ulpianus remind us, the law was *ars boni et aequi* (the art of goodness and fairness).[21] *Aequitas* was the concept on which the *praetor* (the Roman magistrate charged with the application, interpretation, and production of law) grounded most of the changes made in order to *correct* (as many Roman sources literally say) the civil law.[22] It can be affirmed that all the Roman law produced during the Republican age was characterized by the highest level of flexibility.[23] Equity and good faith have been the tools through which new contracts and contractual rules as well as many other juridical institutions were introduced in the Roman legal system.

3. Contemporary perspective about equity

While it should be clear that this concept can, in very general terms, be used to address contemporary challenges, this section offers a more concrete albeit brief overview of contemporary perspectives on equity.

17 See again Harris, 'The Rule of Law' (n 16) 162.

18 See Arnaldo Biscardi, 'L'interpretazione delle legge e la "gnome dikaiotate"' in Arnaldo Biscardi, *Diritto Greco Antico* (Giuffrè 1982) 361ff. See also Bearzot who underlined that *gnome dikaiotate* was even older than the Aristotelian *epieikeia*: Bearzot, 'La *gnome* del giudice' (n 16) 19.

19 See again Bearzot, 'La *gnome* del giudice' (n 16) 19.

20 See Harris, 'How Strictly Did the Athenian Courts Apply the Law?' (n 15) 48.

21 D 1.1.1.pr. For more information about this specific definition of law see Filippo Gallo, *Celso e Kelsen: Per la rifondazione della scienza giuridica* (Giappichelli 2010).

22 See Filippo Gallo, *L'*officium *del pretore nella produzione e applicazione del diritto* (Giappichelli 1997).

23 For a quite complete perspective about this issue, see Laura Solidoro Maruotti, *Tra morale e diritto: Gli itinerari dell'*aequitas*: Lezioni* (Giappichelli 2014).

Perelman's theory of justice is grounded on the conviction that across centuries there has been just one idea of justice – that is, equality.[24] Of course, conceptions of equality have been various. Perelman called these variations 'essential categories'.[25] An example offered by the philosopher himself can make it clearer. An employer should pay all his employees according to the same criteria. To do that he has to choose between two essential categories: 'everybody's salary will be proportionate to their work' or 'everybody's salary will be proportionate to their needs'.[26] So, the concept of justice is still expressed by the idea of equality but the conception of justice changes according to the chosen category.

Even if Perelman is perfectly aware that the essential category choice depends on cultural variables, he stated also that the complexity of reality and our sense of justice inevitably lead us to take into consideration several categories at the same time.[27] This overlapping of categories causes antinomies which can be attenuated by the equity that Perlman defined as the 'law's crutch'.[28]

In what has been said so far, the central role played by judges has been implied. Aristotle charged judges to apply equity as a corrective of the law and so does Perelman, even though he looks at the judges' discretion with the same suspicion that characterized our recent and less recent legal perspective. After all, our inclination to protect the supremacy of the law is strongly corroborated by the need to protect the democratic demands that the law itself in modern times represents. But, in this opposition between law (or lawgiver) and judges, we can recognize the chronic conflict between imposed rule, whoever the legislator is, and the real case.

Maybe a compromise could be possible – perhaps thanks to Dworkin's theory of interaction between rules and principles.[29] According to Dworkin, the law cannot be reduced to a system of rules. Lawgivers are significantly linked to a set of ethical and social principles that can be the points of reference even for judges in order to decide on so-called 'hard cases'.[30] In Dworkin's thought, judges' discretion is conceived as a 'weak discretion' which has to conform to two essential criteria, namely 'coherence' and 'justification'. It has been also argued that these concepts, able to direct law interpretation, seem to be even more important than

24 Chaïm Perelman, *La giustizia* (Liliana Ribet tr, Giappichelli 1959).

25 ibid 32.

26 ibid 58.

27 ibid.

28 ibid 61.

29 Ronald Dworkin, *Taking Rights Seriously* (HUP 1977); Ronald Dworkin, 'Non v'è davvero soluzione corretta nei casi difficili?' in Ronald Dworkin, *Questioni di principio* (Il Saggiatore 1990).

30 Those are the basic ideas for Dworkin's criticism of Hart's positivism and of the so-called 'no right answer thesis'.

the certainty of law.[31] In this perspective, scholars glimpsed exactly the concept of equity.[32]

4. Smart contracts

We will illustrate three issues arising from DLT smart contracts: issues of classification, of creation, and execution. To maintain the focus of this chapter on how traditional concepts such as equity and justice apply to contemporary challenges in the law of obligations, we single out these issues in smart contracts. While aware that this severely limits the scope of our study, we believe the choice is justifiable because the three issues we identify lend themselves well to illustrate the multifaceted applications of equity and justice to contract law.

We will survey a few selected solutions offered by private law scholars and by comparative lawyers, with no other aim than to provide an idea of the nature and the complexity of the legal issues involved. These are, we believe, by no means distinctive to smart contracts. They are instances of the problems created by automatism and formalization – by the 'general and abstract'. It will also be shown that the correction of law is an instance of the Aristotelian notion of justice: the abandonment of the general and abstract in favour of the concrete and appropriate.

4.1 Classification

As for many legal objects, there is no agreed definition of a smart contract. Some consider it a 'normal' contract – subject to the discipline of whatever rules of private law regulate contracts;[33] others have distinct definitions for smart contracts – that is, by focusing on the smart contract *code*.[34] It is clear that an element of novelty can be found in a contract containing blockchain technologies – because 'everything is a little bit different from everything else', as Jon Elster would put it.[35]

In essence, as Jelena Madir has it, a smart contract is a binding agreement whose execution is automatic.[36] Often the 1994 definition of Nick Szabo is

31 Giorgio Bongiovanni, 'Costituzionalismo, democrazia e liberalismo in R. Dworkin' in Alberto Artosi, Giorgio Bongiovanni, and Silvia Vida (eds), *Problemi della produzione e dell'attuazione normativa*, vol 1 (Gedit 2001) 109.

32 See Richard Wasserstrom, 'Equity in the Philosophy of Law' in Alfredo Mordechai Rabello (ed), *Aequitas and Equity: Equity in Civil Law and Mixed Jurisdictions* (Hebrew University of Jerusalem 1993) 163–78.

33 Savelyev (n 5) 120.

34 In this sense, Madir (n 4) 3.

35 Jon Elster accuses Tocqueville of adopting this law in relation to his speculative explanation of religious phenomena: Jon Elster, *Alexis de Tocqueville, the First Social Scientist* (CUP 2009) 4.

36 Madir (n 4) 3.

cited: 'A smart contract is a computerized transaction protocol that executes the terms of a contract.'[37] The contract executed by a vending machine fulfils this definition.[38]

Although they all 'include' some form of automation, smart contracts come on a spectrum. In some cases, the text of the contract may be drafted in computer code. In other cases, the natural language of the contract will incorporate the code/software.

On the other hand, some insist then on the special technology that enables the existence of smart contracts, so Gideon Greenspan defines it as follows: 'A smart contract is a piece of code which is stored on a Blockchain, triggered by Blockchain transactions, and which reads and writes data in that Blockchain's database.'[39] Similarly, Savelyev considers 'Blockchain [as] a "paradigm-shifter" in the sphere of contracting: it allows automation of the process of contractual performance of both parties.'[40]

Savelyev explains, 'if there is no difference in principle between vending machines and Smart contracts, then we will have to admit that Smart contracts are almost as old as Roman law itself',[41] and goes on to provide an example of automated contracts known in the ancient world.[42]

4.2 Creation

But how do we know when a smart contract is valid? For example, does a party need to understand the code (in the same way as a party, in order to express consent, needs to understand what is in the contract they are about to conclude)? If so, to what extent? Finally, in what form should smart contracts be concluded?

There is a relatively easy solution, which seems to be overwhelmingly adopted across the world: namely, to apply the rules for the formation of the contract to determine the validity of smart contracts as well.

This solution is, again, to consider that smart contracts are simply contracts 'written' in a different way. What follows from this determination is that usual rules apply. Offer, acceptance, some commonality of intent over the object/cause of the transaction – depending on the rules of private law applicable in a given jurisdiction.

37 Szabo (n 2).

38 Savelyev (n 5) 120.

39 Gideon Greenspan, 'Beware of the Impossible Smart Contract' (*Blockchain News*, 12 April 2016) <www.the-blockchain.com/2016/04/12/beware-of-the-impossible-smart-contract> accessed 18 November 2019.

40 Savelyev (n 5) 121.

41 ibid.

42 According to Savelyev, Ctesibius, a Greek engineer and mathematician, invented the first 'vending machine', a device which dispensed holy water in the temple when a coin was deposited in. See ibid.

Smart contract code used on a distributed ledger is likely to constitute an offer if other participants on the ledger are entitled to interact with, and execute, the code (i.e. if they the recipient can see what is going to happen if they click on something that says 'pay' or any other similar action). The acceptance can be signalled by any participant in the transaction in a ledger – for example, when they authenticate the action by signing in with their password before clicking 'pay' (or any other similar action).

4.3 Execution

What if conditions change? What if the contract says that it has to be adjusted to reflect 'reasonable commercial practices'?

Is a smart contract self-enforcing? In a sense, it is, because enforceability is automatic and, in fact, independent from the law[43] (it is possible to exclude quite radically that law is a reason for the action of whatever kind for the machine).

The immutability of smart contracts – as they do not self-adjust to include new circumstances – deprives them of the flexibility of 'traditional' contracts. Take as an example the events of June 2016, during the hack of The DAO:

> a fundraising vehicle that raised USD 168 million when it was launched on Ethereum in 2016. When an attacker exploited a smart contract flaw to siphon off over USD 50 million from the DAO, the Ethereum community questioned the principle of maintaining the ledger's immutability.[44]

It leads also to the other issues concerning social justice in contract law, or, anyway, contractual justice. Smart contracts are more than simple contracts: they are products as well, created by only one of the parties involved. The risk of a power's balance switching among contractual parties is clearly undeniable. This risk will be even more dangerous when smart contracts are used to provide essential services.

5. Conclusion

Despite significant efforts to regulate new phenomena such as contracts dependent upon or incorporating sophisticated technology, we are not yet able to cover every possible situation effectively. Likely, as Aristotle taught us, we will never be able to. A historical approach could be useful to understand how much this issue is in fact inherent in the very application of the law. The tension between rigidity (which guarantees certainty and predictability) and flexibility (which may allow a fair result in individual cases) is, as far as

43 Max Raskin, 'The Law and Legality of Smart Contracts' (2017) 1 *Geo L Tech Rev* 305.
44 Madir (n 4) 17.

we know, as old as the law itself. Another manifestation of this tension lies in the different time-frame, so to speak, between law and reality, and this is brought to the fore by the emergence of new technologies: one thing is the written and stable norm, and quite another the constantly evolving reality, which may give rise to situations that are not covered (because they could not be foreseeable) by the law. The tensions to which the regulation of smart contracts give rise can, in fact, be found across virtually all legal systems and millennia and are not distinctive to any one in particular. A reconstruction of the speculation on equity in ancient Greek or Roman legal systems could be a valuable source or point of reference to begin to think about how to address the contemporary law of obligations.

Maybe tools like a general principle of equity, which derives from a moral intuition of fairness, can still play a role in these specific cases. Yet equity is a principle that comes into play in the concrete solution of controversies, and it is applied by judges. For this reason, in order to achieve a practical solution to contemporary legal problems in the law of obligations, probably we will need to face some of our (generally shared) fears regarding judges' role and their discretion. As the contemporary reflection of legal philosophers mentioned in this chapter shows, constitutions (or whatever is the source of general principles in a given legal system) could be the fundamental reference for judges. These general principles tend to represent, usually, the different 'essential categories' (to use Perelman's expression) which a judge may use to guide its decision, a decision which would then be constitutionally guided and thus provide a solution that is not unduly arbitrary. While rules are specific and do not cover the whole extent of possible present or future situations that may arise through the accidents of litigation or future technologies, general principles often reflect millenary categories such as equity and fairness and thus lend themselves to inform the solution of cases where the system would not otherwise offer a satisfactory solution.

The same goes for smart contracts. Where the regulation has not caught up with technological advancements, where the regulation cannot foresee or cover the difficult mathematical ideas that are necessary in a smart contract, or simply where the legislator has decided to leave a void in order not to restrain the creativity of legal operators, general principles such as equity may act as the polar star to lead the conduct of judges.

Bibliography

Aristotle, *Rhetoric* in *Aristotle in 23 Volumes*, vol 22 (Freese JH tr, HUP and William Heinemann Ltd 1926) (Perseus Digital Library <www.perseus.tufts.edu> accessed 23 March 2020)

——— *Nicomachean Ethics* in *Aristotle in 23 Volumes*, vol 19 (Rackham H tr, HUP and William Heinemann Ltd 1934) (Perseus Digital Library <www.perseus.tufts.edu> accessed 23 March 2020)

——— *Rhetoric* in *Ars Rhetorica* (Ross WD ed, Clarendon Press 1959) (Perseus Digital Library <www.perseus.tufts.edu> accessed 23 March 2020)

Bearzot C, *La giustizia nella Grecia antica* (Carocci 2008)

——— 'La *gnome* del giudice nell'oratoria attica' in Vimercati E and Bearzot C (eds), *La giustizia dei greci tra riflessione filosofica e prassi giudiziaria* (Vita e Pensiero 2013)

Biscardi A, 'L'interpretazione delle legge e la "gnome dikaiotate"' in Biscardi A, *Diritto Greco Antico* (Giuffrè 1982)

——— 'On *Aequitas* and *Epieikeia*' in Rabello AM (ed), *Aequitas and Equity: Equity in Civil Law and Mixed Jurisdictions* (Hebrew University of Jerusalem 1993)

Bongiovanni G, 'Costituzionalismo, democrazia e liberalismo in R. Dworkin' in Artosi A, Bongiovanni G, and Vida S (eds), *Problemi della produzione e dell'attuazione normativa*, vol 1 (Gedit 2001)

Bucci O, *Il principio di equità nella storia del diritto* (Giuffré 2000)

Dworkin R, *Taking Rights Seriously* (HUP 1977)

——— 'Non v'è davvero soluzione corretta nei casi difficili?' in Dworkin R, *Questioni di principio* (Il Saggiatore 1990)

Elster J, *Alexis de Tocqueville, the First Social Scientist* (CUP 2009) [DOI: https://doi.org/10.1017/CBO9780511800429]

Gallo F, *L'*officium *del pretore nella produzione e applicazione del diritto* (Giappichelli 1997)

——— *Celso e Kelsen: Per la rifondazione della scienza giuridica* (Giappichelli 2010)

Giancaspro M, 'Is a "Smart Contract" Really a Smart Idea? Insights from a Legal Perspective' (2017) 33 *CLS Rev* 825 [DOI: https://doi.org/10.1016/j.clsr.2017.05.007]

Greenspan G, 'Beware of the Impossible Smart Contract' (*Blockchain News*, 12 April 2016) <www.the-blockchain.com/2016/04/12/beware-of-the-impossible-smart-contract> accessed 18 November 2019

Harris EM, 'The Rule of Law in Athenian Democracy: Reflections on the Judicial Oath' (2006) 9 *Dike* 157

——— 'How Strictly Did the Athenian Courts Apply the Law? The Role of Epieikeia' (2013) 56 *Bull Inst Class Stud* 27 [DOI: https://doi.org/10.1111/j.2041-5370.2013.00049.x]

Madir J, 'Smart Contracts: (How) Do They Fit Under Existing Legal Frameworks?' (2018) <https://ssrn.com/abstract=3301463> accessed 23 March 2020

O'Neil JL, 'Was the Athenian Gnome *Dikaiotate* a Principle of Equity?' (2001) 35 *Antichthon* 20 [DOI: https://doi.org/10.1017/s0066477400001222]

Perelman C, *La giustizia* (Ribet L tr, Giappichelli 1959)

Raskin M, 'The Law and Legality of Smart Contracts' (2017) 1 *Geo L Tech Rev* 305

Savelyev A, 'Contract Law 2.0: "Smart" Contracts as the Beginning of the End of Classic Contract Law' (2017) 26 *I & CTL* 116 [DOI: https://doi.org/10.1080/13600834.2017.1301036]

SenGupta R, 'The Great Integration of Data, Technology and Services' (*Financial Times*, 23 October 2019) <www.ft.com/content/99f6f334-eab7-11e9-85f4-d00e5018f061> accessed 18 November 2019

Solidoro Maruotti L, *Tra morale e diritto: Gli itinerari dell'*aequitas: *Lezioni* (Giappichelli 2014)

Szabo N, 'Smart Contracts' (1994) <www.fon.hum.uva.nl/rob/Courses/InformationInSpeech/CDROM/Literature/LOTwinterschool2006/szabo.best.vwh.net/smart.contracts.html> accessed 23 March 2020

Wasserstrom R, 'Equity in the Philosophy of Law' in Rabello AM (ed), *Aequitas and Equity: Equity in Civil Law and Mixed Jurisdictions* (Hebrew University of Jerusalem 1993)

10 Smart contracts and the evolution of a legal perspective on the protection of human rights

Dino Gliha and Sandra Marković

1. Introduction: blockchain and the digital revolution

The evolution of digital technologies throughout the last decade has changed the way contractual relationship are created, negotiated, concluded, executed, and disputed. New uses, actors, and business models have emerged. Cross-border uses have also intensified and created new opportunities for consumers. These changes have strongly affected the market and confronted regional and national legal systems with new challenges.

A part of this ongoing digital revolution is the exponentially growing interest in the use and wide application of blockchain technologies and smart contracts. The boom in this industry came within the last decade primarily with the development of platforms such as Bitcoin and Ethereum, based on blockchain technology. Although the concept of blockchain was introduced in 2008 through bitcoin,[1] this technology is not a leap in technological progress. The first work on a cryptographically secured chain of blocks dates back to the beginning of 1990s,[2] while public-private key encryption and peer-to-peer public networks were developed in the late 1970s.[3]

1 As is well known, bitcoin is a decentralized digital currency without a central bank or single administrator that can be sent from user to user on the peer-to-peer bitcoin network without the need for intermediaries. Notwithstanding that the idea of having such a free currency without the need for banks and other subjects involved in the financial system gained significant popularity, what is even more interesting is the technology behind it. Bitcoin transactions are verified by network nodes through cryptography and recorded in a public distributed ledger called a blockchain. See Satoshi Nakamoto, 'Bitcoin: A Peer-to-Peer Electronic Cash System' (*Bitcoin Project: Introduction: White Paper*, 31 October 2008) <https://bitcoin.org/en/bitcoin-paper> accessed 29 February 2020.

2 See Aaron Wright and Primavera De Filippi, 'Decentralized Blockchain Technology and the Rise of Lex Cryptographia' (10 March 2015) 5, 10–11 <https://ssrn.com/abstract=2580664> accessed 29 February 2020; Helen Eenmaa-Dimitrieva and Maria José Schmidt-Kessen, 'Creating markets in no-trust environments: The law and economics of smart contracts' (2019) 35 *CLS Rev* 69, 71.

3 See Whitfield Diffie and Martin E Hellman, 'New Directions in Cryptography' (1976) 22 *IEEE Trans Inf Theory* 644; Ronald Linn Rivest, Adi Shamir, and Leonard Adleman, 'A Method for Obtaining Digital Signatures and Public-Key Cryptosystems' (1978) 21

DOI: 10.4324/9781003080596-12

A blockchain is a growing list of records called blocks that are linked using cryptography where each block contains a cryptographic hash of the previous block, a timestamp, and transaction data (generally represented as a Merkle tree).[4] In other words, blockchain is a decentralized, distributed digital ledger that is used to record transactions across many computers so that any involved record cannot be altered retroactively, without the alteration of all subsequent blocks.

At least four types of blockchain may be recognized in practice: (a) a public blockchain (fully decentralized, e.g. bitcoin), (b) a private blockchain (centralized – used within a certain company), (c) a hybrid blockchain (a combination of centralized and decentralized features), and (d) a consortium blockchain (partially decentralized – used by banking consortia). Also, it is possible to differentiate between permissionless and permissioned blockchain, considering whether there is the authority on a network level. Although public blockchains are usually considered to be permissionless while private and consortium blockchains are considered as permissioned blockchains, a combination of all types of blockchains is also possible.[5] The overview of the different types of blockchain is given here only to stress that potential positive application of blockchain technology (and smart contracts) to legal processes goes way beyond platforms such as Bitcoin and Ethereum.

2. The concept and main features of smart contracts

The story with smart contracts started in the 1990s. As is well known, Nick Szabo created the concept of the smart contract and defined it as a computerized transaction protocol executing terms of the contract.[6] However, the genuine development of smart contracts began with the evolution of blockchain technology. Smart contracts fall within the second generation of blockchain applications. They are built on a blockchain by extending the bitcoin

Commun ACM 120; Cat Hope and John Charles Ryan, *Digital Arts: An Introduction to New Media* (Bloomsbury 2014) 161.

4 See Bennett Garner, 'Merkle Tree Hashing: How Blockchain Verification Works' (*Coin Central*, 3 September 2018) <https://coincentral.com/merkle-tree-hashing-blockchain> accessed 29 February 2020; Nathan Reiff, 'Blockchain Explained' (*Investopedia*, 1 February 2020) <www.investopedia.com/terms/b/blockchain.asp> accessed 29 February 2020.

5 Vitalik Buterin, 'On Public and Private Blockchains' (*Ethereum Foundation Blog*, 7 August 2015) <https://blog.ethereum.org/2015/08/07/on-public-and-private-blockchains> accessed 29 February 2020; Shermin Voshmgir and Valentin Kalinov, 'Blockchain: A Beginners Guide' (BlockchainHub Berlin 2017) 13–17 <https://blockchainhub.net/blockchain-technology> accessed 29 February 2020; Rob Marvin, 'Blockchain: The Invisible Technology That's Changing the World' (*PCMag Australia*, 30 August 2017) <https://au.pcmag.com/features/46389/blockchain-the-invisible-technology-thats-changing-the-world> accessed 29 February 2020.

6 Nick Szabo, 'Smart Contracts' (1994) <www.fon.hum.uva.nl/rob/Courses/InformationInSpeech/CDROM/Literature/LOTwinterschool2006/szabo.best.vwh.net/smart.contracts.html> accessed 29 February 2020.

script languages, in some instances into a Turing complete system. Such extended script languages allow complex payment transactions. Some examples are payment conditional on external input confirming receipt of an item or sending out a signal that interrupts the starter of a car in the event that an interim payment for a car has not been received.[7]

Although blockchain technology is mostly underlying smart contracts, other forms of distributed ledgers may also be feasible with the concept of smart contracts.[8] Taking into consideration the current state of the art, this research primarily analyzes smart contracts based on a public blockchain such as the Ethereum; however, most of the discussion and conclusions presented within this chapter can be generalized to any contract concluded and/or executed via smart contracts systems.

There is no universally accepted definition of a smart contract. However, it is usually described as 'a computer code that programmatically executes transactions in accordance with pre-defined terms',[9] '[agreement] that [is] encoded in computer code and placed on a decentralized virtual structure',[10] 'a consensual arrangement between at least two parties for an automated, independent commercial result from the satisfaction or non-satisfaction, determined objectively through code, of a specific factual condition',[11] 'a special protocol intended to contribute, verify or implement the negotiations or performance of the contract without the interference of third parties in a traceable and irreversible manner',[12] or 'a sort of computer code which is operated by a computer and is self-executing and self-enforcing'.[13]

The idea behind smart contracts is to satisfy common contractual conditions, minimize exceptions both malicious and accidental, and minimize the need for trusted intermediaries such as banks or other kinds of agents.[14]

The concept of a smart contract is comparable to a concept of simple vending machines. One party sets up a vending machine on a public location. Another party wants a product from the vending machine. To collect the product, the party has to insert money into the machine. If a sufficient

7 See ibid; Eric Tjong Tjin Tai, 'Formalizing contract law for smart contracts' (2017) *Tilburg Private Law Working Paper Series* 6/2017, 2 <https://ssrn.com/abstract=3038800> accessed 29 February 2020.

8 Tjong Tjin Tai (n 7) 1.

9 Chamber of Digital Commerce, '"Smart Contracts" Legal Primer' (2018) 1 <https://digitalchamber.org/policy-positions/smart-contracts> accessed 29 February 2020.

10 Eenmaa-Dimitrieva and Schmidt-Kessen (n 2) 71.

11 David M Adlerstein, 'Are Smart Contracts Smart? A Critical Look at Basic Blockchain Questions' (*Coindesk*, 26 June 2017) <www.coindesk.com/when-is-a-smart-contract-actually-a-contract> accessed 29 February 2020.

12 Mateja Durovic and André Janssen, 'Formation of Smart Contracts under Contract Law' in Larry A DiMatteo, Michel Cannarsa, and Cristina Poncibò (eds), *The Cambridge Handbook of Smart Contracts, Blockchain Technology and Digital Platforms* (CUP 2019) 63.

13 ibid.

14 Szabo (n 6).

amount of money is inserted, the machine automatically releases the product the second party chose (clicked the button), while the first party will eventually collect money inserted into the vending machine. Smart contracts essentially work in the same way: they automatically enforce themselves once certain conditions are met.

There are several features smart contracts have or may have that may be appealing for various sectors of industry such as self-execution, anonymity, security, intermediation, and transparency.

Self-execution – that is, automatic execution of a contract by a computer program when a consensus has been reached – may be especially useful in situations where legal enforcement is not practical or is too costly for various reasons (other party unknown, situated far away, etc.). Specifically, parties do not have the freedom to breach the conditions of the contract, as it is executed remotely and in real-time.[15] Further on, unlike in traditional contracting relations, the use of smart contracts allows parties to preserve their identity while contracting with each other. Transactions made with public blockchain technology are public and shared. That creates transparency which has been considered to support the trustworthiness and security of the technology for accounting and transactions. At the same time, privacy is protected to an extent since users' identity is hidden behind pseudonyms.[16] Also, security is guaranteed since the distributed ledger is impregnable and immune to alteration. Many parties see the exclusion of the need for intermediary subjects, such as banks, lawyers, notaries, as very attractive. Also, smart contract technology creates an environment of trust as the logic and information in the contract is visible to all participants in the blockchain network.

By looking one-sidedly to potential positive features of smart contracts, some even go as far as seeing smart contracts as a complete replacement for lawyers and legal instruments. Such thinking is usually based on several claims such as: since the contract is constructed in a scripting language instead of in legally valid terms, this would allow the creation of contracts without the need for legal expertise; payment due to the contract could be executed automatically in the virtual currency, which would bypass traditional banks or other payment intermediaries; execution of the contract could be performed automatically without the possibility of interference by any party, and without the need for legal enforcement; as execution is performed on the blockchain, which arguably is difficult to influence by ordinary state force, the code of smart contracts is immutable by law and thereby operates outside of and in place of law.[17]

15 Maciej Hulicki, 'The Legal Framework and Challenges of Smart Contract Applications' (Sixteenth International Conference on Artificial Intelligence and Law, Workshop on Blockchain, Smart Contracts and Law, London, June 2017) 5 <www.cs.bath.ac.uk/smartlaw2017> accessed 29 February 2020.

16 Eenmaa-Dimitrieva and Schmidt-Kessen (n 2) 71.

17 See Tjong Tjin Tai (n 7) 2.

If generalized, such claims are completely unfounded and sometimes even dangerous. There are several concerns connected with the use and wide application of smart contracts. Such concerns are usually derived from the fact that smart contracts need to be translated in computer code, that no ex-post modification or deliberate breach is possible once a smart contract is placed on the blockchain, and that smart contracts may not comply with mandatory rules in contract law.[18]

First, smart contracts need to be written in a code which means that a computer expert is required for the translation of an agreement from human to computer language. That reintroduces an instance of intermediation that could possibly neutralize efficiency gains from automation. Further on, the coding of contracts precludes parties from adopting clauses that allow for desirable and necessary flexibility for adaptations of contracts to unforeseeable future scenarios. Often, and especially in the case of more complex relations, the meaning of certain provisions must not be interpreted literally and needs to be adjusted with reasonable expectations, fairness, protection of weaker parties, and other interests that appear to find political and social support.[19] Also, there is a risk that the code might not run as envisaged due to potential bugs or imprecise coding.[20]

Second, self-execution is one of the features of smart contracts that is usually presented as one of its main benefits. However, smart contracts also have an immutable character. Once a smart contract is placed on a blockchain it is practically unstoppable – neither parties nor courts can effectively intervene ex-post regardless of possible changing circumstances. In the event of hardship, there is practically no way of stopping the execution of a contract when a trigger is evoked. Also, there is no feasible technical solution to remedy automatic performance gone wrong.[21, 22]

Third, there is a significant problem regarding the execution of invalid and illegal contracts and remedial issues. Due to their specific features, the use of smart contracts facilitates the execution of contracts that would be deemed invalid or illegal under contract law.[23] Thus, smart contracts seem to be at-

18 Eenmaa-Dimitrieva and Schmidt-Kessen (n 2) 74.

19 Tjong Tjin Tai (n 7) 4.

20 Eenmaa-Dimitrieva and Schmidt-Kessen (n 2) 74; Hulicki (n 15) 6.

21 See Eenmaa-Dimitrieva and Schmidt-Kessen (n 2) 74.

22 After the hacker attack in 2016, when a hacker or group of hackers drained funds from The DAO, hard fork was implemented on the blockchain system as a safeguard to protect the investors. Although the concept of a hard fork mechanism was shown to be efficient, that experience proved that legal businesses conducted through blockchain are not completely autonomous and adequately self-(un)regulated, and hence require effective legal protection. See Tjong Tjin Tai (n 7) 2. On Ethereum hard fork and return of DAO funds, see Michael del Castillo, 'Ethereum Executes Blockchain Hard Fork to Return DAO Funds' (*Coindesk*, 20 July 2016) <www.coindesk.com/ethereum-executes-blockchain-hard-fork-return-dao-investor-funds> accessed 29 February 2020.

23 See Mark Giancaspro, 'Is a "smart contract" really a smart idea? Insights from a legal perspective' (2017) 33 *CLS Rev* 825, 829; Eenmaa-Dimitrieva and Schmidt-Kessen (n 2) 74.

tractive method used by terrorists, smugglers, hackers, and other groups for their illegal activities.[24]

There are also some other critiques raised regarding the application of smart contracts such as the issue of confidentiality and unreliable inputs.[25] Nevertheless, if used in accordance with an established legal system and needs of a certain relationship in the market, smart contracts may improve particular legal mechanisms and have certain benefits for society in general.

3. The application of smart contracts to legal relations

The term 'smart contract' is far from being a proper term that would adequately describe what lies behind it. It is frequently misunderstood and used incorrectly, which creates unnecessary and potentially harmful confusion, especially from the legal perspective.

As it could be inferred from the above, smart contracts are neither smart nor legal contracts per se. It should be noted that the term 'smart contract' was not chosen by lawyers or other professionals directly involved in legal systems but by IT developers and other progressive thinkers who found the merging of law and code appealing.[26, 27]

On the one side, smart contracts have not achieved high artificial intelligence technology to develop their own 'thinking'. They do not possess (and cannot learn by themselves) necessary knowledge of contract law to safeguard the expectations and interests of parties, and how contract law rules might or might not be implemented in smart contracts.[28] On the other side, smart contracts do not automatically fulfil obligations law requirements for the formation of a contract.[29]

As well as the technology behind it, the idea of combining such reactive software agents with certain legal processes is not a novelty. Such a concept had already been discussed before in the literature on artificial intelligence and technology, independently of the sudden recent popularity of the application

24 Ari Juels, Ahmed Kosba, and Elaine Shi, 'The Ring of Gyges: Using Smart Contracts for Crime' in 'Association for Computing Machinery, CCS '16: Proceedings of the 2016 ACM SIGSAC Conference on Computer and Communications Security' (ACM 2016); Giancaspro (n 22) 833.

25 See Manjunatha G Kukkuru, 'Smart Contracts: Introducing A Transparent Way to Do Business' (*Infosys*) <www.infosys.com/insights/digital-future/smart-contracts.html> accessed 29 February 2020.

26 See Florian Idelberger, 'Connected Contracts Reloaded – Smart Contracts as Contractual Networks' in Stefan Grundmann (ed), *European Contract Law in the Digital Age* (Intersentia 2018) 215.

27 Some authors suggest even a new term 'lex cryptographia' to denote an emerging branch of law comprising self-enforcing contracts and decentralized autonomous organizations. See Wright and De Filippi (n 2) 48–51.

28 See Tjong Tjin Tai (n 7) 4.

29 Merit Kõlvart, Margus Poola, and Addi Rull, 'Smart Contracts' in Tanel Kerikmäe and Addi Rull (eds), *The Future of Law and eTechnologies* (Springer 2016) 140.

of blockchain technologies.[30] In the 1990s, there was research about how to display or digitalize legal agreements, such as semantic formats and ontologies/knowledge-bases designed to make legal rules accessible to machines, and the first notions of digital agents acting in a legal capacity were introduced, but without the networked, decentralized system for record-keeping, security, and enforcement. This concept was potentially the predecessor of what we discuss today under smart contracts. Later, in technical research, the term 'agreement technologies' was coined. It describes technologies used to negotiate or conclude agreements between physical or digital agents, independently of whether somewhere along the line a contract is concluded or not.[31]

Legal systems tend to be slow in comparison to technology development. Whereas the development of the first is linear, the development of the latter is exponential. Nevertheless, through time many technological novelties have been recognized and accepted. Thus, nowadays use of email and video communication, instant messaging, e-contracting, digital databases, software applications, etc. has become a normal occurrence in law, while bitcoin was acknowledged as a contractual mean of payment[32] – all of which was exotic at the time it was developed. There is no reason why the use of smart contracts should be any different.

Still, it should be noted that smart contracts are not congruent with contracts in a legal sense and therefore should not be automatically identified with the law (or be seen as an alternative to the legal system). Smart contracts should be recognized within the law as contracts or part of a contract only under certain circumstances – if they fulfil prescribed requirements to produce legal effects. Even where the use of smart contracting might exclude the need to enforce contract terms in a court, it does not set aside the jurisdiction. There should always be a possibility for a party to protect its right before a competent court or other body.[33]

4. Smart contracts within contract law

One of the main principles of the contract law system is private autonomy and freedom of contract.

Legal systems have already acknowledged various forms for the conclusion of agreements other than written on paper or oral. Thus, contracts may

30 See Giovanni Sartor, 'Cognitive Automata and the Law: Electronic Contracting and the Intentionality of Software Agents' (2009) 17 *AI&L* 253; Giovanni Sartor, 'Intentional compliance with normative systems' (2012) *EUI Working Paper Law* 27/2012 <https://ssrn.com/abstract=2201459> accessed 29 February 2020.

31 See Idelberger (n 26) 218.

32 See Case C-264/14 *Skatteverket v David Hedqvist* [2015] ECLI:EU:C:2015:718; Georgios Dimitropoulos, 'Global Currencies and Domestic Regulation: Embedding through Enabling?' in Philipp Hacker and others (eds), *Regulating Blockchain: Techno-Social and Legal Challenges* (OUP 2019) 122–24.

33 See Kõlvart, Poola, and Rull (n 29) 137.

be concluded via telephone, email, instant messenging, video calls, online platforms, by conduct, etc. What contract law systems in general require is that statement of willingness is made freely and in a serious manner. Formal requirements for contracts are relatively rare and are prescribed only for specific contractual relationships to preserve and protect the interests of certain parties.

Accordingly, there is no reason why a contract concluded via a reactive software agent, such as a smart contract, would not be valid and recognized in a legal system. However, whether such a contract would satisfy a qualified written or notarized form, required for some contractual relations, is a further question and is still disputable. For instance, if a simple financial transaction is concluded and executed via smart contract, it should already be valid under the applicable law. However, as to the question whether a real-estate purchase could be concluded and executed via smart contract, the answer is probably no at this moment, at least in systems that require written form (which even then may be considered to be satisfied) and entry into a land registry. It is probable that competent authorities would also take similar positions for other contracts that require entry into public registers or notarized forms. Nevertheless, it is still necessary to develop sufficient practice to take some solid standpoints on this matter.

For a smart contract to become a legal contract the legal requirements prescribed by contract law must be fulfilled. During the last couple of years, many papers have been written on this subject and it should be clear by now that smart contracts are not parallel to or exempt from the national law of obligations. For example, in the Croatian legal system, an obligation law contract is a two (or more) sided legal act directed at the creation of obligation law relationship.[34] The Croatian Obligations Act prescribes that a contract is concluded when the contracting parties have reached an agreement on the essential elements of the contract.[35] Formation of a contract generally requires an offer and acceptance, mutual intent to create a legal relationship, and capacity. Similar provisions regulating the formation of a contract can be found in comparative legislations, as well as in the United Nations Convention on Contracts for the International Sale of Goods (CISG), UNIDROIT Principles of International Commercial Contracts (UPICC), Principles of European Contract Law (PECL), and Draft Common Frame of Reference (DCFR). If a smart contracting solution is used in a legal contract, the obligation law rules must be taken into consideration. Otherwise, a smart contract would not form a contract and therefore would not be legally binding. A smart contract is only binding if the parties have agreed upon the essential requirements needed for the conclusion of a contract.

34 Petar Klarić and Mladen Vedriš, *Građansko pravo* (13th edn, Narodne novine 2012) 401.
35 Obligations Act (*Zakon o obveznim odnosima*), *NN* 35/2005, 41/2008, 125/2011, 78/2015, 29/2018, Art 247.

Such general requirements of contract law may be found in contracts concluded via smart contracts. The posting of the on-chain smart contract on the blockchain can be considered as an offer since the binary code posted on a blockchain precisely specifies the terms of the transaction. Once the proposed smart contract is posted on the blockchain, it is capable of acceptance by the offeree. This acceptance can also be done by conduct. The action of uploading digital asset (cryptocurrency, money, or a digital representation of an offline asset) provides an unequivocal communication of acceptance. Thus, acceptance can occur either by performance or by authorization of transfer through putting in the special cryptographic key. Further, to be valid and enforceable, smart contracts must contain a certain exchange of promises. Since smart contracts usually entail the exchange of digital assets for certain content of offer, such conceptually and pragmatically sufficient consideration will normally be present. Such contracts may be comparable to conditioned contracts. The intention is generally presumed. Capacity is not discussed, but can be subject to ex-post evaluation.[36]

Herein it should also be noted that smart contracts may be used for the conclusion and execution of the contract as well as only for the execution of the contract concluded without the use of smart contract technology. Thus, it is possible to differentiate fully automated or pure smart contracts and partially automated or execution smart contracts.[37] Having in mind limitations of coding and underlying algorithms, fully automated or pure smart contracts might only be suitable for simple contractual relationships – at least until more sophisticated artificial intelligence technology is implemented in smart contract systems. On the other side, partially automated or execution smart contracts can already be used as an effective tool for contract enforcement besides the actual legal contract.

All in all, it seems that there is no need for special regulation of smart contracts. Smart contracts are definitely not contracts per se. Only if a contract concluded via smart contract fulfilled all necessary requirements of contract law would that contract be qualified as a legally binding contract or as a mean of execution of a contract. It is true that legal systems are sluggish and often are unprepared for challenges brought up by technological development. However, any ad hoc solutions are not preferable. Most legal systems already have solid obligations law regulation and it is only necessary to widen understanding of smart contracts and blockchain technology primarily among lawyers so that proper interpretation of existing legal provisions may be applied to potential cases dealing with this specific subject matter.

36 On requirements of smart contracts on contract formation see Durovic and Janssen (n 12).

37 See ibid; Kristian Lauslahti, Juri Matilla, and Timo Seppälä, 'Smart Contracts – How Will Blockchain Technology Affect Contractual Practices?' (2017) *ETLA Reports* 68/2017, 21–22 <https://ssrn.com/abstract=3154043> accessed 29 February 2020.

Some countries such as Italy[38] and Liechtenstein[39] have already introduced special legislation on smart contracts. However, such legal intervention is not necessarily needed. What may be useful is to have a uniform terminology and defined concepts for the application of smart contracts and blockchain technology. Thus, for EU Member States, rather than enacting specific regulations on a national level, the most practical solution might be to introduce a soft law document which would provide uniform terminology and general definition of concepts and processes involved in smart contracting and the application of blockchain technology.

5. Application of smart contracts

There is vast scope for the application of smart contracts to various industries and relationships in the market. Smart contracts have the potential to introduce radical changes in the way international business and trade is executed by speeding up transactions, reducing paperwork, and making processes cost-efficient.

Generally, smart contracts may be used for the conclusion of a simple contract but are not suitable, due to their limitations, to regulate complex relations. However, smart contracts may be used as an auxiliary method for more efficient and less costly execution of agreements. In such a way even more complex agreements may benefit from smart contract technology.

Several industries have already recognized the potential of smart contracts, although there is still much potential left for further growth in their importance and application. Nowadays, smart contracts based on public permissionless blockchain are mostly discussed. However, there are some indications that smart contracts based on permissioned blockchain technology should have a more important role than they have now, especially when they are custom-tailored for specific industry sectors. They might be used for payment of music royalties to authors and other rights holders, for sharing of health data in the public sector, for clearing and settlements in the banking sector, for creating an immutable record of goods along the supply chain,[40] and even for distribution of compensation for suffered damages resulting from the exercise of flight passengers' rights. For future application, it may also be useful if the platforms that host smart contracts would accept payments in all currencies instead of just cryptocurrency, which could potentially open some new markets suitable for smart contracts. In any event, the spread of smart

38 See Law Decree 135, 'Urgent provisions on support and simplification for businesses and the public administration' (*Decreto-legge* 135, '*Disposizioni urgenti in materia di sostegno e semplificazione per le imprese e per la pubblica amministrazione*'), *GU* 290 of 14 December 2018.

39 See Token and TT Service Providers Act (*Gezetz* of 3 October 2019 *über Token und VT-Dienstleister*), *LGBl* 301/2019.

40 Eenmaa-Dimitrieva and Schmidt-Kessen (n 2) 74.

contract application provides incentives for further growth and development of legal systems and society in general.

6. Smart contracts and human rights

As seen from the previous sections, there is still much discussion on whether and which rules of the legal system apply to smart contracts. The law is certainly applicable to relations entered or executed through smart contracts. If a certain violation occurs, one should not be deprived of legal protection. However, whether or not the legal framework and practice can be improved is a completely different question which should be put in focus. The use of smart contracts is still a relatively new business practice. Legal practice is very scarce – there is practically no concrete case law on this subject matter. For now, commentators are mostly focused on obligation law aspects of smart contracts. In all discussions of the pros and cons of smart contracts and their place in the legal system, one aspect is persistently neglected – that is, the issue of human rights and fundamental freedoms affected by the use of smart contracts.

With the development of technology and globalization, the subject of the protection of human rights and fundamental freedoms (with certain new formulations provided through international and national legal acts) only gains on its significance. In the European Union, the protection of fundamental rights is a horizontal question that affects all areas of activity of the EU. In other words, all competent bodies of the EU, regardless of their level and fields of competence, must take fundamental rights into consideration.[41]

The issue of the protection of human rights may not stay out of the context of digitalization and modernization of the human environment. Since many new ways have emerged to violate certain human rights, lawyers and practitioners must take additional efforts to interpret the existing legal acts and apply the relevant provisions to new occurrences emerging from the era of digitalization and development of new technologies, as well as to find an adequate response in the protection of human rights. Lawyers and especially human right experts should not run from advancement, nor that is possible. Yet it is necessary to actively participate in development so that law can promptly follow technological advancement to the benefit of society, especially in the field of human rights, which is often neglected.

Wide application of smart contracts opens the issue of protection of privacy. Privacy as a human right has been established through several international treaties. It is protected by Art 12 of the Universal Declaration of Human Rights[42] and Art 17 of the International Covenant on Civil and Po-

41 There is also a specialized body within the EU dealing with all matters directly connected with fundamental rights: Working Party on Fundamental Rights, Citizens Rights and Free Movement of Persons (FREMP).

42 Universal Declaration of Human Rights (adopted 10 December 1948) UNGA Res 217 A(III).

litical Rights.[43] Article 8 of the European Convention on Human Rights[44] guarantees 'right to respect for private and family life'. Similar to Art 8(1) ECHR, Art 7 of the Charter of Fundamental Rights of the European Union[45] states: 'Everyone has the right to respect for his or her private and family life, home and communications.' The Charter also provides special provisions on the protection of personal data that define the position of the person whose data is collected.[46] Standards of protection of privacy and protection of personal data are additionally regulated within national legislation.[47]

Unquestionably, technologies might help in the protection of human rights. Protection of personal data and the right to respect family life are important fundamental human rights and are not connected only to disturbances. Whether a right to privacy is adequately protected may significantly affect whether citizens would be willing to participate in the application of smart technologies. Protection of personal data is a fundamental right in the framework of the European Union law. The European Council and Parliament have proposed a legal package for the reform and modernization of personal data protection.[48] Thus, without strong protection of human rights and fundamental freedoms, the chances of the effective long-term application of smart contract technology are significantly reduced. If users start to feel threatened by the use of new technologies, they would surely avoid using them.

Due to the above-mentioned digital progress, the legal framework and case law are also gradually developing and adapting. Protection of human rights is faced with the new challenges in the fields of privacy, security, freedom of expression, among others. Also, some new fields are emerging such as the right to be forgotten, protection of identity, and anonymity. All of these are substantial issues that, in their initial phase of development, were considered as less important; however, in time they have gained a wider context and are

43 International Covenant on Civil and Political Rights (adopted 16 December 1966, entered into force 23 March 1976) 999 *UNTS* 171.

44 Convention for the Protection of Human Rights and Fundamental Freedoms (Rome, 4 November 1950), as amended (European Convention on Human Rights, ECHR).

45 Charter of Fundamental Rights of the European Union [2012] *OJ* C326/391 (Charter).

46 Charter, Art 8 reads:

1. Everyone has the right to the protection of personal data concerning him or her.
2. Such data must be processed fairly for specified purposes and on the basis of the consent of the person concerned or some other legitimate basis laid down by law. Everyone has the right of access to data which has been collected concerning him or her, and the right to have it rectified.
3. Compliance with these rules shall be subject to control by an independent authority.

47 For instance, Art 35 of the Constitution of the Republic of Croatia (*Ustav Republike Hrvatske, NN* 56/1990, 135/1997, 113/2000, 28/2001, 76/2010, 5/2014) guarantees everyone respect and the legal protection of one's personal and family life, dignity, and reputation.

48 See Council of the EU, 'Human rights and democracy in the world: 2018 EU annual report adopted' (Press release, 13 May 2019) 346/19.

gradually becoming part of the legal purview. Over the last couple of years, some important changes have occurred in the area of protection of privacy by the entering into force of GDPR.[49] Despite characteristics of smart contracts such as anonymity, security, and transparency, history has shown that even the most solid digital technologies have eventually been hacked. Thus, it is important not to neglect the privacy issue even in the use of smart contracts.

This wide presentation of the impact of digitalization and modernization of technology leads to a certain wariness of practitioners regarding smart contracts, primarily due to ignorance of the modalities for the protection of rights in the challenges of new technologies. One of the questions that emerges from the use of smart contract technology is the protection of the right of ownership. The conventional and constitutional aspect imposes discussions about the impact of smart contracts on potential breaches of ownership right protected by Art 1 of Protocol 1 to the ECHR. Blockchain is practically a giant spreadsheet for the registration of property and an accounting system for business on a global scale, which may include all kinds of property possessed by users around the world. Such a system demands reflection on the levels and protections of ownership, which may be brought into question due to the immutable character of smart contracts.

7. Conclusion

Taking into consideration all the pros and cons, generally the application of smart contracts may encourage the development of the legal system and society in general. However, smart contracts do not seem suitable for complex relationships. Thus, contracts concluded through smart contracts should only be used for simple transactions, while for more complex relations smart contracts seem like an efficient tool for the execution of regular contracts, especially in situations where regular legal enforcement is not practical or too costly.

The current legal regulation applicable to the use of smart contracts is solid and there is no need for a completely new regulatory system. What should be improved is the general understanding of smart contracts and blockchain technology especially among lawyers. The system is effective and has future potential; however, it does have flaws and, as always, disputes do and will occur. Soft law documents, preferably on the EU level, may help competent courts and other bodies to understand the concept of smart contracts and how to approach them in case of a dispute.

After several pieces of research in that field, the obligations law aspect of the smart contract seems clear. What still remains completely undiscussed is the human rights aspect of smart contracts. In the application of smart

49 Regulation (EU) 2016/679 of the European Parliament and of the Council of 27 April 2016 on the protection of natural persons with regard to the processing of personal data and on the free movement of such data, and repealing Directive 95/46/EC (General Data Protection Regulation) [2016] *OJ* L119/1 (GDPR).

contracts, several concerns may raise potential human rights and fundamental freedoms violations. Some of them are likely to be the right to privacy and the right to ownership. Therefore, more focus should be put on those specific aspects of the law in future research.

Bibliography

Adlerstein DM, 'Are Smart Contracts Smart? A Critical Look at Basic Blockchain Questions' (*Coindesk*, 26 June 2017) <www.coindesk.com/when-is-a-smart-contract-actually-a-contract> accessed 29 February 2020

Buterin V, 'On Public and Private Blockchains' (*Ethereum Foundation Blog*, 7 August 2015) <https://blog.ethereum.org/2015/08/07/on-public-and-private-blockchains> accessed 29 February 2020

Chamber of Digital Commerce, '"Smart Contracts" Legal Primer' (2018) 1 <https://digitalchamber.org/policy-positions/smart-contracts> accessed 29 February 2020

Council of the EU, 'Human rights and democracy in the world: 2018 EU annual report adopted' (Press release, 13 May 2019) 346/19

Del Castillo M, 'Ethereum Executes Blockchain Hard Fork to Return DAO Funds' (*Coindesk*, 20 July 2016) <www.coindesk.com/ethereum-executes-blockchain-hard-fork-return-dao-investor-funds> accessed 29 February 2020

Diffie W and Hellman ME, 'New Directions in Cryptography' (1976) 22 *IEEE Trans Inf Theory* 644 [DOI: https://doi.org/10.1109/tit.1976.1055638]

Dimitropoulos G, 'Global Currencies and Domestic Regulation: Embedding through Enabling?' in Hacker P and others (eds), *Regulating Blockchain: Techno-Social and Legal Challenges* (OUP 2019)

Durovic M and Janssen A, 'Formation of Smart Contracts under Contract Law' in DiMatteo LA, Cannarsa M, and Poncibò C (eds), *The Cambridge Handbook of Smart Contracts, Blockchain Technology and Digital Platforms* (CUP 2019) [DOI: https://doi.org/10.1017/9781108592239.004]

Eenmaa-Dimitrieva H and Schmidt-Kessen MJ, 'Creating markets in no-trust environments: The law and economics of smart contracts' (2019) 35 *CLS Rev* 69 [DOI: https://doi.org/10.1016/j.clsr.2018.09.003]

Garner B, 'Merkle Tree Hashing: How Blockchain Verification Works' (*Coin Central*, 3 September 2018) <https://coincentral.com/merkle-tree-hashing-blockchain> accessed 29 February 2020

Giancaspro M, 'Is a "smart contract" really a smart idea? Insights from a legal perspective' (2017) 33 *CLS Rev* 825 [DOI: https://doi.org/10.1016/j.clsr.2017.05.007]

Hope C and Ryan JC, *Digital Arts: An Introduction to New Media* (Bloomsbury 2014)

Hulicki M, 'The Legal Framework and Challenges of Smart Contract Applications' (Sixteenth International Conference on Artificial Intelligence and Law, Workshop on Blockchain, Smart Contracts and Law, London, June 2017) 5 <www.cs.bath.ac.uk/smartlaw2017> accessed 29 February 2020

Idelberger F, 'Connected Contracts Reloaded – Smart Contracts as Contractual Networks' in Grundmann S (ed), *European Contract Law in the Digital Age* (Intersentia 2018) [DOI: https://doi.org/10.1017/9781780686431.007]

Juels A, Kosba A, and Shi E, 'The Ring of Gyges: Using Smart Contracts for Crime' in 'Association for Computing Machinery, CCS '16: Proceedings of the 2016 ACM SIGSAC Conference on Computer and Communications Security' (ACM 2016) [DOI: https://doi.org/10.1145/2976749.2978362]

Klarić P and Vedriš M, *Građansko pravo* (13th edn, Narodne novine 2012)

Kõlvart M, Poola M, and Rull A, 'Smart Contracts' in Kerikmäe T and Rull A (eds), *The Future of Law and eTechnologies* (Springer 2016) [DOI: https://doi.org/10.1007/978-3-319-26896-5_7]

Kukkuru MG, 'Smart Contracts: Introducing A Transparent Way to Do Business' (*Infosys*) <www.infosys.com/insights/digital-future/smart-contracts.html> accessed 29 February 2020

Lauslahti K, Matilla J, and Seppälä T, 'Smart Contracts – How Will Blockchain Technology Affect Contractual Practices?' (2017) *ETLA Reports* 68/2017 <https://ssrn.com/abstract=3154043> accessed 29 February 2020

Marvin R, 'Blockchain: The Invisible Technology That's Changing the World' (*PCMag Australia*, 30 August 2017) <https://au.pcmag.com/features/46389/blockchain-the-invisible-technology-thats-changing-the-world> accessed 29 February 2020

Nakamoto S, 'Bitcoin: A Peer-to-Peer Electronic Cash System' (*Bitcoin Project: Introduction: White Paper*, 31 October 2008) <https://bitcoin.org/en/bitcoin-paper> accessed 29 February 2020

Reiff N, 'Blockchain Explained' (*Investopedia*, 1 February 2020) <www.investopedia.com/terms/b/blockchain.asp> accessed 29 February 2020

Rivest RL, Shamir A, and Adleman L, 'A Method for Obtaining Digital Signatures and Public-Key Cryptosystems' (1978) 21 *Commun ACM* 120 [DOI: https://doi.org/10.1145/359340.359342]

Sartor G, 'Cognitive Automata and the Law: Electronic Contracting and the Intentionality of Software Agents' (2009) 17 *AI&L* 253 [DOI: https://doi.org/10.1007/s10506-009-9081-0]

—— 'Intentional compliance with normative systems' (2012) *EUI Working Paper Law* 27/2012 <https://ssrn.com/abstract=2201459> accessed 29 February 2020

Szabo N, 'Smart Contracts' (1994) <www.fon.hum.uva.nl/rob/Courses/InformationInSpeech/CDROM/Literature/LOTwinterschool2006/szabo.best.vwh.net/smart.contracts.html> accessed 29 February 2020

Tjong Tjin Tai E, 'Formalizing contract law for smart contracts' (2017) *Tilburg Private Law Working Paper Series* 6/2017 <https://ssrn.com/abstract=3038800> accessed 29 February 2020

Voshmgir S and Kalinov V, 'Blockchain: A Beginners Guide' (BlockchainHub Berlin 2017) <https://blockchainhub.net/blockchain-technology> accessed 29 February 2020

Wright A and De Filippi P, 'Decentralized Blockchain Technology and the Rise of Lex Cryptographia' (10 March 2015) <https://ssrn.com/abstract=2580664> accessed 29 February 2020

Part III

Digital contracts, accounts, and services

11 How do terms of service agreements, as contracts of adhesion, influence users' digital accounts and their content?

Dubravka Klasiček

1. Introduction

During the course of a lifetime, a person concludes numerous contracts of adhesion, often without even being aware that a contract is being made. In today's society, many of these contracts are made online when a future user wants to open an account with an online service provider (OSP). There has to be a set of rules that govern a relationship between a user and an OSP concerning the account, its content, and everything else related. Since people from all over the world open accounts with OSPs located in different countries, the only possible way to conclude a contract containing these rules is to do it online in the form of a contract of adhesion. This type of contract is concluded after a user accepts a set of terms that are dictated by an OSP. There are a lot of advantages to concluding a contract this way, but there are also a lot of problems that derive from it.

The first part of this chapter will bring a short overview of contracts of adhesion in general, especially the rules of the Croatian Obligations Act (*Zakon o obveznim odnosima*,[1] ZOO) that pertain to them. The second part will deal with wrap contracts as a particular kind of contract of adhesion that are being concluded online. The third part will explain OSPs' stand on the (un)inheritability of a digital account and its content, according to their terms of service (TOS) agreements and the reasons behind these rules. The fourth part will explain what rights a user might have over digital content – does the user become its owner or something else?

2. Contracts of adhesion

Contracts of adhesion are contracts shaped by one party that has stronger bargaining power and are accepted by another party, usually with a weaker bargaining power (consumer in need of goods or services). The weaker party usually does not have the power to negotiate or influence the terms of the

1 *NN* 35/2005, 41/2008, 125/2011, 78/2015, 29/2018.

DOI: 10.4324/9781003080596-14

contract.[2] These types of contracts allow cheap and swift mass distribution of goods and services to a large number of consumers since contractual parties do not have expenses that are usually associated with the conclusion of ordinary contracts.[3] Contracts of adhesion have become the norm during the last century, first concerning the transportation of goods and persons, then in banking and insurance, now to become one of the principal ways to conclude contracts in most areas of business.[4]

In the Croatian legal system, Arts 295 and 296 ZOO outline contracts of adhesion. The offer to conclude a contract of adhesion is never directed to a certain person or persons, as is usually the case, but to an indeterminate number of people, because it is used by parties that conclude a large number of identical contracts, usually on a daily basis.[5] Their clauses cannot change – the party wanting to attain goods or services has to either accept all of the conditions set in the contract or decline it – the 'take it or leave it' principle.[6]

According to Art 295(4) ZOO, the conditions set in contracts of adhesion have to be communicated in a 'usual' or 'customary' manner to a party that is agreeing to them. Also, these contracts will be binding only if that party was or could have been aware of the conditions he or she is accepting.[7] One of the main characteristics of these types of contracts is a significant difference in the positions of the contracting parties: the party that is agreeing to conditions set in contracts of adhesion is usually a consumer in need of goods or services, with much weaker bargaining power compared to another party. Also, this weaker party usually feels the urgency to acquire the desired goods and services. The stronger party is therefore in a position to determine, without exception, the conditions under which a contract will be concluded.[8] All of this often results in consumers not being aware of the rules set in contracts of adhesion, either because the terms are not communicated in a 'usual' or a 'customary' way or because the party agreeing to them did not even read them, for whatever reason. These problems will be dealt with in more detail in the next part of the chapter.

2 Margaret Jane Radin, 'Online Standardization and the Integration of Text and Machine' (2002) 70 *Fordham L Rev* 1125, 1139–40. See also 'Adhesion Contract (Contract of Adhesion)' *Wex: Legal Dictionary & Encyclopedia* <www.law.cornell.edu/wex/adhesion_contract_(contract_of_adhesion)> accessed 27 February 2020.

3 Silvija Petrić, 'O nepravičnim klauzulama općih uvjeta ugovora u pravu Europske unije' (2002) 39 *Zbor Rad Prav Fak Split* 59, 60.

4 ibid 59; David Horton, 'Flipping the Script: Contra Proferentem and Standard Form Contracts' (2009) 80 *U Colo L Rev* 431, 438–47.

5 Petar Klarić and Martin Vedriš, *Građansko pravo* (14th edn, Narodne novine 2014) 407.

6 Natalie M Banta, 'Inherit the Cloud: The Role of Private Contracts in Distributing or Deleting Digital Assets at Death' (2014) 83 *Fordham L Rev* 799, 822.

7 ZOO, Art 295(5).

8 Zvonimir Slakoper, 'Nevaljanost pojedinih odredbi općih uvjeta ugovora s posebnim osvrtom na potrošačke ugovore' (2002) 22 *Zbor Prav Fak Rijeka* 181, 182.

However, for these reasons, it is very important for legislators to try to protect the consumer as a weaker party. When it comes to other types of contracts, the parties' freedom to contract, primarily to decide what will or will not be a part of their contract, prevents legislators from meddling too much into the contents of the contract.[9] However, with contracts of adhesion, there is an actual need to create mandatory rules on what clauses, if put in these contracts, will cause them to become null and void. This is exceptionally important since contracts of adhesion are concluded with a large number of consumers on a daily basis. If their content is not in accordance with the basic principles of law, these contracts might harm many people every day.[10]

Accordingly, in Croatian law, ZOO determines that the provisions of contracts of adhesion which, contrary to the principle of good faith, cause apparent inequality in the rights and obligations of the parties, to the detriment of the party that is agreeing to conditions set in the contract or to jeopardize the achievement of the purpose of the contract, will be null and void. This will even be the case if the conditions contained in the contract of adhesion were approved by the competent authority.[11] According to Art 296(3) ZOO, this will not be applied to those provisions the contents of which were taken from the legal regulations or negotiated individually prior to the conclusion of the contract so the other party may have influenced their content, and to the provisions concerning the object and the price of the contract if these were clear, understandable, and easily discernible.

Article 320 ZOO also states that in the case that the contract has been concluded according to the previously printed content or when the contract was otherwise prepared and proposed by one contracting party, if there are any unclear provisions, they will be interpreted in favour of the other party (in the case of contracts of adhesion, in favour of the consumer).[12]

3. Terms of service agreements – wrap contracts

In the twenty-first century, contracts of adhesion are becoming more and more relevant, largely due to the increased number of digitally signed contracts and 'wrap' contracts.[13] When a person wants to open an account with a certain OSP, he or she has to agree to the rules determined by an OSP that are set in TOS agreements. These rules govern the user's relationship with an OSP.[14] TOS agreements are contracts of adhesion that are concluded usually

9 ZOO, Art 2; Klarić and Vedriš (n 5) 8.
10 Petrić (n 3) 61.
11 ZOO, Art 296(1).
12 See also Horton, 'Flipping the Script' (n 4) 437.
13 See 'Adhesion Contract' (n 2).
14 Suzanne B Walsh, 'Coming Soon to a Legislature Near You: Comprehensive State Law Governing Fiduciary Access to Digital Assets' (2014) 8 *Charleston L Rev* 429, 431. Among other things, TOS agreements contain clauses that determine the applicable law, the

after a user clicks 'I agree' at the bottom of these terms or if a user continues to browse a certain web page containing a link that can take him or her to the TOS.[15]

It is undeniable that it would be impossible to make a contract between a user and an OSP in any other way than the one they are made in.[16] A TOS agreement made in the form of a digital contract of adhesion certainly benefits users, for it enables them to access various online platforms from the comfort of their homes. But these agreements benefit OSPs even more, since by drafting them OSPs protect themselves from lawsuits, limit their liability, and reduce risks and uncertainty that are associated with new technologies and business models.[17]

TOS agreements are usually referred to as wrap contracts and there are two basic types of wrap contracts (or agreements) – clickwrap and browsewrap.[18] Clickwrap agreements are concluded when the user accepts all of the conditions, which in no case means that the user has actually read them. The user will accept these conditions by clicking at the bottom that he or she is

---

possibility of transfer of an account to other persons, deletion after a certain period of inactivity, and the rights that the user has over digital content. Sometimes a TOS agreement decides the fate of an account after its holder dies. See Tyler G Tarney, 'A Call for Legislation to Permit the Transfer of Digital Assets at Death' (2012) 40 *Cap U L Rev* 773, 779; Ashley F Watkins, 'Digital Properties and Death: What Will Your Heirs Have Access to After You Die?' (2014) 62 *Buff L Rev* 193, 216; Nancy S Kim, 'The Wrap Contract Morass' (2014) 44 *Sw L Rev* 309.

15 Tin Matić, 'Formularni ugovori u elektroničkom obliku (Sklapanje ugovora klikom miša – elektroničkim očitovanjem volje putem Interneta na web stranici – *click wrap* i *browse wrap* ugovori)' (2008) 58 *Zbor Prav Fak Zagreb* 779; Anthony C Eichler, '"Owning" What You "Buy": How iTunes Uses Federal Copyright Law to Limit Inheritability of Content, and the Need to Expand the First Sale Doctrine to Include Digital Assets' (2016) 16 *Hous Bus & Tax LJ* 208, 217–18.

16 Adam Gatt, 'Electronic Commerce – Click-Wrap Agreements: The Enforceability of Click-Wrap Agreements' (2002) 18 *CLS Rev* 404, 405.

17 Nancy S Kim, 'Exploitation by Wrap Contracts – Click "Agree"' (2014) 39 *California Bar IP Journal* 10; Kim, 'The Wrap Contract Morass' (n 14) 315.

18 Other than clickwrap and browsewrap agreements, there are also shrinkwrap agreements that are used especially for computer games and software. These agreements are packed with the product in a shrinkwrap plastic wrapping and can be read only after the product has arrived and been unwrapped by the purchaser (thus the name, shrinkwrap). A contract is made if the buyer remains passive and fails to reject the terms. See Matić (n 15) 786–89; Horton, 'Flipping the Script' (n 4) 434. There are also combinations of these types of contracts, called multi-wrap contracts: click-browsewrap (eg Facebook Terms of Use). (They are like browsewrap agreements because the terms are visible only if a user clicks on a hyperlink, but also like clickwrap agreements because a user has to click 'Sign Up' to assent to the terms viewed on a hyperlink.) There are also rolling clickwrap agreements that combine the form of shrinkwrap agreements, but its terms are presented in a clickwrap or browsewrap form. See Nancy S Kim, 'Wrap Contracting and the Online Environment: Causes and Cures' in John A Rothchild (ed), *Research Handbook on Electronic Commerce Law* (Edward Elgar 2016) 25–26; Allison S Brehm and Cathy D Lee, 'Click Here to Accept the Terms of Service' (2015) 31 *Comm Law* 4, 4–6.

agreeing to them, and therefore he or she is consenting to TOS in a direct way, as one would by signing a document.[19] With browsewrap agreements, it is implied that the user is agreeing to TOS merely by browsing the web page of an OSP (primary page) which contains the link that can take him or her to the page containing TOS (secondary page), regardless of whether he or she has actually clicked on it.[20] With browsewrap agreements, the user's consent is not given in a direct way and can only be deduced from his or her behaviour.[21]

No matter what format TOS agreements are made in, it should come as no surprise that they are seldom read. Maybe two people in a thousand actually read TOS agreements and most of those that do so read only certain parts.[22] Because of this, consumers are not aware of how these types of contracts affect their rights.[23] There are many reasons for users not reading TOS agreements. They are usually long, unclear to an average person, and their content might be scattered all over the web page on various hyperlinks.[24] Also, TOS agreements have no real alternative because users cannot influence their content. Therefore, users see no sense in reading them, since there is nothing they could do to change them. They can consent to them or forego the web page altogether.[25]

19 Kim, 'Wrap Contracting and the Online Environment' (n 18) 18-21.

20 Matić (n 15) 779; Joseph Ronderos, 'Is Access Enough?: Addressing Inheritability of Digital Assets Using the Three-Tier System Under the Revised Uniform Fiduciary Access to Digital Assets Act' (2017) 18 *Tenn J Bus L* 1031, 1052.

21 Kim, 'Wrap Contracting and the Online Environment' (n 18) 21-23.

22 Kristina Sherry, 'What Happens to Our Facebook Accounts When We Die?: Probate Versus Policy and the Fate of Social-Media Assets Postmortem' (2012) 40 *Pepp L Rev* 185, 205; Sandi S Varnado, 'Your Digital Footprint Left Behind at Death: An Illustration of Technology Leaving the Law Behind' (2014) 74 *La L Rev* 719, 747-48. Kim differentiates between the ordinary 'reasonable' people, who do not read TOS agreements and 'judicially constructed, hyper-vigilant and entirely fictitious versions of "reasonable" people', who read it: Kim, 'The Wrap Contract Morass' (n 14) 316.

23 For example, in 2013, Google announced that it would use its user's information in paid advertisements, so when a user of one of Google's services endorsed or followed a certain company, that endorsement can show up on another one of Google's sites. They claimed that the users consented to it because they consented to TOS, regardless of the fact that this was a new feature and was introduced in Google's updated TOS. The users were not aware of the implications this change in TOS has, until they saw their faces being used to advertise something they had no intention of advertising to a broad audience. See Kim, 'Exploitation by Wrap Contracts' (n 17) 10.

24 Nancy S Kim, 'The Duty to Draft Reasonably and Online Contracts' in Larry A DiMatteo and others (eds), *Commercial Contract Law: Transatlantic Perspectives* (CUP 2013) 198; Eichler (n 15) 217; Ronderos (n 20) 1055-56.

25 Radin (n 2) 1135; Shelly Kreiczer-Levy and Ronit Donyets-Kedar, 'Better Left Forgotten: An Argument against Treating Some Social Media and Digital Assets as Inheritance in an Era of Platform Power' (2019) 84 *Brook L Rev* 703, 722–23.

Furthermore, most users are optimistic and do not believe they will suffer any harm from an OSP to whose TOS they are agreeing.[26] Users might not even be aware of the existence of TOS or they simply believe these terms are harmless. Besides, users are usually eager to acquire goods and services, so they click 'I agree' without reading what they are agreeing to, in order to obtain what they want as soon as possible.[27] Likewise, even if a diligent user reads a TOS agreement, an OSP can change it without notifying the user or asking for his or her consent to changes, which is one more reason for users not bothering to read these agreements.[28]

Despite users not reading TOS agreements and despite them being presented in a way that might obscure their legally binding nature, TOS agreements are binding contracts between users and OSPs.[29] An important issue, when it comes to the content of TOS agreements, is the fact that OSPs often fill them with terms that give them an advantage over users, but which might not have anything to do with what the user is anticipating from an OSP; or they try to hide crucial provisions that regulate the user's rights over digital content among other, more harmless provisions.[30] It often seems that OSPs draft these types of contracts in ways to obscure their content.[31] They could certainly draft them in a way to make them more noticeable and transparent, but choose not to do so, since wrap contracts obviously reflect the favouring of OSPs over individual interests.[32] And as futile as it is to read a TOS agreement, the burden to do so is placed upon the user, who cannot later justify him or herself by stating that he or she did not read the TOS agreement.[33]

26 Kim, 'Exploitation by Wrap Contracts' (n 17) 11.

27 ibid.

28 Banta, 'Inherit the Cloud' (n 6) 819; Laura McCarthy, 'Digital Assets and Intestacy' (2015) 21 *BU J Sci & Tech L* 384, 390–91; Kim, 'Wrap Contracting and the Online Environment' (n 18) 12–13.

29 Kim, 'The Duty to Draft Reasonably' (n 24) 181; McCarthy (n 28) 390.

30 Gatt (n 16) 408; Kim, 'The Duty to Draft Reasonably' (n 24) 182; Kim, 'The Wrap Contract Morass' (n 14) 310; Eichler (n 15) 218–20; Andrej Savin, *EU Internet Law* (2nd edn, Edward Elgar 2017) 274, fn 33. For example, users who want to buy goods from a web page are not aware that, in turn, they are giving an OSP a permission to access their private information and use it. Users probably believe that they are agreeing to policies defining the sale and delivery of goods, not to something that has nothing to do with what they think is the purpose of said OSP. For example, see Amazon, 'Amazon Privacy Notice' (Amazon: Legal Policies, last updated 1 January 2020) <www.amazon.com/gp/help/customer/display.html?nodeId=468496> accessed 26 February 2020.

31 Kim, 'The Duty to Draft Reasonably' (n 24) 200.

32 Kim, 'The Wrap Contract Morass' (n 14) 312, 319. There are a number of ways in which OSPs can make TOS more transparent. See Brehm and Lee (n 18) 6–7.

33 Kim, 'The Duty to Draft Reasonably' (n 24) 187–88; Eichler (n 15) 219. Kim states that not only users but businesses also are to blame for users not reading TOS agreements, since they feel no great need to make reading convenient. The duty to draft these agreements reasonably (instead of merely giving reasonable notice of the existence of TOS) would move the burden from the user to an OSP, who is in a much better position to deal with it. See Kim, 'The Duty to Draft Reasonably' (n 24) 189–94.

4. Inheritability of digital accounts and its content (digital assets[34])

Not so long ago, many items that now exist in a digital form, such as photos, documents, receipts, bills, music, and videos, were tangible or were fixed on a tangible media such as CDs or DVDs. When somebody died, all of these tangible items were part of their estate and were passed on to their heirs.[35] Now, it is common for these items to be digitized and stored on computers, smartphones, flash drives, email accounts, clouds, social media, blogs, etc.[36] All of these items (and more) constitute digital assets.[37]

Most people view themselves as owners of their digital assets, which is not inaccurate for a lot of them.[38] However, when it comes to digital assets stored on OSPs' servers (digital accounts and their content, which this part of the chapter is dealing with), it is obvious that traditional principles of property and succession law cannot be applied, as long as contracts like TOS agreements, shaped entirely by OSPs, determine what can or cannot be done with them. To clarify: on one hand, these digital assets are certainly some form of a 'thing' with 'property-like' aspects, so it is not surprising that the users view them as their property; on the other hand, they are also a 'creature of contract' because they are created by TOS agreements and moulded solely by the needs and policies of OSPs.[39]

Before this chapter starts dealing with ways OSPs handle digital assets' inheritability, one question should be answered: should these assets be inheritable at all? Most authors agree that they should and proceed to state numerous advantages to this. For example, many digital assets have real monetary value (blog contents, manuscripts, music or videos in a digital form, characters for online computer games,[40] domain names, sellers' eBay accounts, contents of

34 In this section, the term 'digital assets' refers only to digital accounts opened with an OSP and its content.

35 Michael D Walker, 'The New Uniform Digital Assets Law: Estate Planning and Administration in the Information Age' (2017) 52 *Real Prop Tr & Est LJ* 51, 52.

36 Dubravka Klasiček, 'Digital Inheritance' in Dražen Barković and others, *IMR 2018: Interdisciplinary Management Research XIV* (Josip Juraj Strossmayer University of Osijek, Faculty of Economics 2018) 105.

37 For more on what constitutes digital assets, see Gerry W Beyer and Naomi Cahn, 'When You Pass on, Don't Leave the Passwords Behind: Planning for Digital Assets' (2012) 26 *Probate Prop* 40, 41; Sherry (n 22) 193–204; Jamie P Hopkins, 'Afterlife in the Cloud: Managing a Digital Estate' (2013) 5 *Hastings Sci & Tech LJ* 209, 211–12; Banta, 'Inherit the Cloud' (n 6) 801–2.

38 This is true for locally stored assets – assets stored on devices owned by the decedent. Matthew Slaughter, 'The Barriers of Facebook's Terms of Service Agreement: Hardship Placed on Fiduciaries Access to Digital Assets' (2015) 24 *I & CTL* 183, 187.

39 Natalie M Banta, 'Property Interests in Digital Assets: The Rise of Digital Feudalism' (2017) 38 *Cardozo L Rev* 1099, 1101.

40 When it comes to online games, it is interesting to mention that a few years ago, the most valuable digital assets sold was a virtual space station on Entropia Universe, which is an online gaming platform. It was sold for $635,000. Sasha A Klein and Mark R Parthemer,

a celebrity's social media profile).[41] Even if they were worthless, they certainly have great emotional value to friends and family of the decedent.[42] Also, copyright is inheritable, so if an artist had artwork in a digital form, his or her heirs will inherit copyright, but will not be able to access the decedent's creations and control their distribution, if the artist's digital account and its content are not inheritable.[43]

Furthermore, social media is used as a coping mechanism for a decedent's family and friends. After a person dies, his or her family and friends will often seek answers and closure by accessing the decedent's email and social media accounts.[44] In addition, nowadays, there are fewer and fewer tangible items containing information about people's lives, finances, and businesses, since they are usually in a digital form. It is reasonable to expect that it will soon be impossible to go through probate proceedings without having access to the decedent's digital accounts. Data stored on digital accounts might provide valuable estate and property information, both known and unknown to heirs.[45] This is extraordinarily important if a decedent conducted his or her business exclusively online.[46] Likewise, many people receive their utility and other bills online. If the decedent's accounts are not accessed, these bills might keep coming, without anybody knowing about them. In that case,

---

'Who Will Delete the Digital You: Understanding Fiduciary Access to Digital Assets' (2016) 30 *Probate Prop* 3, 32.

41 Lilian Edwards and Edina Harbinja, 'Protecting Post-Mortem Privacy: Reconsidering the Privacy Interests of the Deceased in a Digital World' (2013) 32 *Cardozo Arts & Ent LJ* 101, 106; Banta, 'Inherit the Cloud' (n 6) 814; Matt Borden, 'Covering Your Digital Assets: Why Stored Communications Act Stands in the Way of Digital Inheritance' (2014) 75 *Ohio St LJ* 405, 429; Edina Harbinja, 'Virtual Worlds – a Legal Post-Mortem Account' (2014) 11 *SCRIPTed* 273, 286; Edina Harbinja, 'Virtual Worlds Players – Consumers or Citizens' (2014) 3 (4) *Internet Pol'y Rev* 1, 4–5 <https://policyreview.info/articles/analysis/virtual-worlds-players-consumers-or-citizens> accessed 26 February 2020.

42 Robert E Calem, 'What Happens to Your Online Accounts When You Die' (*Techlicious*, 29 June 2010) <www.techlicious.com/how-to/what-happens-to-your-online-accounts-when-you-die> accessed 27 February 2020; Edwards and Harbinja (n 41) 107; Slaughter (n 38) 185.

43 Borden (n 41) 431; Edina Harbinja, 'Post-Mortem Social Media: Law and Facebook After Death' in David Mangan and Lorna E Gillies, *The Legal Challenges of Social Media* (Edward Elgar 2017) 191–92; McCarthy (n 28) 387; Walker (n 35) 54–55.

44 Borden (n 41) 431–32. A decedent's loved ones sometimes create online memorial sites to serve as emotional outlets: Carrie Arnold, 'How to Manage Your Digital Afterlife' (*Scientific American*, 1 September 2013) <www.scientificamerican.com/article/how-to-manage-your-digital-afterlife> accessed 27 February 2020; Jed R Brubaker and Vanessa Callison-Burch, 'Legacy Contact: Designing and Implementing Post-mortem Stewardship at Facebook' in *CHI '16: Proceedings of the 2016 CHI Conference on Human Factors in Computing Systems* (Association for Computing Machinery 2016) 2908.

45 Banta, 'Inherit the Cloud' (n 6) 811; Naomi Cahn, 'Probate Law Meets the Digital Age' (2014) 67 *Vand L Rev* 1697, 1705; McCarthy (n 28) 396–98.

46 Tarney (n 14) 785–87; Walker (n 35) 70–71.

these will accumulate and stay unpaid, which might result in penalties.[47] All of this, and more, is the reason why most agree that inheritability of digital assets is extremely important.

4.1 Ownership of an account and its content

Treating digital assets stored on OSPs servers as ordinary property might be questionable.[48] However, it cannot be denied that users have a number of rights that amount to rights any owner has over his or her things. This is probably why users consider these digital assets to be their property and thus inheritable.[49]

For example, users have the right to possess digital assets – when they are logged into an account, but even when they are not.[50] Users also have the right to use their accounts for the reason they were designed for – to transmit data, store and share documents, videos, or pictures, modify accounts, delete content. They can, likewise, exclude others from using and accessing their digital assets, which is often prescribed by the TOS agreement itself – users are usually prohibited from sharing their log-in information with anybody.[51]

One of the typical rights an owner has is the right to dispose of an asset (e.g. to sell, donate, or leave to one's heirs). With digital assets, one has to differentiate between two objects: account content and the account itself. While users usually have the right to transfer digital content – often, that is the very nature of it – the account itself cannot be transferred (even while users

47 Gerry W Beyer, 'Estate planning for digital assets' (*Estate Planning Studies*, 5 January 2015) <https://montecito.bank/articles> accessed 27 February 2020; Walker (n 35) 71–72.

48 Kreiczer-Levy and Doeyets-Kedar (n 25) 733-38.

49 In Croatian property law, some typical rights an owner has, according to Art 30(2) of the Act on Ownership and Other Proprietary Rights (*Zakon o vlasništvu i drugim stvarnim pravima* (ZVDSP), *NN* 91/1996, 68/1998, 137/1999, 22/2000, 73/2000, 129/2000, 114/2001, 79/2006, 141/2006, 146/2008, 38/2009, 153/2009, 143/2012, 152/2014) are the right to possess, to use (with or without having the right to collect earnings from the asset), to dispose of (which includes the right to devise), to exclude others from intervening into one's ownership. Obviously, digital assets are intangible, but that should have nothing to do with preventing them from being owned or inherited. For example, in Croatian property law, dematerialized shares are equalized to tangible items and are treated as such. See Nikola Gavella, *Stvarno pravo* (Narodne novine 2007) 79 (fn 50), 94–95, 387. This is also applied to the proportional share of a co-owner and the right to build, both intangible entities: ZVDSP, Arts 37(3) and 280(2).

50 Since users know their passwords, they can log in whenever they want to, which is enough for the right to possess to be exercised: Banta, 'Property Interests in Digital Assets' (n 39) 1116. Possession is a factual physical connection that a person has over a tangible item: Gavella (n 49) 151. However, in Croatian law of property, there are situations when a person can possess something without actually having any physical connection to the item he or she possesses. That type of possession is called an 'ideal possession', ideal meaning imaginary or fictitious. See Gavella (n 49) 174–83.

51 Banta, 'Property Interests in Digital Assets' (n 39) 1114–18.

are alive) and this is usually categorically stated in most TOS agreements.[52] Non-transferability of an account is not, for the most part, an issue while the user is still alive. Most users probably want to exclude everyone else from accessing their accounts and their content while they still live. However, if they want these digital assets to be inherited by their heirs, that will probably not be possible under most OSPs' rules, as will be shown in the next section.

4.2 Inheritability of digital accounts and their content

Theoretically, there are several possible ways in which OSPs might deal with inheritability (and transfer in general) of an account and its content. Any transfer could either be expressly prohibited or it could be prohibited as a general rule, but an OSP might allow it under certain conditions. The transfer might also be explicitly allowed or a TOS agreement could be silent about the account's transferability *post mortem*.[53] Also, an OSP might have the policy to terminate an account and delete its content after a certain period of inactivity.[54] Consequently, after a user dies, digital assets might either transfer back to OSPs' control, be deleted (if inheritability is prohibited), or become a part of the user's estate (if inheritability is allowed).[55] Despite the prohibition of transfer and deletion being the most extreme and alarming solutions, they are the ones that are usually chosen by OSPs. Also, many of them are completely silent about transfer *post mortem*.[56]

When it comes to deletion, it is important to note that even if the TOS declare that an account will be deleted after a period of inactivity, it is not certain deletion will actually happen. This was proven in much-publicized Ellsworth case after Justin Ellsworth's father was denied access to his deceased son's Yahoo! account. Ellsworth's father sued Yahoo! and in the end obtained a court order which forced Yahoo! to give him access to the emails in the

52 Kreiczer-Levy and Doeyets-Kedar (n 25) 712.

53 For examples of some popular OSPs rules, see Walsh (n 14) 435–37.

54 Deletion might also happen in the event that a user violates a TOS agreement, and trying to leave an account login information to the user's heirs would certainly amount to violation of TOS agreement. Slaughter (n 38) 194; Alberto B Lopez, 'Death and the Digital Age: The Disposition of Digital Assets' (2016) 3 *Savannah L Rev* 77, 81.

55 Natalie M Banta, 'Death and Privacy in the Digital Age' (2016) 94 *NC L Rev* 927, 949; Banta, 'Property Interests in Digital Assets' (n 39) 1152.

56 Banta, 'Inherit the Cloud' (n 6) 834; Watkins (n 14) 197, 199, 211, 214, 218; Banta, 'Property Interests in Digital Assets' (n 39) 1102. Also see Verizon Media TOS: '[W]e may, without notice, temporarily or permanently suspend or cancel your account or impose limits on or restrict your access to parts or all of your account or the Services [...] (4) if your account shows extended periods of inactivity in accordance with our account deletion policy.' Verizon Media, 'Verizon Media Terms of Service' (*Verizon Media*) <www.verizonmedia.com/policies/us/en/verizonmedia/terms/otos> accessed 27 February 2020. Some OSPs deal with transfer of digital assets after its user dies not in their TOS but elsewhere. However, since the user agreed to the TOS, he or she also agreed to all of the OSP's policy supplements, no matter where they are located. Banta, 'Inherit the Cloud' (n 6) 816–17.

account. What is interesting here is that, several months after Ellsworth's death, the account was not deleted regardless of it being inactive and regardless of Yahoo!'s deletion policy.[57]

If an OSP does not have a deletion policy but prohibits inheritability, a question arises: what will happen to the decedent's account and its content? It is entirely plausible for an OSP to claim ownership and do with an account and its content whatever it wants.[58] Another possibility is to leave account content to linger on the OSP's server forever, without benefiting anybody. Since some of the most popular OSPs mentioned in this chapter are situated in the US (Facebook, Google, Amazon, Apple, and Yahoo!), this part of the chapter will explain why these OSPs deny heirs access to decedents' accounts. The reason for this is the Stored Communications Act (SCA) of 1986, which prohibits electronic service providers and remote computing services from disclosing account content to unauthorized individuals.[59] The SCA does not actually mention ownership and inheritability of these digital assets; its primary focus is privacy and the prohibition of unauthorized access to digital accounts and their content.[60] A probable reason for the SCA not mentioning inheritability is that at the time it was enacted, nobody could have predicted that these assets would be capable of being inherited or that anybody would want to inherit them, in the first place.[61] Therefore, it is probable that the SCA was never meant to apply to the inheritability of an account.[62] Regardless, US-based OSPs have chosen to interpret it in a way that would minimize their potential liability. Therefore, they have adopted policies that prevent anyone from accessing someone else's account, including account holders' heirs, due to protection of decedents' privacy.[63]

Consequently, all the rights a user has had over his or her digital account and its content, which are akin to those owners have over their things, will not be transferred to his or her heirs. So, even if a user stated in his or her will that digital assets should be inherited by his or her heirs, that would not be possible, since the user agreed to TOS prohibiting the transfer, probably long before he or she made a will.[64] This is obviously contrary to the principle of freedom of testation which states that the decedent is free to decide who will inherit which parts of his or her inheritance, tangible or intangible.[65] TOS

57 Olivia Y Truong, 'Virtual Inheritance: Assigning More Virtual Property Rights' (2009) 21 *Syracuse Sci & Tech L Rep* 57, 83–84; Banta, 'Death and Privacy' (n 55) 961–62.

58 Banta, 'Death and Privacy' (n 55) 964.

59 18 USC, Ch 121, §§ 2701 to 2712.

60 SCA, § 2702; Banta, 'Inherit the Cloud' (n 6) 840–42; Cahn (n 45) 1701.

61 Slaughter (n 38) 198.

62 Banta, 'Inherit the Cloud' (n 6) 841; Cahn (n 45) 1697, 1701; David Horton, 'The Stored Communications Act and Digital Assets' (2014) 67 *Vand L Rev* 1729, 1731–34.

63 Borden (n 41) 417-22; Banta, 'Death and Privacy' (n 55) 960.

64 Horton (n 64) 1736.

65 For Croatian law see Nikola Gavella and Vlado Belaj, *Nasljedno pravo* (Narodne novine 2008) 123.

agreements are in discord with the rules on intestacy, as well, because if the decedent did not leave a will, it is presumed that he or she wanted his or her immediate family (testate heirs) to inherit his or her estate[66] – which will not be possible under most TOS agreements.

Of course, contracts limiting the inheritability of a person's property are not unheard of. Probably in most legal systems, there are examples of contracts that are used for this reason. In Croatia, one can make a donation contract that will take effect after the donor dies (*donatio mortis causa*),[67] or a contract on support for life or support until death that is used to transfer the owner's property to an individual who has taken care of him or her until death.[68] The consequence of these contracts is that the property included in these contracts will not be inheritable, because it will be transferred to the decedent's contractual party which has priority over heirs.[69] However, all of these contracts are aimed at circumventing the heirs and transferring the property to certain persons, according to the owner's wishes.

TOS agreements limit the inheritability of digital assets in a similar way, but with a completely different outcome: these agreements circumvent heirs as well, but they do not allow anyone else of the user's choosing to access and benefit from the account and its content. Rather, OSPs will destroy these assets or keep them on their servers indefinitely, to whatever end. Thus, the main differences between other contracts that influence inheritability and TOS agreements are: (a) TOS agreements explicitly prohibit the transfer of personal property, rather than promote it, and (b) the terms of the transfer are controlled solely by an OSP and not by the owner, which is normally the case with other contracts that limit inheritability.[70]

To conclude this part, the author wants to mention a very interesting point that was made by others who have also dealt with this topic: if contracts drafted by OSPs alone are allowed to determine what will happen to digital assets, a dangerous precedent might be set – in the future, the same thing might happen to tangible assets or to any new type of property that might be developed.[71] TOS agreements might increase users' tolerance for oppressive terms, which might pave the way to even more oppressive terms. Because, if users keep accepting terms that encroach on their rights, for whatever reason, OSPs will assume users will continue to click 'I agree' to even more and more

66 For Croatian law, see Art 8 of the Inheritance Act (*Zakon o nasljeđivanju*), *NN* 48/2003, 163/2003, 35/2005, 127/2013, 33/2015, 14/2019.

67 ZOO, Art 491.

68 ZOO, Arts 579 to 589.

69 If somebody has the right to acquire a part or whole of the decedent's property after he or she dies, based on a valid contract made between himself or herself and the decedent, that property is not inheritable. It transfers to that person after decedent's death. See Gavella and Belaj (n 65) 61.

70 Banta, 'Inherit the Cloud' (n 6) 810, 823.

71 ibid 827–29; Banta, 'Property Interests in Digital Assets' (n 39) 1157.

rights-encroaching terms.[72] All of this certainly paints a grim picture of our future online.

5. Which rights does the user have over digital content – ownership or licence?

There are two answers to this question: OSPs either state that the user is an owner of digital content or that he or she has acquired a licence to use it.[73] A user usually owns whatever he or she creates, uploads, and stores on OSPs' platforms.[74] However, even if a user retains ownership and copyright of the above-mentioned digital content, OSPs limit it by establishing, for example, a 'worldwide license to use, host, store, reproduce, modify, create derivative works [...] communicate, publish, publicly perform, publicly display and distribute such content',[75] or a 'non-exclusive, transferable, sub-licensable, royalty-free, and worldwide license to host, use, distribute, modify, run, copy, publicly perform or display, translate, and create derivative works of your content'.[76]

With purchased digital assets, such as music, videos, or books, the rules change dramatically. These items are not actually purchased, since to purchase something means to buy it.[77] And OSPs that sell digital content do not actually sell it with the intention of transferring ownership of digital content; rather, they sell a licence that allows purchasers to merely use digital content. Therefore, a user is prohibited to 'redistribute, transmit, assign, sell, broadcast, rent, share, lend, repurpose, modify, adapt, edit, license or otherwise transfer' digital content.[78]

72 Zev J Eigen, 'Norm shifting by contract' (2014) 44 *Sw L Rev* 231, 235.

73 Cahn (n 45) 1705; Banta, 'Property Interests in Digital Assets' (n 39) 1105–7.

74 Banta, 'Property Interests in Digital Assets' (n 39) 1005. See eg Google TOS: 'Some of our Services allow you to upload, submit, store, send or receive content. You retain ownership of any intellectual property rights that you hold in that content. In short, what belongs to you stays yours.' Google, 'Content in Google services' (Google: Terms of Service, last updated on 22 January 2019) <https://policies.google.com/terms?hl=en#toc-content> accessed 27 February 2020. See also Facebook TOS: 'You own the intellectual property rights (things like copyright or trademarks) in any such content that you create and share on Facebook and the other Facebook Company Products you use. Nothing in these Terms takes away the rights you have to your own content. You are free to share your content with anyone else, wherever you want.' Facebook, 'Terms of Service' (Facebook, last updated on 31 July 2019) <www.facebook.com/legal/terms> accessed 27 February 2020.

75 Google TOS (n 74).

76 Facebook TOS (n 74).

77 Eichler (n 15) 210, 212.

78 Amazon, 'Amazon Music Terms of Use' (Amazon, last updated on 1 October 2019) <www.amazon.com/gp/help/customer/display.html?nodeId=201380010> accessed 27 February 2020. See also eg Apple, 'Apple Media Services Terms and Conditions' (Apple: Legal, last updated on 13 May 2019) <www.apple.com/legal/internet-services/itunes/us/terms.html> accessed 27 February 2020.

Users who purchase digital content have similar rights over digital content to those of any other owner. For example, they have the right to exclude others from accounts they used to purchase digital content and they also have the right to exclude others from the content they purchased. Users also have the right to possess and use what they purchased.[79] This is similar to what a person would be able to do if he or she actually bought a physical book, CD, or DVD.

However, when it comes to transferring purchased digital content, the fact that a user actually purchased a licence becomes obvious. After a person buys a physical item containing copyright, he or she can sell it, donate it, and borrow it – all of this under first sale doctrine.[80] On the other hand, if a book, music, or a video was purchased in a digital form, only a user can use it, since only he or she purchased a licence to use it. Most TOS agreements expressly forbid users to transfer, in any way, purchased digital content. By doing that, TOS agreements are actually circumventing the first sale doctrine, since it obviously does not apply to digital content.[81]

It is important to note that the price of digital media is mostly equal to the price of its physical copy, so OSPs cannot justify the fact that the purchaser does not acquire ownership over digital media by stating that it was cheaper.[82] The actual reason behind the OSPs prohibition of transfer is copyright protection. To elaborate: in order to transfer a digital file from one device to another, the RAM (random-access memory) of the recipient's computer has to create a new copy of the file that is being transferred, since it cannot be transferred in any other way. This copy actually violates the copyright owner's reproduction right, because if anybody wants to make a copy of copyright owner's creation, he or she has to have permission from the creator and has to reimburse him or her for it.[83]

TOS agreements that regulate the rights users have over the purchased digital content in most cases do not mention what will happen to that content after its user dies.[84] This problem is solved on a 'case-by-case' basis, so if heirs are persistent enough, they might obtain access to digital content purchased by the decedent.[85] According to one author, there are at least two ways in which inheritability of purchased digital content could be achieved,

79 Banta, 'Property Interests in Digital Assets' (n 39) 1126–28.

80 This doctrine is incorporated in Croatian law by Art 20(2) of the Copyright and Related Rights Act (*Zakon o autorskom pravu i srodnim pravima*, ZAPDSP), *NN* 167/2003, 79/2007, 80/2011, 125/2011, 141/2013, 127/2014, 62/2017, 96/2018. See also Eichler (n 15) 221–22.

81 Kim, 'The Wrap Contract Morass' (n 14) 313; Eichler (n 15) 223; Banta, 'Property Interests in Digital Assets' (n 39) 1129.

82 Banta, 'Property Interests in Digital Assets' (n 39) 1155.

83 In Croatia, reproduction and distribution rights of copyright owners are in regulated by ZAPDSP, Arts 19 and 20. See also Eichler (n 15) 222.

84 Amazon or Apple are silent about this. See Banta, 'Property Interests in Digital Assets' (n 39) 1130, 1145. Others might prohibit transfer. See Watkins (n 14) 207.

85 Benjamin Mayo, 'Digital property after death issues continue as Apple requires court order for widow to get late husband's Apple ID password' (9to5Mac, 19 January 2016)

without violating copyright law. First, the ownership of the decedent's account could be switched to his or her heirs, so that they own the same copy as the decedent, and, second, the digital content could be transferred to the decedent's heirs, but the original copy could be deleted after the transfer, so only one copy of a digital asset exists.[86] This is because inheritability of digital content should not be treated like any other transfer, since the decedent is not trying to sell or redistribute property or create a new copy of digital content. After the decedent's death, heirs take his or her place and inherit all of the decedent's belongings, rights, and obligations, as they existed when he or she was alive (apart from those that cease at death). This has nothing to do with other ways of transferring assets from one person to another and that is why, since Roman times, singular succession has been distinguished from universal succession.

The confusion concerning rights that the users have over digital content illustrates, in the best way, the fact that most of them do not read TOS and have no idea how important they are and how they influence the user's relationship with an OSP. Because of that, most people who have purchased digital content online are certain they own it and can do with it whatever they want. They treat digital content exactly as they would that same content if it were fixed on a tangible medium, and that could not be more wrong. This situation really shows that users do not take TOS agreements seriously, but the burden to read them lies solely on them and they cannot later justify themselves by stating they did not know what they were agreeing to.

6. Conclusion

Some might take a stand that if a user agreed to TOS, which prevent inheritability of digital assets or give him or her a mere licence, instead of ownership over digital content, then there is nothing more to talk about. If a user did not wish for that to happen, he or she should not have consented to TOS agreements. However, things are not as straightforward as that. First, users do not have any alternative to TOS and they do not have choices between them – most OSPs have the same rules when it comes to issues discussed in this chapter and they will never allow users to negotiate and change them. If one did not want to consent to these rules, one would be forced to live one's life offline. Second, users are often not aware what they are consenting to, either because they did not read TOS or because TOS agreements were made in such a way as to obscure what is really specified by them. Third, even if users were aware of what they consented to and still went through with clicking 'I agree', it is questionable whether TOS agreements should have effect since

<https://9to5mac.com/author/benjaminmayo> accessed 27 February 2020; Banta, 'Property Interests in Digital Assets' (n 39) 1130.

86 Eichler (n 15) 224.

their provisions violate some of the basic principles of civil law and an issue of their fairness and enforceability therefore arises.

No one can know what the future holds. What seemed impossible only a few years ago exists today. How things will progress when it comes to digital assets and possibly new types of intangible property that might emerge in the future is anybody's guess. Therefore, we should all be extremely wary of what we are agreeing to today, because soon we may find ourselves in a world where our rights over these assets are severely limited by contracts that we are forced to enter into, which we cannot influence, and which we do not like at all.

Bibliography

——— 'Adhesion Contract (Contract of Adhesion)' *Wex: Legal Dictionary & Encyclopaedia* <www.law.cornell.edu/wex/adhesion_contract_(contract_of_adhesion)> accessed 27 February 2020.

Amazon, 'Amazon Music Terms of Use' (Amazon, last updated on 1 October 2019) <www.amazon.com/gp/help/customer/display.html?nodeId=201380010> accessed 27 February 2020.

Amazon, 'Amazon Privacy Notice' (Amazon: Legal Policies, last updated 1 January 2020) <www.amazon.com/gp/help/customer/display.html?nodeId=468496> accessed 26 February 2020.

Apple, 'Apple Media Services Terms and Conditions' (Apple: Legal, last updated on 13 May 2019) <www.apple.com/legal/internet-services/itunes/us/terms.html> accessed 27 February 2020.

Arnold C, 'How to Manage Your Digital Afterlife' (*Scientific American*, 1 September 2013) <www.scientificamerican.com/article/how-to-manage-your-digital-afterlife> accessed 27 February 2020.

Banta NM, 'Inherit the Cloud: The Role of Private Contracts in Distributing or Deleting Digital Assets at Death' (2014) 83 *Fordham L Rev* 799.

——— 'Death and Privacy in the Digital Age' (2016) 94 *NC L Rev* 927.

——— 'Property Interests in Digital Assets: The Rise of Digital Feudalism' (2017) 38 *Cardozo L Rev* 1099.

Beyer GW and Cahn N, 'When You Pass on, Don't Leave the Passwords Behind: Planning for Digital Assets' (2012) 26 *Probate Prop* 40.

——— 'Estate planning for digital assets' (*Estate Planning Studies*, 5 January 2015) <https://montecito.bank/articles> accessed 27 February 2020.

Borden M, 'Covering Your Digital Assets: Why Stored Communications Act Stands in the Way of Digital Inheritance' (2014) 75 *Ohio St LJ* 405.

Brehm AS and Lee CD, 'Click Here to Accept the Terms of Service' (2015) 31 *Comm Law* 4.

Brubaker JR and Callison-Burch V, 'Legacy Contact: Designing and Implementing Post-mortem Stewardship at Facebook' in *CHI '16: Proceedings of the 2016 CHI Conference on Human Factors in Computing Systems* (Association for Computing Machinery 2016) [DOI: https://doi.org/10.1145/2858036.2858254].

Cahn N, 'Probate Law Meets the Digital Age' (2014) 67 *Vand L Rev* 1697.

Calem RE, 'What Happens to Your Online Accounts When You Die' (Techlicious, 29 June 2010) <www.techlicious.com/how-to/what-happens-to-your-online-accounts-when-you-die> accessed 27 February 2020.

Edwards L and Harbinja E, 'Protecting Post-Mortem Privacy: Reconsidering the Privacy Interests of the Deceased in a Digital World' (2013) 32 *Cardozo Arts & Ent LJ* 101 [DOI: https://doi.org/10.2139/ssrn.2267388].

Eichler AC, '"Owning" What You "Buy": How iTunes Uses Federal Copyright Law to Limit Inheritability of Content, and the Need to Expand the First Sale Doctrine to Include Digital Assets' (2016) 16 *Hous Bus & Tax LJ* 208.

Eigen ZJ, 'Norm shifting by contract' (2014) 44 *Sw L Rev* 231.

Facebook, 'Terms of Service' (Facebook, last updated on 31 July 2019) <www.facebook.com/legal/terms> accessed 27 February 2020.

Gatt A, 'Electronic Commerce – Click-Wrap Agreements: The Enforceability of Click-Wrap Agreements' (2002) 18 *CLS Rev* 404 [DOI: https://doi.org/10.1016/s0267-3649(02)01105-6].

Gavella N, *Stvarno pravo* (Narodne novine 2007).

——— and Vlado Belaj, *Nasljedno pravo* (Narodne novine 2008).

Google, 'Content in Google services' (Google: Terms of Service, last updated on 22 January 2019) <https://policies.google.com/terms?hl=en#toc-content> accessed 27 February 2020.

Harbinja E, 'Virtual Worlds – a Legal Post-Mortem Account' (2014) 11 *SCRIPTed* 273 [DOI: https://doi.org/10.2966/scrip.110314.273].

——— 'Virtual Worlds Players – Consumers or Citizens' (2014) 3 (4) *Internet Pol'y Rev* 1, 4–5 <https://policyreview.info/articles/analysis/virtual-worlds-players-consumers-or-citizens> accessed 26 February 2020 [DOI: https://doi.org/10.14763/2014.4.329].

——— 'Post-Mortem Social Media: Law and Facebook After Death' in Mangan D and Gillies LE, *The Legal Challenges of Social Media* (Edward Elgar 2017) [DOI: https://doi.org/10.4337/9781785364518.00023].

Hopkins JP, 'Afterlife in the Cloud: Managing a Digital Estate' (2013) 5 *Hastings Sci & Tech LJ* 209.

Horton D, 'Flipping the Script: Contra Proferentem and Standard Form Contracts' (2009) 80 *U Colo L Rev* 431.

——— 'The Stored Communications Act and Digital Assets' (2014) 67 *Vand L Rev* 1729.

Kim NS, 'The Duty to Draft Reasonably and Online Contracts' in DiMatteo LA and others (eds), *Commercial Contract Law: Transatlantic Perspectives* (CUP 2013) [DOI: https://doi.org/10.1017/cbo9781139235662.012].

——— 'Exploitation by Wrap Contracts – Click "Agree"' (2014) 39 *California Bar IP Journal* 10.

——— 'The Wrap Contract Morass' (2014) 44 *Sw L Rev* 309.

——— 'Wrap Contracting and the Online Environment: Causes and Cures' in John A Rothchild (ed), *Research Handbook on Electronic Commerce Law* (Edward Elgar 2016) [DOI: https://doi.org/10.4337/9781783479924.00010].

Klarić P and Vedriš M, *Građansko pravo* (14th edn, Narodne novine 2014).

Klasiček D, 'Digital Inheritance' in Barković D and others, *IMR 2018: Interdisciplinary Management Research XIV* (Josip Juraj Strossmayer University of Osijek, Faculty of Economics 2018).

Klein SA and Parthemer MR, 'Who Will Delete the Digital You: Understanding Fiduciary Access to Digital Assets' (2016) 30 *Probate Prop* 3.

Kreiczer-Levy S and Donyets-Kedar R, 'Better Left Forgotten: An Argument against Treating Some Social Media and Digital Assets as Inheritance in an Era of Platform Power' (2019) 84 *Brook L Rev* 703.

Lopez AB, 'Death and the Digital Age: The Disposition of Digital Assets' (2016) 3 *Savannah L Rev* 77.

Matić T, 'Formularni ugovori u elektroničkom obliku (Sklapanje ugovora klikom miša – elektroničkim očitovanjem volje putem Interneta na web stranici – *click wrap* i *browse wrap* ugovori)' (2008) 58 *Zbor Prav Fak Zagreb* 779.

Mayo B, 'Digital property after death issues continue as Apple requires court order for widow to get late husband's Apple ID password' (9to5Mac, 19 January 2016) <https://9to5mac.com/author/benjaminmayo> accessed 27 February 2020.

McCarthy L, 'Digital Assets and Intestacy' (2015) 21 *BU J Sci & Tech L* 384.

Petrić S, 'O nepravičnim klauzulama općih uvjeta ugovora u pravu Europske unije' (2002) 39 *Zbor Rad Prav Fak Split* 59.

Radin MJ, 'Online Standardization and the Integration of Text and Machine' (2002) 70 *Fordham L Rev* 1125.

Ronderos J, 'Is Access Enough?: Addressing Inheritability of Digital Assets Using the Three-Tier System Under the Revised Uniform Fiduciary Access to Digital Assets Act' (2017) 18 *Tenn J Bus L* 1031.

Savin A, *EU Internet Law* (2nd edn, Edward Elgar 2017) [DOI: https://doi.org/10.4337/9781784717971].

Sherry K, 'What Happens to Our Facebook Accounts When We Die?: Probate Versus Policy and the Fate of Social-Media Assets Postmortem' (2012) 40 *Pepp L Rev* 185.

Slakoper Z, 'Nevaljanost pojedinih odredbi općih uvjeta ugovora s posebnim osvrtom na potrošačke ugovore' (2002) 22 *Zbor Prav Fak Rijeka* 181.

Slaughter M, 'The Barriers of Facebook's Terms of Service Agreement: Hardship Placed on Fiduciaries Access to Digital Assets' (2015) 24 *I & CTL* 183 [DOI: https://doi.org/10.1080/13600834.2015.1042569].

Tarney TG, 'A Call for Legislation to Permit the Transfer of Digital Assets at Death' (2012) 40 *Cap U L Rev* 773.

Truong OY, 'Virtual Inheritance: Assigning More Virtual Property Rights' (2009) 21 *Syracuse Sci & Tech L Rep* 57.

Varnado SS, 'Your Digital Footprint Left Behind at Death: An Illustration of Technology Leaving the Law Behind' (2014) 74 *La L Rev* 719.

Verizon Media, 'Verizon Media Terms of Service' (Verizon Media) <www.verizonmedia.com/policies/us/en/verizonmedia/terms/otos> accessed 27 February 2020.

Walker MD, 'The New Uniform Digital Assets Law: Estate Planning and Administration in the Information Age' (2017) 52 *Real Prop Tr & Est LJ* 51.

Walsh SB, 'Coming Soon to a Legislature Near You: Comprehensive State Law Governing Fiduciary Access to Digital Assets' (2014) 8 *Charleston L Rev* 429.

Watkins AF, 'Digital Properties and Death: What Will Your Heirs Have Access to After You Die?' (2014) 62 *Buff L Rev* 193.

12 Online peer-to-peer accommodation services

The ECJ's judgment in Case C-390/18, *Airbnb Ireland*

Kosjenka Dumančić

1. Introduction

In the last decade, the collaborative economy[1] has expanded to include a variety of social and also legally binding relationships and activities. Initially, the collaborative economy originated within the merchandising industry (e.g. eBay, Craigslist) and in the area of services related to music and videos (e.g. YouTube), knowledge (e.g. Wikipedia), and personal information (e.g. Facebook), and to date it evolved to also covering transportation (e.g. Uber, BlaBlaCar) and accommodation (e.g. Airbnb, Couchsurfing). It is also growing in all other activities and areas where the service can be provided with the support of an internet digital platform.[2]

According to some authors, the collaborative economy as a part of the Fourth Industrial Revolution (or Industry 4.0) does not create a need for specific regulation. Most of the platforms are self-regulated[3] and they are still subject to the 'traditional' legal framework that regulates the specific relationship between service providers and users with the intermediation of the digital platform. On the other hand, at the EU level, the need for the regulation of digital platforms is strongly emphasized in the activities led by the European Commission relating to the modernization of the legal framework for digital services as part of the announced Digital Services Act package. The European Commission President Ursula von der Leyen addressed the challenges and opportunities of the digital world in her inaugural political

1 In addition to the term collaborative economy, terms such as sharing economy, demand economy, peer-to-peer economy, and gig economy are used as equivalent. The author uses the term collaborative economy as used in the European Commission Agenda for the Collaborative Economy: European Commission, 'A European Agenda for the Collaborative Economy' (Communication) COM (2016) 356 final (EC Agenda for the Collaborative Economy).

2 See eg Organisation for Economic Co-operation and Development (OECD), 'Protecting Consumers in Peer Platform Markets: Exploring the Issues' (2016) *OECD Digital Economy Papers* 253/2006 <www.oecd-ilibrary.org/science-and-technology/protecting-consumers-in-peer-platform-markets_5jlwvz39m1zw-en> accessed 17 March 2020.

3 Vassillis Hatzopoulos, *The Collaborative Economy and EU Law* (Hart Publishing 2018) 200.

DOI: 10.4324/9781003080596-15

guidelines and promised that 'a new Digital Services Act will upgrade our liability and safety rules for digital platforms, services, and products'.[4]

In the early stage of the development of collaborative economy models, the collaborative economy was created to allow individuals to use untapped or surplus resources without paying a special fee.[5] The collaborative economy was understood as an opportunity for entrepreneurship for everyone, not only entrepreneurs but all individuals. By further developing technology, especially mobile applications, the collaborative economy contributed to an increase in individuals' personal income, but also to a reduction in the cost of goods and services. As a consequence, a large number of individuals who have not previously engaged in entrepreneurial activity have joined the competition.[6] An interesting point is that the collaborative economy platforms as a model of sharing instead of ownership transform anything into services.[7]

The definition of a collaborative economy, provided in the EC Agenda for the Collaborative Economy, states that the term 'refers to business models where activities are facilitated by collaborative platforms that create an open marketplace for the temporary usage of goods and services often provided by private individuals'.[8] The collaborative economy platforms operating in five key sectors of the EU's collaborative economy (peer-to-peer accommodation, peer-to-peer transport, on-demand household activities, on-demand professional services, and collaborative finances) generated revenues of 3.6 billion euros in 2015.[9] The potential of the collaborative economy is significant. With annual growth exceeding 25%,[10] it is estimated that, in theory, the economic profits associated with better capacity utilization made possible by the collaborative economy could exceed 572 billion euros.[11] There are no studies on the value of the collaborative economy after the year 2015.

4 Ursula von den Leyen, 'Political Guidelines for the Next European Commission 2019–2024: A Union that strives for more: My agenda for Europe' (2019) 13 <https://op.europa.eu/en/publication-detail/-/publication/43a17056-ebf1-11e9-9c4e-01aa75ed71a1> accessed 15 October 2020.

5 European Commission, 'More than Profit: A Collaborative Economy with a Social Purpose' (European Commission 2016) 8 <https://ec.europa.eu/docsroom/documents/18443> accessed 15 October 2020.

6 James Manyika and others, 'Disruptive technologies: Advances that will transform life, business, and the global economy' (McKinsey Global Institute 2016) <www.mckinsey.com/business-functions/mckinsey-digital/our-insights/disruptive-technologies#> accessed 17 March 2020.

7 Vera Demary, 'Competition in the Sharing Economy' (2015) *IW Policy Paper* 19/2015 <www.iwkoeln.de/studien/iw-policy-papers/beitrag/vera-demary-competition-in-the-sharing-economy-235445.html> accessed 17 March 2020.

8 EC Agenda for the Collaborative Economy (n 1) 3.

9 Based on estimates of PwC Consulting as part of a study contracted by the European Commission: ibid 2.

10 Pierre Goudin, *The Cost of Non-Europe in the Sharing Economy: Economic, Social and Legal Challenges and Opportunities* (European Parliamentary Research Service 2016) 8.

11 ibid 38. Other research indicates that, by 2025, the total value of transactions in Europe in the five most important sectors of the collaborative economy could rise to 335 billion

2. Key regulatory issues regarding the collaborative economy

In the last few years, the debate about regulating the relationships between actors in a collaborative economy relationship has been raised between practitioners and scientists.[12] One of the biggest challenges is the cross-border character of the services provided based on an agency relationship with the digital platform.

The existing EU legal framework applicable to collaborative economy includes the E-Commerce Directive,[13] the Information Society Services Directive,[14] the Digital Content and Services Directive,[15] the Sale of Goods Directive,[16] the General Data Protection Regulation,[17] Services Directive,[18] the Consumer Rights Directive,[19] the Working Time Directive,[20]

US dollars: Robert Vaughan and Raphael Daverio, 'Assessing the Size and Presence of the Collaborative Economy in Europe' (European Commission 2016) 9.

12 See Timm Teubner, 'Thoughts on the Sharing Economy' in Piet Kommers and others, *Proceedings of International Conferences on the ICT, Society and Human Beings 2014, Web Based Communities and Social Media 2014, e-Commerce 2014, Information Systems Post-Implementation and Change Management 2014 and e-Health 2014* (International Association for Development of the Information Society 2014) 322; Molly Cohen and Arun Sundararajan, 'Self-Regulation and Innovation in the Peer-to-Peer Sharing Economy' (2015) 82 *U Chi L Rev Online* 116 <https://chicagounbound.uchicago.edu/uclrev_online/vol82/iss1/8> accessed 17 March 2020.

13 Directive 2000/31/EC of the European Parliament and of the Council of 8 June 2000 on certain legal aspects of information society services, in particular electronic commerce, in the Internal Market ('Directive on electronic commerce') [2000] *OJ* L178/1 (E-Commerce Directive).

14 Directive (EU) 2015/1535 of the European Parliament and of the Council of 9 September 2015 laying down a procedure for the provision of information in the field of technical regulations and of rules on Information Society services [2015] *OJ* L241/1.

15 Directive (EU) 2019/770 of the European Parliament and of the Council of 20 May 2019 on certain aspects concerning contracts for the supply of digital content and digital services [2019] *OJ* L136/1.

16 Directive (EU) 2019/771 of the European Parliament and of the Council of 20 May 2019 on certain aspects concerning contracts for the sale of goods, amending Regulation (EU) 2017/2394 and Directive 2009/22/EC, and repealing Directive 1999/44/EC [2019] *OJ* L136/28.

17 Regulation (EU) 2016/679 of the European Parliament and of the Council of 27 April 2016 on the protection of natural persons with regard to the processing of personal data and on the free movement of such data, and repealing Directive 95/46/EC (General Data Protection Regulation) [2016] *OJ* L119/1.

18 Directive 2006/123/EC of the European Parliament and of the Council of 12 December 2006 on services in the internal market [2006] *OJ* L376/36 (Services Directive).

19 Directive 2011/83/EU of the European Parliament and of the Council of 25 October 2011 on consumer rights, amending Council Directive 93/13/EEC and Directive 1999/44/EC of the European Parliament and of the Council and repealing Council Directive 85/577/EEC and Directive 97/7/EC of the European Parliament and of the Council [2011] *OJ* L304/64.

20 Directive 2003/88/EC of the European Parliament and of the Council of 4 November 2003 concerning certain aspects of the organisation of working time [2003] *OJ* L299/9.

the Transparent and Predictable Working Conditions Directive,[21] and the Professional Qualifications Directive.[22] The existing regulatory framework, which applies wholly, or in part, to the collaborative economy relationships, lately has often been questioned.[23] One of the goals of the European Commission should be establishing a regulatory framework at EU level that offers the sector certainty for the long term.[24] Besides the regulatory issues such as consumer protection and worker rights, there are also topics on taxation,[25] competition,[26] and other issues that have to be taken in concern.

The E-Commerce Directive applies to collaborative economy services when these are 'information society services', as defined by the Art 1(1)(b) of the Information Society Services Directive.[27] The challenge exists where the service provided is not a digital service itself. The ECJ has dealt with the issue of qualification of the provided services in two sectors of the collaborative economy: transport[28] and, recently, accommodation.[29]

21 Directive (EU) 2019/1152 of the European Parliament and of the Council of 20 June 2019 on transparent and predictable working conditions in the European Union [2019] *OJ* L186/105.

22 Directive 2005/36/EC of the European Parliament and of the Council of 7 September 2005 on the recognition of professional qualifications [2005] *OJ* L255/22, as amended by Directive 2013/55/EU of the European Parliament and of the Council of 20 November 2013 amending Directive 2005/36/EC on the recognition of professional qualifications and Regulation (EU) No 1024/2012 on administrative cooperation through the Internal Market Information System ('the IMI Regulation') [2013] *OJ* L354/132.

23 See Goudin (n 10) 23ff.

24 ibid 23.

25 Since taxation is part of national law, there is a regulatory problem in providing services cross-border in the situation where the platform is not service provider itself.

26 When analyzing competition rules the main starting point is the market definition what makes the issues related to collaborative economy more complicated since it is questionable which criteria should be used: digital platform market or underlying service market. See more in Hatzopoulos (n 3) 107; Ana Pošćić, 'Europsko pravo tržišnog natjecanja i ekonomija dijeljenja – odabrana pitanja' (2019) 40 *Zbor Prav Fak Rijeka* 237, 248. Poščić also mentions the definition of undertaking as a key question; however, the author of this chapter sees the market definition as the main problem.

27 Information Society Services Directive, Art 1(1)(b) reads:

> 'service' means any Information Society service, that is to say, any service normally provided for remuneration, at a distance, by electronic means and at the individual request of a recipient of services.
>
> For the purposes of this definition:
>
> (i) 'at a distance' means that the service is provided without the parties being simultaneously present;
>
> (ii) 'by electronic means' means that the service is sent initially and received at its destination by means of electronic equipment for the processing (including digital compression) and storage of data, and entirely transmitted, conveyed and received by wire, by radio, by optical means or by other electromagnetic means;
>
> (iii) 'at the individual request of a recipient of services' means that the service is provided through the transmission of data on individual request.

28 Case C-526/15 *Uber Belgium BVBA v Taxi Radio Bruxellois NV* [2016] ECLI:EU:C:2016:830; Case C-434/15 *Asociación Profesional Elite Taxi v Uber Systems Spain, SL* [2017] ECLI:EU:C:2017:981; Case C-320/16 *Criminal proceedings against Uber France* [2018] ECLI:EU:C:2018:221.

29 Case C-390/18 *Criminal proceedings against X* [2019] ECLI:EU:C:2019:1112 (*Airbnb Ireland*).

3. Peer-to-peer accommodation services

3.1 Participants in peer-to-peer accommodation relationship

The EC Agenda for the Collaborative Economy defines three categories of participants: service providers, users, and collaborative platforms.[30] Service providers are persons who share things, resources, time, or skills, and they are either natural persons offering services occasionally ('peers') or professional service providers. The second category of involved actors is service users, while the third is collaborative platforms, intermediaries that connect service providers and users through online platforms and facilitate transactions between them.[31] In terms of the language used by Airbnb, the service providers who provide accommodation services are hosts, while accommodation services users are guests. The third actor is the platform itself: the facilitator of the network. The role between these three actors and their mutual relationships have an impact on the applicable legal rules.

From the legal perspective, there are specific legal relationships between the involved actors in collaborative economy transactions that arise (a) between the Airbnb platform and hosts (accommodation service providers), (b) between the Airbnb platform and guests (accommodation service users), and (c) between hosts and guests.[32]

However, when assessing the application of the applicable regulation to this basically *tripartite* relationship, the question of the nature of the service provided by the platform itself arises. Thus, in the practice of the ECJ, two different directions of application of law are drawn, depending on whether a platform only mediates the provision of the service or the service of the platform is an essential and inseparable part of the service itself. This was the starting point for the analysis and application of the law initiated in the proceedings in *Airbnb Ireland*.[33]

For the purpose of further analysis, the first distinction should be based on the specifics of the host. When a host is a professional and provides services in his professional capacity, rules on consumer protection law will apply. The consumer protection law[34] is harmonized at the EU level and has priority in application over national law. When the provider of the service is not a

30 EC Agenda for the Collaborative Economy (n 1) 3.

31 See also Dianne Dredge and others, 'Impact of regulatory approaches to the collaborative economy in the tourism accommodation sector: Barcelona, Berlin, Amsterdam and Paris' (2016) *Impulse Paper* 9/2016 <https://ec.europa.eu/growth/content/impact-regulatory-approaches-collaborative-economy-tourism-accommodation-sector-barcelona-0_en> accessed 12 January 2020.

32 See Hatzopoulos (n 3) 22.

33 *Airbnb Ireland* (n 29), para 40.

34 See Hans-W Micklitz, Norbert Reich, and Peter Rott, *Understanding EU Consumer Law* (Intersentia 2009); Stephen Weatherill, *EU Consumer Law and Policy* (2nd edn, Edward Elgar 2013); Christoph Busch and others, 'The Rise of the Platform Economy: A New Challenge for EU Consumer Law?' (2016) 5 *EuCML* 3; Vassilis Hatzopoulos and Sofia Roma, 'Caring for Sharing? The Collaborative Economy under EU Law' (2017) 54 *CML Rev* 81.

professional but a peer – an ordinary person[35] – there is no prerequisite for the application of consumer law and, instead, the law of obligations of the state where the service is provided will apply. The problem in differentiation between a professional and non-professional provider of peer-to-peer (P2P) accommodation service arises from the applicable administrative law which regulates short-term rent in Member States.[36] The possibility to rent an accommodation which later grew into the possibility of becoming a non-professional host resulted in the diversity of hosts ranging from ordinary people who rent their own apartment, or even a spare room, to hotels and commercial real estate companies which can achieve a higher return on investment through short-term than through long-term rental.[37]

P2P accommodation causes a disturbance in the global market which is also seen through the relationship with other competitors in the market. In theory, this problem is also considered through the application of competition law, where the question of defining the relevant market is raised – that is, whether a collaborative platform creates a new market or whether it competes with the service providers in the existing market.[38]

The study conducted by Koolhoven and others gives answers to what extent competition in the tourism sector varies within Member States.[39] Intermediation (by e.g. Airbnb) in the housing sector could give rise to unfair competition between intermediary platforms and professional agents who need a diploma or professional insurance to engage in such activity. On the other hand, consumer accommodation providers might be in unfair competition with the professional hotels which are subject to permits and safety regulations.

3.2 Airbnb business model

Airbnb was one of the first digital platforms to provide peer-to-peer services in the field of accommodation. Initially, the idea was to offer accommodation properties that were not in use, such as holiday homes, apartments, guest houses, spare rooms, and the like. With time, activities were extended to hostels, hotel rooms, apartments, and other accommodation that is leased solely to provide accommodation services. The digital platform connects people who want to rent their accommodation with people seeking accommodation.

35 Alina Geiger, Chris Horbel, and Claas Christian Germelmann, '"Give and Take": How Notions of Sharing and Context Determine Free Peer-to-Peer Accommodation Decisions' (2018) 35 *J Travel Tour Mark* 5.

36 Hatzopoulos (n 3) 40.

37 Geiger, Horbel, and Germelmann (n 35) 5.

38 Hatzopoulos (n 3) 107.

39 Rosalie Koolhoven and others, 'Impulse Paper on Specific Liability Issues Raised by the Collaborative Economy in the Accommodation Sector: Paris – Amsterdam – Barcelona' (European Commission 2016).

It is not important whether accommodation providers are 'peers' or professionals.[40] Airbnb is considered a collaborative economy platform through which transactions between service providers and service users are conducted on a one-to-one basis that provides temporary access to fee-based accommodation. The platform is not the owner of the accommodation. The platform adds value to the traditional accommodation service by providing a range of additional services, including transactions and administrative services, customer checks, and advertising, and can influence pricing.[41]

What is common to all Airbnb hosts is their motivation which is always connected with the profit motives. At the same time, they are simultaneously taking advantage of the communal bonding aspects afforded to them when they offer their services. Both guests and providers engage with one another and, aside from financial compensation, other forms of reciprocation often emerge.[42] In contrast to Airbnb, which is an example of P2P accommodation platform for profit, there are also other platforms such as Couchsurfing[43] that are facilitating a free P2P accommodation hosting community where members offer underutilized space in their homes to other travellers and gain access themselves to underutilized space in other people's homes when they travel.[44]

Airbnb calls itself an 'online marketplace', but it is essentially an intermediary platform that allows accommodation supply and demand to be linked. It acts as an intermediary between hosts and guests whose rights and obligations are defined by the Terms of Service (for European users)[45] that are an integral part of the future contract between parties. This is also confirmed by the method of commission collection since Airbnb charges 3% commission on every booking from hosts, and between 6% and 12% from guests.[46] As a prerequisite to access the Airbnb webpage, potential hosts and guests have to initially register through creating a personal profile. Once accepted as the host of the property, the platform provides space for recommendations from

40 Traditional providers of accommodation services as tourism services are professionals or private owners who provide accommodation services on a permanent basis. In the new circumstances, with the competition of 'peer' providers that are using the platform as their only mean of communication with guests, their business faces pressures such as increased competition, unequal regulatory burdens, etc.

41 Pierre Hausemer and others, 'Exploratory Study of Consumer Issues in Online Peer-to-Peer Platform Markets: Final Report' (European Commission 2017) 53.

42 Mohammad Reza Habibi, Alexander Davidson, and Michel Laroche, 'What Managers Should Know About the Sharing Economy' (2017) 60 *Bus Horiz* 113, 115.

43 Couchsurfing offers accommodation and social networking available at the web page and a mobile application that works based on the principle 'if I host you, I expect you to host me'.

44 Geiger, Horbel, and Germelmann (n 35) 6; Hatzopoulos (n 3) 15.

45 Airbnb, 'Terms of Service for European Users' (*Airbnb*, last updated on 1 November 2019) <www.airbnb.co.uk/terms> accessed 7 December 2019.

46 Rules and guidelines are explained at the official Airbnb web page <www.airbnb.com/help/article/271> accessed 7 December 2019.

former guests, a response rating, and a private messaging system. Hosts do not pay for their listing page but will be charged a 3% 'service fee' once a reservation has been confirmed. Since it has to be paid after the reservation confirmation, the 'service fee' is the sign that the contractual obligation of intermediation of the platform has been fulfilled.

In its Terms of Service, Airbnb as the provider of the Airbnb Platform states that it does not organize or retail travel packages and consequently its activity does not fall under Directive (EU) 2015/2302.[47, 48] It is clear from analysis of this provision that Airbnb does not consider itself to be a professional travel package provider which exempts it from the applicable EU rules connected with travel arrangements, including consumer protection rules.[49]

Before concluding the main contract – the accommodation contract – the future service provider and user communicate exclusively via the platform. After the conclusion of the accommodation contract between the service provider and service user, the platform takes a commission, as explained above, from both the service provider and service user.

The Airbnb business model was adapted to local and national regulations,[50] primarily in the EU Member States. The business model includes the establishment of daughter companies in different states so that users enter into a contract with Airbnb of the particular state for the use of the site (placing of a listing, reservations), on the one hand, and with Airbnb Payments UK for payments made through that site, on the other hand.[51]

Precisely due to the lack of European and national regulation, an important role is given to self-regulation.[52] On the one hand, the success of the collaborative economy self-regulatory solution is in the sufficient control and compliance with rules developed by the platform, while, on the other hand,

47 Airbnb, 'Terms of Service' (n 45), Art 1.2.

48 Directive (EU) 2015/2302 of the European Parliament and of the Council of 25 November 2015 on package travel and linked travel arrangements, amending Regulation (EC) No 2006/2004 and Directive 2011/83/EU of the European Parliament and of the Council and repealing Council Directive 90/314/EEC [2015] *OJ* L326/1 (Package Travel Directive).

49 Recital 1 of the new Package Travel Directive states that the directive lays down a number of important consumer rights. In European law theory and practice, a traveller is generally considered as a consumer. To avoid application of the Package Travel Directive rules on package travel and linked travel arrangements on the Airbnb business model, Airbnb's Terms of Service strictly exclude the application of the Package Travel Directive in the Airbnb model and the possible application of the consumer protection rights in the relationship between Airbnb and the 'guests'.

50 Cohen and Sundararajan (n 12) 119; Homa Hajibaba and Sara Dolnicar, 'Regulatory Reactions Around the World' in Sara Dolnicar (ed), *Peer-to-Peer Accommodation Networks* (Goodfellow Publishers 2017) 120.

51 Case 390/18 *Criminal proceedings against X* [2019] ECLI:EU:C:2019:336, Opinion of AG Szpunar, para 33.

52 Cohen and Sundararajan (n 12) 119.

the credibility of the host is self-regulated by the rating given by guests.[53] The self-regulation of the platforms is considered as one possible way to 'put things in order' until a common solution is found.[54]

The European Commission has argued that 'for the sharing economy in general, it would be beneficial to have specific legislation in various industries', in order to avoid a 'lack of clarity because existing legislation does not cover certain activities and transactions' or the possibility that 'legislation developed for conventional industries is wrongfully applied to markets in the sharing economy'.[55]

For the purpose of preparing the EU regulation on the collaborative economy, different stakeholders were consulted, also including Airbnb. Airbnb reports were used[56] since the company produces reports regularly with numbers on different aspects of the company's business. But the main critic of this European Commission approach was that a public authority cannot rely on reports based on data given by the platform since the data cannot be checked.[57] Also, the data could be presented with a vested interest of the company that has an interest in policymaking.

According to Haar,[58] lobbyists for the accommodation platforms pressed the Commission to interpret the EU rules as strictly as possible. Regulatory fragmentation was one of the biggest challenges for the Airbnb business model in the EU. In 2015, after European cities started to tighten up the regulation on short-term rentals, Airbnb began developing a European response with the help of European institutions and the potential to solve the problem of applicable law. In order to get an objective analysis of the market, the European Commission DG GROW produced its own statistics in April 2016 by mapping hosts' activities. In it, many obstacles were encountered. As discussed earlier in this chapter, since hosts are not 'service providers' in the classical sense, they are not members of the European consumer associations. For that reason, they could not be represented adequately during the consultations which preceded the EC Communication. For the Commission, that work was actually finished with EC Agenda for the Collaborative Economy from June 2016,[59] but it was to continue in another form.

53 Sara Dolnicar, 'Unique Features of Peer-to-Peer Accommodation Networks' in Sara Dolnicar (ed), *Peer-to-Peer Accommodation Networks* (Goodfellow Publishers 2017) 5.

54 Arun Sundararajan, 'Peer-to-Peer Businesses and the Sharing (Collaborative) Economy: Overview, Economic Effects and Regulatory Issues' (Committee on Small Business of the United States House of Representatives, 14 January 2014) <https://republicans-smallbusiness.house.gov/uploadedfiles/1-15-2014_revised_sundararajan_testimony.pdf> accessed 7 December 2019.

55 Goudin (n 10) 23.

56 Kenneth Haar, 'UnFairbnb: How Online Rental Platforms Use the EU to Defeat Cities' Affordable Housing Measures' (Corporate Europe Observatory 2018) 4.

57 ibid.

58 ibid.

59 EC Agenda for the Collaborative Economy (n 1) 3.

In the process that preceded the EC Agenda for the Collaborative Economy, the discussion between two opposite sides was initiated. On one side were Airbnb and other P2P accommodation platforms lobbyists that are small in number when compared to other sectors, but whose influence at the European Commission is considerable,[60] claiming for the single digital market and openness of the businesses. On the opposite side were representatives of Member States and local governments generally defending measures taken by cities: ensuring the availability and affordability of local housing was seen as a legitimate policy that must be allowed to override the restrictions in the Services Directive and the E-Commerce Directive. Local governments have already noticed in early-stage what disruption in the market can be caused by the P2P accommodation platforms and their entrance into the previously regulated market.[61] The main discussion was raised based on the right to affordable housing and the potential to turn cities into 'only for tourists' places. The idea was to start the pan-European campaign but it turned out that the so-called P2P accommodation platforms are 'bigger players' and 'better lobbyists'[62] (it is often cited that Airbnb is the world's largest accommodation provider which does not own a single property or apartment).

Since the EC Agenda for the Collaborative Economy is a document that sets the principles and not the regulatory framework for P2P accommodation, applicable rules are still based on the above-mentioned directives (which both date from the time before the expansion of the P2P accommodation platforms). The E-Commerce Directive was adopted in 2000, at a time when the internet was flourishing and there were no other rules at the EU level regulating the issue. P2P accommodation was at that time still not enabled by the platforms.

When applying the E-Commerce Directive to P2P accommodation, there are some limitations such as for the cities where checking listings at web providers (i.e. digital platforms) is not allowed. The E-Commerce Directive applies to 'information society services', as defined by Art 1(1)(b) of the Information Society Services Directive.[63] Nevertheless, the actual challenge is that the service provided is not digital service itself. Another directive applicable to P2P accommodation is the Services Directive. It applies to accommodation in the terms that state that the authorities have the right to require permits, licences, or authorization when it is necessary but measures

60 Daniel Guttentag, 'Airbnb: Disruptive Innovation and the Rise of an Informal Tourism Accommodation Sector' (2015) 18 *Curr Issues Tour* 1192.

61 Shirley Nieuwland and Rianne van Melik, 'Regulating Airbnb: How Cities Deal with Perceived Negative Externalities of Short-Term Rentals' (2020) 23 *Curr Issues Tour* 811.

62 Haar (n 56) 11.

63 See n 27.

should be justified, proportionate, and non-discriminatory.[64] On the other side, service providers as well as service users are protected by the EU law.[65]

4. The ECJ judgment in *Airbnb Ireland*

The platform 'intervention' to the European Commission policy led to the so-called *Airbnb* cases and finally in 2019 to the ECJ judgment in the *Airbnb Ireland* case.[66] This was especially caused by the fact that in the absence of regulation in EU law of a particular legal issue, it is the practice of the Court of Justice of the European Union (CJEU) that is used as a source.[67]

The judgment in *Airbnb Ireland* is at the moment the most relevant document regarding the P2P accommodation sector in the EU.

The dilemma as it was discussed in the judgment was the definition of the 'information society service' and its applicability to the service provided by the Airbnb platform. This position was raised since in the *Uber* cases it was clear that if the service itself could be classified as an 'information society service', the EU law will be applicable.[68] In its judgment in *Airbnb Ireland*, the ECJ followed the Opinion of AG Szpunar,[69] and regarding the legal status of the Airbnb platform, showed an opposite direction to what was given before in *Uber* cases.[70]

The *Airbnb Ireland* case placed in the centre of the discussion the company Airbnb Ireland, which is a company established in Ireland under Irish law as a part of the Airbnb Group, made up of several companies directly or indirectly owned by Airbnb Inc., which is established in the United States. According to the ECJ judgment, Airbnb Ireland offers an electronic platform the purpose of which is, on payment of a commission, to establish contact, in particular in France, between, on the one hand, hosts, whether professionals or private individuals, with accommodation to rent and, on the other, people looking for such accommodation. Airbnb Payments UK Ltd, a company

64 According to the well-established practice of the ECJ in the interpretation of Arts 56, 49, and 18 of the Treaty on the Functioning of the European Union [2012] *OJ* C326/47 (TFEU), the measures that restrict free movement of services when EU law is applicable should be justified where they serve overriding reasons relating to the general interest, are suitable for securing the attainment of the objective which they pursue, and do not go beyond what is necessary in order to attain it.

65 TFEU, Art 56.

66 *Airbnb Ireland* (n 29).

67 Case law of the CJEU is considered as a supplementary source of law which is not specifically mentioned in the treaties and it is applicable when there is no other source of law.

68 In short, the *Uber* cases closed the possibility for application of EU law since the service provided by Uber was classified as a transport service and therefore exempted from the application of EU law. The idea in the *Airbnb* case was to defend the thesis that the Airbnb platform is providing a service which is different from the Uber service and that the EU law should be applicable.

69 See n 51.

70 See n 28.

established in London under the law of the United Kingdom, provides online payment services as part of that contact service and manages the payment activities of the Airbnb Group in the European Union. Also, Airbnb France SARL, a company established under French law and a supplier to Airbnb Ireland, is responsible for promoting that platform among users in the French market by organizing, *inter alia*, advertising campaigns for target audiences.[71]

In particular, the French Association for Professional Tourism and Accommodation complained that Airbnb Ireland does not respect French property laws and that Airbnb Ireland acts as a real estate agent without a permit, violating a local act known as the Hoguet Law. Airbnb Ireland argued that the company was designed so that people could rent spare rooms or entire real estate in the short term, and that they were protected by EU laws on 'electronic commerce'. According to the European Commission, a case-by-case analysis ought to be performed in order to set the legal nature of the platform's activities. Highlighting the enduring legal uncertainty surrounding such a definition is the case of Airbnb, an online platform that does not provide a service by itself but is however deemed a professional trader.

In practice, Airbnb Ireland enables guests to identify a place where they wish to go to and the period and number of persons of their choice. On that basis, Airbnb Ireland provides them with a list of available accommodation matching those criteria so that the users can select the accommodation of their choice and proceed to reserve it online.[72] Users of the electronic platform, both hosts and guests, conclude a contract with Airbnb Ireland for the use of that platform and with Airbnb Payments UK for the payments made via that platform.[73]

The main dilemma for the ECJ in *Airbnb Ireland* was whether the Airbnb service falls under the Services Directive or whether instead that service must be qualified as an 'information society service', within the meaning of Art 2(a) of E-Commerce Directive, as amended by the Information Society Services Directive. Under Art 1(1)(b) of Information Society Services Directive, the concept of an 'information society service' covers 'any service normally provided for remuneration, at a distance, by electronic means and at the individual request of a recipient of services'. Relating to the question of whether the Airbnb service is provided 'at a distance' and 'by electronic means', AG Szpunar illustrated his point as follows:

> AIRBNB Ireland does not physically meet the recipients of its services: neither the hosts nor the guests. As is apparent from the preliminary observations concerning AIRBNB Ireland's activities, the host is not required to approach AIRBNB Ireland in person in order to publish his

71 *Airbnb Ireland* (n 29), para 18.
72 ibid, para 20.
73 ibid, para 21.

> accommodation on the platform. Furthermore, a user of the platform managed by AIRBNB Ireland may rent an accommodation at a distance, without having to be physically in contact with that service provider. However, it is clear that the connection of users of the platform managed by AIRBNB Ireland results in the use of an accommodation, which may be regarded as a non-electronic component of the service provided by that company.[74]

Following the Opinion of AG Szpunar, the ECJ found that the Airbnb Ireland intermediation service meets the four cumulative conditions provided in Art 1(1)(b) of the Information Society Services Directive, and thus constitutes an 'information society service' within the meaning of the E-Commerce Directive.[75] Moreover, the ECJ determined that the Airbnb Ireland intermediation service cannot be regarded as forming an integral part of the overall service, the main component of which is the provision of accommodation.[76] The ECJ concluded that Art 2(a) of E-Commerce Directive, which refers to Art 1(1)(b) of the Information Society Services Directive

> must be interpreted as meaning that an intermediation service which, by means of an electronic platform, is intended to connect, for remuneration, potential guests with professional or non-professional hosts offering short-term accommodation services, while also providing a certain number of services ancillary to that intermediation service, must be classified as an 'information society service' under Directive 2000/31.[77]

Interestingly, the ECJ in its judgment also made a distinction between Airbnb and Uber. In December 2017, the ECJ ruled that the car-sharing company Uber was a taxi company, not just an 'information society service'.[78] But in the *Airbnb Ireland* judgment, the ECJ said that the case against Airbnb Ireland was unlike the case against Uber, as it cannot be established that Airbnb Ireland has a 'decisive influence' over the conditions for the provision of the accommodation services to which its intermediation service relates.[79] This differentiation is also in accordance with the European Commission idea that each sector should be regulated by a specific 'tailor-made' regulation.

The differentiation in the classification of the service itself was caused by the reaction of the national legislation to the *Uber* judgment and was explained by the analysis of the Airbnb business model. Airbnb does not determine

74 *Airbnb Ireland*, Opinion of AG Szpunar (n 51), para 41.
75 *Airbnb Ireland* (n 29), para 49.
76 ibid, para 57.
77 ibid, para 69.
78 Case C-434/15, *Asociación Profesional Elite Taxi* (n 28).
79 *Airbnb Ireland* (n 29), para 68.

the rental price charged for the property and allows buyers to choose which house to rent. In contrast, Uber sets a price for the ride in its application and assigns a driver to each passenger. Analysis of the policy document shows that significant documents and recommendations in the area of collaborative economy exist, but significant issues remain that require consideration.[80]

In the lack of the particular regulation of the P2P accommodation provided by the digital platforms, and while waiting for new 'policy guidance' or 'a charter', the local restrictions on short-term rental accommodation are, at the moment, determined at the EU level by the ECJ judgment in *Airbnb Ireland*.

5. Conclusion

The European executive has repeatedly pointed to the obstacles in the existing national laws of Member States that could impede the measures taken in cities across Europe. Whether it is about registration procedures, enforcement, or rules ensuring that large chunks of the existing or potential market are available for regular rent to locals, the Commission is finding many ways to ensure that the activities of collaborative platforms are not restricted at the national or local level. Since the EC Agenda for the Collaborative Economy was meant to be applied to all collaborative platforms, and not specifically to P2P accommodation platforms, the question of whether the P2P accommodation platforms are information society services providers had to be decided by the ECJ. In its judgment in the *Airbnb Ireland* case, the ECJ proclaimed *in concreto* Airbnb as a digital platform and its service as an 'information society service'. Consequently, the EU law is applicable which is essentially based on the freedom to provide a digital service in the entire market, while the national restrictions should be evaluated by the CJEU. The judgment in the *Airbnb Ireland* case ended the debate on the nature of the service provided and it is to be expected that national legislation will follow that path.

Bibliography

Airbnb, 'Terms of Service for European Users' (Airbnb, last updated on 1 November 2019) <www.airbnb.co.uk/terms> accessed 7 December 2019

Busch C and others, 'The Rise of the Platform Economy: A New Challenge for EU Consumer Law?' (2016) 5 *EuCML* 3

Cohen M and Sundararajan A, 'Self-Regulation and Innovation in the Peer-to-Peer Sharing Economy' (2015) 82 *U Chi L Rev Online* 116 <https://chicagounbound.uchicago.edu/uclrev_online/vol82/iss1/8> accessed 17 March 2020

Demary V, 'Competition in the Sharing Economy' (2015) *IW Policy Paper* 19/2015 <www.iwkoeln.de/studien/iw-policy-papers/beitrag/vera-demary-competition-in-the-sharing-economy-235445.html> accessed 17 March 2020

80 Goudin (n 10) 106.

Dolnicar S, 'Unique Features of Peer-to-Peer Accommodation Networks' in Dolnicar S (ed), *Peer-to-Peer Accommodation Networks* (Goodfellow Publishers 2017) [DOI: https://doi.org/10.23912/9781911396512-3599]

Dredge D and others, 'Impact of regulatory approaches to the collaborative economy in the tourism accommodation sector: Barcelona, Berlin, Amsterdam and Paris' (2016) *Impulse Paper* 9/2016 <https://ec.europa.eu/growth/content/impact-regulatory-approaches-collaborative-economy-tourism-accommodation-sector-barcelona-0_en> accessed 12 January 2020

European Commission, 'A European Agenda for the Collaborative Economy' (Communication) COM (2016) 356 final

——— 'More than Profit: A Collaborative Economy with a Social Purpose' (European Commission 2016) 8 <https://ec.europa.eu/docsroom/documents/18443> accessed 15 October 2020

Geiger A, Horbel C, and Germelmann CC, '"Give and Take": How Notions of Sharing and Context Determine Free Peer-to-Peer Accommodation Decisions' (2018) 35 *J Travel Tour Mark* 5 [DOI: https://doi.org/10.1080/10548408.2016.1231101]

Goudin P, *The Cost of Non-Europe in the Sharing Economy: Economic, Social and Legal Challenges and Opportunities* (European Parliamentary Research Service 2016) [DOI: http://doi.org/10.2861/26238]

Guttentag D, 'Airbnb: Disruptive Innovation and the Rise of an Informal Tourism Accommodation Sector' (2015) 18 *Curr Issues Tour* 1192 [DOI: https://doi.org/10.1080/13683500.2013.827159]

Haar K, 'UnFairbnb: How Online Rental Platforms Use the EU to Defeat Cities' Affordable Housing Measures' (Corporate Europe Observatory 2018)

Habibi MR, Davidson A, and Laroche M, 'What Managers Should Know About the Sharing Economy' (2017) 60 *Bus Horiz* 113 [DOI: https://doi.org/10.1016/j.bushor.2016.09.007]

Hajibaba H and Dolnicar S, 'Regulatory Reactions Around the World' in Dolnicar S (ed), *Peer-to-Peer Accommodation Networks* (Goodfellow Publishers 2017) [DOI: https://doi.org/10.23912/9781911396512-3609]

Hatzopoulos V, *The Collaborative Economy and EU Law* (Hart Publishing 2018) [DOI: https://doi.org/10.5040/9781509917167]

——— and Roma S, 'Caring for Sharing? The Collaborative Economy under EU Law' (2017) 54 *CML Rev* 81

Hausemer P and others, 'Exploratory Study of Consumer Issues in Online Peer-to-Peer Platform Markets: Final Report' (European Commission 2017) [DOI: https://doi.org/10.2838/779064]

Koolhoven R and others, 'Impulse Paper on Specific Liability Issues Raised by the Collaborative Economy in the Accommodation Sector: Paris – Amsterdam – Barcelona' (European Commission 2016)

Manyika J and others, 'Disruptive technologies: Advances that will transform life, business, and the global economy' (McKinsey Global Institute 2016) <www.mckinsey.com/business-functions/mckinsey-digital/our-insights/disruptive-technologies#> accessed 17 March 2020

Micklitz H-W, Reich N, and Rott P, *Understanding EU Consumer Law* (Intersentia 2009)

Nieuwland S and Melik R van, 'Regulating Airbnb: How Cities Deal with Perceived Negative Externalities of Short-Term Rentals' (2020) 23 *Curr Issues Tour* 811 [DOI: https://doi.org/10.1080/13683500.2018.1504899]

Organisation for Economic Co-operation and Development (OECD), 'Protecting Consumers in Peer Platform Markets: Exploring the Issues' (2016) *OECD Digital Economy Papers* 253/2006 <www.oecd-ilibrary.org/science-and-technology/protecting-consumers-in-peer-platform-markets_5jlwvz39m1zw-en> accessed 19 March 2020 [DOI: https://doi.org/10.1787/5jlwvz39m1zw-en]

Pošćić A, 'Europsko pravo tržišnog natjecanja i ekonomija dijeljenja – odabrana pitanja' (2019) 40 *Zbor Prav Fak Rijeka* 237 [DOI: https://doi.org/10.30925/zpfsr.40.1.9]

Sundararajan A, 'Peer-to-Peer Businesses and the Sharing (Collaborative) Economy: Overview, Economic Effects and Regulatory Issues' (Committee on Small Business of the United States House of Representatives, 14 January 2014) <https://republicans-smallbusiness.house.gov/uploadedfiles/1-15-2014_revised_sundararajan_testimony.pdf> accessed 7 December 2019

Teubner T, 'Thoughts on the Sharing Economy' in Kommers P and others, *Proceedings of International Conferences on the ICT, Society and Human Beings 2014, Web Based Communities and Social Media 2014, e-Commerce 2014, Information Systems Post-Implementation and Change Management 2014 and e-Health 2014* (International Association for Development of the Information Society 2014)

Vaughan R and Daverio R, 'Assessing the Size and Presence of the Collaborative Economy in Europe' (European Commission 2016) [DOI: http://doi.org/10.2873/971404]

Von den Leyen U, 'Political Guidelines for the Next European Commission 2019–2024: A Union that strives for more: My agenda for Europe' (2019) <https://op.europa.eu/en/publication-detail/-/publication/43a17056-ebf1-11e9-9c4e-01aa75ed71a1> accessed 15 October 2020

Weatherill S, *EU Consumer Law and Policy* (2nd edn, Edward Elgar 2013) [DOI: https://doi.org/10.4337/9780857936981]

Index

Note: Page numbers followed by "n" denote endnotes.

Lightning Source UK Ltd.
Milton Keynes UK
UKHW050659220822
407581UK00004BA/21

9 780367 512705